grzimek's
Student Animal Life Resource

• • • •

grzimek's
Student Animal Life Resource

• • • •

Insects and Spiders
volume 2

Webspinners to Pauropods

Arthur V. Evans, D.Sc., author

Madeline S. Harris, project editor
Neil Schlager and Jayne Weisblatt, editors

THOMSON

GALE

Detroit • New York • San Francisco • San Diego • New Haven, Conn. • Waterville, Maine • London • Munich

Grzimek's Student Animal Life Resource: Insects

Arthur V. Evans, D.Sc

Project Editor
Madeline S. Harris

Editorial
Kathleen J. Edgar, Melissa Hill,
Heather Price

Indexing Services
Synapse, the Knowledge Link
Corporation

Rights and Acquisitions
Sheila Spencer, Mari Masalin-Cooper

Imaging and Multimedia
Randy Bassett, Michael Logusz, Dan
Newell, Chris O'Bryan, Robyn Young

Product Design
Tracey Rowens, Jennifer Wahi

Composition
Evi Seoud, Mary Beth Trimper

Manufacturing
Wendy Blurton, Dorothy Maki

LIBRARY OF CONGRESS CATALOGING-IN-PUBLICATION DATA

Evans, Arthur V.
Grzimek's student animal life resource. Insects and spiders / Arthur V. Evans ;
Neil Schlager and Jayne Weisblatt, editors.
    p. cm.
  Includes bibliographical references and index.
  ISBN 0-7876-9243-3 (hardcover 2 vol. set : alk. paper) — ISBN 0-7876-9244-1
(vol. 1) — ISBN 0-7876-9245-X (vol. 2)
  1. Insects—Juvenile literature. 2. Spiders—Juvenile literature. I. Schlager, Neil,
1966- II. Weisblatt, Jayne. III. Title.
  QL467.2.E36 2005
  595.7—dc22
                                                                    2005000144

ISBN 0-7876-9402-9 (21-vol set), ISBN 0-7876-9243-3 (2-vol set), ISBN 0-7876-9244-1 (vol 1), ISBN 0-7876-9245-X (vol 2)

This title is also available as an e-book
Contact your Thomson Gale sales representative for ordering information.

Printed in Canada
10 9 8 7 6 5 4 3 2 1

Contents

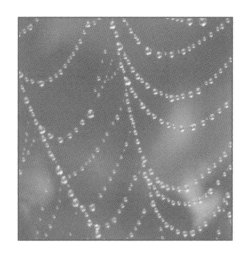

INSECTS AND SPIDERS: VOLUME 2

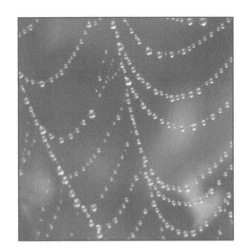

Reader's Guide

Grzimek's Student Animal Life Resource: Insects and Spiders offers readers comprehensive and easy-to-use information on Earth's insects and spiders. Entries are arranged by taxonomy, the science through which living things are classified into related groups. Each entry includes sections on physical characteristics; geographic range; habitat; diet; behavior and reproduction; animals and people; and conservation status. All entries are followed by one or more species accounts with the same information as well as a range map and photo or illustration for each species. Entries conclude with a list of books, periodicals, and Web sites that may be used for further research.

ADDITIONAL FEATURES

Each volume of *Grzimek's Student Animal Life Resource: Insects and Spiders* includes a pronunciation guide for scientific names, a glossary, an overview of Insects and Spiders, a list of species in the set by biome, a list of species by geographic range, and an index. The set has 236 full-color maps, photos, and illustrations to enliven the text, and sidebars provide additional facts and related information.

NOTE

Grzimek's Student Animal Life Resource: Insects and Spiders has standardized information in the Conservation Status section. The IUCN Red List provides the world's most comprehensive inventory of the global conservation status of plants and animals. Using a set of criteria to evaluate extinction risk, the IUCN recognizes the following categories: Extinct, Extinct in the Wild, Critically Endangered, Endangered, Vulnerable, Conservation Dependent, Near Threatened, Least Concern, and Data Deficient. These terms are defined where they are used in the text, but for a complete explanation of each category, visit the IUCN web page at http://www.iucn.org/themes/ssc/redlists/RLcats2001booklet.html.

ACKNOWLEDGEMENTS

Gale would like to thank several individuals for their assistance with this set. Dr. Arthur V. Evans wrote the entire text. At Schlager Group Inc., Neil Schlager and Jayne Weisblatt coordinated the writing and editing of the set, while Marcia Merryman Means and Leah Tieger also provided valuable assistance.

Special thanks are also due for the invaluable comments and suggestions provided by the *Grzimek's Student Animal Life Resource: Insects and Spiders* advisors:

- Mary Alice Anderson, Media Specialist, Winona Middle School, Winona, Minnesota
- Thane Johnson, Librarian, Oklahoma City Zoo, Oklahoma City, Oklahoma
- Debra Kachel, Media Specialist, Ephrata Senior High School, Ephrata, Pennsylvania
- Nina Levine, Media Specialist, Blue Mountain Middle School, Courtlandt Manor, New York
- Ruth Mormon, Media Specialist, The Meadows School, Las Vegas, Nevada

COMMENTS AND SUGGESTIONS

We welcome your comments on *Grzimek's Student Animal Life Resource: Insects and Spiders* and suggestions for future editions of this work. Please write: Editors, *Grzimek's Student Animal Life Resource: Insects and Spiders*, U•X•L, 27500 Drake Rd., Farmington Hills, Michigan 48331-3535; call toll free: 1-800-877-4253; fax: 248-699-8097; or send e-mail via www.gale.com.

Pronunciation Guide for Scientific Names

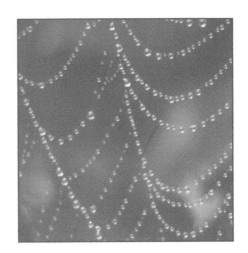

Acherontia atropos ah-KER-on-tee-uh at-TRUH-pohs

Acyrthosiphon pisum as-er-THOS-ih-fon PY-sum

Aedes aegypti ay-EE-deez ee-JIP-ty

Allopauropus carolinensis al-oh-puh-ROP-uhs kar-uh-LINE-en-sis

Anthophiloptera dryas an-thoh-FILL-op-tuh-ruh DRY-uhs

Apis mellifera AY-puhs muh-LIF-uh-ruh

Arachnida uh-RAK-nuh-duh

Atta sexdens ATE-tuh SEKS-dunz

Attacus atlas AT-uh-kuhs AT-luhs

Basilia falcozi buh-SIL-ee-ay FAL-koh-zy

Blatta orientalis BLAY-tuh or-ee-EN-tuh-lis

Blattella germanica BLAY-tell-uh jer-MAN-ih-kuh

Blattodea BLAD-uh-dee

Bombyx mori BOM-biks MOR-ee

Carausius morosos kuh-RAW-see-uhs muh-ROH-suhs

Ceratitis capitata sair-uh-TID-is kap-ih-TOT-ah

Chelifer cancroides KEL-uh-fer kan-KROY-deez

Chilopoda ky-LOP-uh-duh

Chiloporter eatoni ky-LOP-uh-der ee-uh-TOH-ny

Cimex lectularius SY-meks lek-choo-LAR-ee-uhs

Coleoptera KOH-lee-OP-tuh-ruh

Collembola kuh-LEM-buh-luh

Colossendeis megalonyx KALL-uh-SEN-days MEG-uh-LON-iks

Columbicola columbae kuh-lim-BIH-koh-luh kuh-LUM-bay

Conocephalus discolor KON-oh-SEF-uh-luhs dis-KUH-ler

Corydalus cornutus kuh-RID-uh-luhs KOR-nuh-tuhs

Cubacubana spelaea KYOO-buh-kyoo-BAH-nuh spuh-LAY-ee-uh

Cyrtodiopsis dalmanni ser-toh-DY-op-sis DALL-muh-nee

Demodex folliculorum DEM-uh-deks fuh-LIK-yuh-LOR-um

Dermacentor andersoni DER-muh-SEN-ter an-der-SOH-ny

Dermaptera der-MOP-tuh-ruh

Deroplatys lobata der-OP-luh-teez LOH-bah-duh

Diapheromera femorata DY-uh-FER-ah-mer-uh fem-uh-RAW-tuh

Diplopoda duh-PLAW-puh-duh

Diplura duh-PLER-uh

Diptera DIP-tuh-ruh

Dorcadia ioffi dor-KAY-dee-uh EYE-oh-fee

Dynastes hercules DY-nuh-steez her-KYOO-leez

Dytiscus marginalis dy-TIS-cuhs MAR-gih-NAL-is

Embioptera EM-bee-OP-tuh-ruh

Ephemera vulgata uh-FEM-uh-ruh vuhl-GAW-tuh

Ephemeroptera uh-FEM-uh-ROP-tuh-ruh

Euclimacia torquata YOO-kluh-MAY-see-uh tor-KWAH-tuh

Eumenes fraternus YOO-muh-neez fruh-TER-nuhs

Extatosoma tiaratum EK-stat-TOH-suh-muh TEE-ar-uh-tum

Forficula auricularia for-FIK-yoo-luh oh-RIK-yoo-LAR-ee-uh

Frankliniella occidentalis FRANK-lin-ee-EL-luh AWK-sih-DEN-tuh-lis

Galeodes arabs GAY-lee-OH-deez AIR-rubs

Glomeris marginata GLAW-mer-is mar-GIH-nah-tuh

Glossina palpalis glaw-SEE-nuh pal-PUH-lis

Gongylus gongylodes GON-jih-luhs gon-JIH-loh-DEEZ

Grylloblatta campodeiformis GRIL-oh-BLAH-duh KAM-poh-DAY-for-mis

Grylloblattodea GRILL-oh-BLAD-uh-DEE

Halictophagus naulti huh-LIK-tuh-FAY-guhs NALL-ty

Halobates micans huh-LOH-buh-teez MY-kunz

Hemiptera heh-MIP-tuh-ruh

Heteropteryx dilitata HED-er-OP-ter-iks DIL-uh-TAH-tuh

Holijapyx diversiuguis huh-LIJ-uh-piks dih-VER-see-uh-gwis

Hymenoptera HY-muh-NOP-tuh-ruh

Hymenopus coronatus HY-muh-NAW-puhs KUH-ruh-NAW-tuhs

Inocellia crassicornis IN-uh-SEE-lee-uh KRAS-sih-KOR-nis

Isoptera eye-SOP-tuh-ruh

Labidura herculeana luh-BIH-der-uh her-KYOO-lee-ah-nuh

Lepidoptera LEP-uh-DOP-tuh-ruh

Lepisma saccharina luh-PIZ-muh SAK-uh-REE-nuh

Lethocerus maximus luh-THAW-suh-ruhs mak-SIH-muhs

Limulus polyphemus lim-YUH-luhs PAW-lih-FUH-muhs

Liposcelis bostrychophila LIP-uh-SEL-is buh-STRIK-uh-FEE-lee-uh

Lucanus cervus LOO-kah-nuhs SER-vuhs

Lymantria dispar LY-mon-tree-uh DIS-per

Macrotermes carbonarius MAK-roh-TER-meez KAR-buh-NAR-ee-uhs

Maculinea arion MAK-yoo-LIN-ee-uh uh-REE-uhn

Magicicada septendecim MAJ-uh-SIK-uh-duh SEP-ten-DEE-sum

Mallada albofascialis muh-LAH-duh AL-boh-FOS-ee-uh-lis

Mantis religiosa MAN-tuhs ruh-LIH-jee-OH-suh

Mantodea man-TOH-dee-uh

Mantophasmotodea MAN-tuh-FAZ-muh-TOH-dee-uh

Mastigoproctus giganteus MAS-tuh-goh-PROK-tuhs JY-gan-TEE-uhs

Mecoptera meh-KOP-tuh-ruh

Megalithone tillyardi MEG-uh-LITH-uh-NEE til-YER-dy

Megaloprepus caerulatus MEG-uh-LAH-prih-puhs kee-ROO-lah-tuhs

Megaloptera MEG-uh-LOP-tuh-ruh

Megarhyssa nortoni MEG-uh-RY-suh NOR-tuh-ny

Merostomata MER-uh-STOH-muh-duh

Microcoryphia MY-kroh-KUH-rih-fee-uh

Mimetica mortuifolia MIH-meh-TIH-kuh mor-CHOO-ih-FOH-lee-uh

Morpho menelaus MOR-foh MEN-uh-LAY-uhs

Mutilla europaea myoo-TIL-uh yer-OH-pee-uh

Myrmeleon formicarius mer-MUH-lee-uhn for-MUH-kar-ee-uhs

Nasutitermes nigriceps nuh-SOO-duh-ter-meez NY-gruh-seps

Nemoptera sinuata nuh-MOP-tuh-ruh sin-YOO-ah-tuh

Neuroptera new-ROP-tuh-ruh

Nicrophorus americanus ny-KRAW-fuh-ruhs uh-MAIR-uh-KAN-uhs

Notonecta sellata NOD-uh-NEK-tuh SUH-lah-tuh

Ocypus olens AH-sih-puhs OH-lenz

Odonata OH-duh-NOD-uh

Oligotoma saundersii uh-LIG-uh-TOH-muh sawn-DER-see-eye

Orthoptera ar-THAP-tuh-ruh

Pandinus imperator pan-DEE-nuhs im-PAIR-uh-tor

Panorpa nuptialis puh-NOR-puh nup-CHEE-ah-lis

Pantala flavescens pan-TUH-luh fluh-VEH-sunz

Pauropoda pah-ROP-uh-duh

Pediculus humanas peh-DIK-yoo-luhs HYOO-mah-nuhs

Pepsis grossa PEP-suhs GRAH-suh

Periplaneta americana PAIR-uh-pluh-NEH-tuh uh-MAIR-ih-KAN-uh

Petrobius brevistylis PUH-troh-BEE-uhs bruh-VIS-tuh-lis

Phalangium opilio fuh-LAN-jee-um oh-PIL-ee-oh

Phasmida FAZ-mih-duh

Pholcus phalangioides FALL-kuhs fuh-LAN-jee-OY-deez

Phrynus parvulus FRY-nuhs PAR-vuh-luhs

Phthiraptera ther-OP-tuh-ruh

Phyllium bioculatum FIL-ee-um by-AWK-yoo-LAY-dum

Plecoptera pluh-COP-tuh-ruh

Plodia interpunctella PLOH-dee-uh IN-ter-PUNK-tel-luh

Polyancistrus serrulatus PAW-lee-AN-sis-truhs suh-ROO-lah-tuhs

Polydesmus angustus paw-LEE-deez-muhs an-GUS-tuhs

Praedatophasma maraisi pre-DAT-uh-FAZ-muh muh-RAY-sy

Protura PRUH-tyer-uh

Psocoptera soh-KOP-tuh-ruh

Pteronarcys californica TAIR-uh-NAR-seez KAL-ih-FOR-nih-kuh

Pycnogonida PIK-nuh-GON-uh-duh

Raphidioptera ruh-FID-ee-OP-tuh-ruh

Reticulitermes flavipes ruh-TIK-yoo-luh-TER-meez FLAV-uh-peez

Rhabdotogryllus caraboides RAB-doh-TAH-grih-luhs KAR-uh-BOY-deez

Rhyparobia maderae RY-puh-ROH-bee-uh muh-DER-ee

Salticus scenicus SALL-tih-kuhs SEN-ih-kuhs

Scarabaeus sacer SKAR-uh-BEE-uhs SAY-ser

Scolopendra morsitans SKALL-uh-PEN-druh MOR-sih-TAWNZ

Scutigera coleoptrata SKYOO-tij-er-uh KOH-lee-OP-truh-tuh

Scutigerella immaculata skyoo-TIJ-uh-REL-uh ih-MAK-yoo-LAH-duh

Sinetomon yoroi SY-nuh-TOH-mun YOR-oy

Siphonaptera SY-fuh-NOP-tuh-ruh

Sminthuris viridis smin-THOOR-uhs vuh-RID-is

Strepsiptera strep-SIP-tuh-ruh

Supella longipalpa SOO-pel-uh LAWN-gih-PALL-puh

Symphyla SIM-fuh-luh

Tabanus punctifer tuh-BAY-nus PUNK-tih-fer

Tachycines asynamorus TAK-uh-SEE-neez A-sih-NAW-muh-ris

Tenodera aridifolia sinensis tuh-NAH-duh-ruh uh-RID-uh-FOH-lee-uh sih-NEN-sis

Termes fatalis TER-meez FAY-tal-is

Thysanoptera THY-suh-NOP-tuh-ruh

Thysanura THY-suh-NER-uh

Tipula paludosa TIP-yuh-luh PAL-uh-DOH-suh

Trachelophorus giraffa TRAK-uh-luh-FOR-uhs jih-RAF-uh

Triaenodes bicolor try-ee-NUH-deez BY-kuh-ler

Trialeurodes vaporariorum TRY-uh-LER-uh-deez VAY-poh-rar-ee-OR-um

Trichoptera truh-KOP-tuh-ruh

Trissolcus basalis TRIH-sohl-KUHS BAS-uh-lis

Tunga Penetrans TUNG-uh PEN-uh-tronz

Zonocerus variegatus ZOH-nuh-SUH-ruhs VAIR-ee-uh-GAH-tuhs

Zootermopsis laticeps ZOO-der-MOP-sis LAD-ih-seps

Zoraptera zuh-ROP-tuh-ruh

Zorotypus hubbardi ZOR-uh-TIP-is huh-BAR-dy

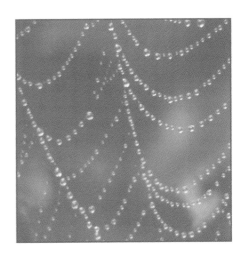

Words to Know

A

Adaptations: Physical features, behaviors, and other characteristics that help an organism to survive and reproduce.

Agile: Able to move quickly and with grace.

Algae: Tiny plantlike organisms that live in water and lack true roots, stems, or leaves.

Ametabolous: Lacking metamorphosis; larvae resemble small versions of wingless adults and are unable to reproduce.

Anamorphosis: A type of metamorphosis where the larva hatches with fewer abdominal segments than the adult.

Antennae: Structures that act like "feelers," or sense organs; sensitive to smell or touch.

Aposematic coloration: Bright or distinctive colors that serve as a warning.

Appendages: Mouthparts, antennae, legs, wings, and tail-like projections.

Aquatic: Living in water.

Arachnologist: A scientist who studies spiders and their relatives.

Arthropod: An animal with a hard outer skeleton and several pairs of jointed limbs.

B

Bacteria: Tiny living things that are made up of only one cell.

Bay: An inlet of the sea.

Binocular vision: The ability to use two eyes to focus on objects.

Biodiversity: The diversity of all life at all levels in a particular place.

Biological control: Using a pest's own natural enemies, such as predators, parasites, parasitoids, and diseases, to control it.

Bioluminescence: Light produced by living organisms.

Bioluminescent: Describing organisms that produce their own light.

Brackish: Salty.

Bristles: Short, stiff hairs.

C

Carapace: An upper platelike shield that covers all or part of certain arachnids; a shield-like plate covering the body of some animals.

Carnivore: An animal that eats the flesh of other animals.

Carnivorous: Meat eating.

Chimera: A single organism that has features of two or more species.

Chitin: A material similar to fingernails that is the main component of the outer skeletons of some animals.

Cholesterol: A substance in animals' cells and body fluids that "cleans" the blood; too much of it can be unhealthy.

Chrysalis: The pupa of a butterfly.

Clutch: A group of eggs.

Coevolution: Description of two or more groups of organisms that influence each other's evolution.

Colony: A grouping of animals that typically lives in a cluster, or mass; such groups of sea organisms are found together on a solid object, such as a coral reef.

Compound eyes: Eyes made up of many lenses.

Contamination: The act of making impure, or dirty, by adding a harmful substance.

Coral: A tiny sea-dwelling animal whose hard skeleton, also called coral, forms reefs in the ocean, often pinkish rose in color.

Courtship: An animal's activities that are meant to attract a mate.

Cove: A small, sheltered inlet of the sea.

Critically Endangered: Facing an extremely high risk of extinction in the wild in the near future.

Crustacean: An animal that lives in water and has a soft, segmented body covered by a hard shell, such as lobsters and shrimp.

Crypsis: A form of camouflage in which an animal imitates specific objects in the environment.

D

Decomposed: Decayed, rotted, disintegrated.

Deforestation: Clearing land of trees to use the timber or to make room for human settlement or farming.

Detritus: Tiny bits of plant and animal remains that have decomposed, or disintegrated.

Diapause: A period of rest or inactivity.

Digestive organs: The body parts that break down food and take it into the body.

Distribution: Geographic range of an animal, where it roams and feeds.

E

Ectoparasite: Parasitic organism that lives on the outside of its host organism.

Eggs: The reproductive cells that are made by female animals and that are fertilized by sperm, or reproductive cells of male animals.

Elytra: The hard, leathery forewings of beetles.

Endangered: Facing a very high risk of extinction in the wild.

Endoparasite: Parasitic organism that lives on the inside of its host organism.

Engorge: To fill up with blood.

Entomologist: A scientist who studies insects.

Estuary: The wide part at the lower end of a river, where the river meets the sea.

Evolution: Gradual process of change over time.

Exoskeleton: An animal's outer covering or supportive structure; the external skeleton or hard outer covering of some animal, especially arthropods.

Extinct: No longer alive.

F

Forage: To search for food.

Fossils: The remains, or parts, of animals that lived long ago, usually found preserved in rock or earth, amber, or other materials.

G

Galls: Abnormal plant growths caused by insects, mites, funguses, and disease.

Ganglia (sing. ganglion): Masses of nerve cells.

Geologist: A scientist who studies the history of Earth through rocks.

Gill: An organ for obtaining oxygen from water.

Gynandromorph: An individual having both male and female characteristics.

H

Hair follicle: A small cavity surrounding the root of a hair.

Harvest: To collect or gather.

Herbivore: A plant-feeding animal.

Heredity: Physical features passed from parent to offspring through genes.

Hibernation: A period of inactivity during the winter.

Hormones: Chemicals that circulate in the blood that stimulate tissues and organs.

Hydrozoans: A group of water-dwelling organisms without backbones that includes jellyfish.

Hypermetamorphosis: Development of insect larvae that have two or more distinctive body forms.

I

Instar: The stage between molts in arthropods.

Invertebrate: An animal without a backbone, such as an insect or earthworm.

Invertebrate zoologist: A scientist who studies animals without backbones.

L

Larva (plur. larvae): The early, or young, form of an animal, which must go through metamorphosis, or certain changes in form, before becoming an adult.

Lek: A group of animals gathered together to find mates.

Lichens: Plantlike growths of funguses and algae living together.

Loamy: Used in reference to soil and meaning soil that is made up of bits of plant material, clay, sand, and silt.

M

Metamorphosis: Process of change, development, and growth in animals.

Migrate: To move from one area or climate to another to breed or feed.

Migration: Movement from one area or climate to another to breed or feed.

Mimics: Organisms that imitate the appearance of another species.

Molt: To shed feathers, shell, or some other outer body part, typically at certain times of the year.

Myiasis: Disease or injury inside or outside the body caused by an infestation of fly larvae.

Myriapodologist: A scientist who studies millipedes, centipedes, and their kin.

N

Near Threatened: At risk of becoming threatened with extinction in the future.

Nymph: A young arachnid; replaced by larva in insects.

O

Omnivore: An animal that eats plants and animals.

Omnivorous: Feeding on both plant and animal materials.

Overwinter: Last through the winter weather; survive.

Ovipositor: The egg-laying tube on the abdomen of many insects and some arachnids.

Ovoviviparity: Act of retaining eggs inside the body until they hatch.

P

Paleontologist: A scientist who studies fossils of plants and animals.

Palp: Fingerlike appendages associated with mouthparts of many arthropods.

Paralyze: To make helpless or unable to move.

Parasite: An animal that lives on another organism, called a "host," from which it obtains its food; the host is seldom killed.

Parasitic: Living on another plant or animal without helping it and often harming it.

Parasitoid: A parasite that slowly kills its host.

Parthenogenesis: Development of young from unfertilized eggs.

Pedipalps: Leg-like appendages of the mouthparts of arthropods.

Pheromones: Chemicals produced by animals that affect the behavior of other individuals in the same species.

Polar: Referring to the cold regions of the world that are farthest north (the Arctic) and farthest south (the Antarctic), where temperatures never rise above 50°F (10°C).

Pollution: Poison, waste, or other material that makes the environment dirty and harmful to health.

Postures: Body positions.

Predator: An animal that hunts and kills other animals for food.

Prey: An animal hunted and caught for food.

Proboscis: A long, flexible, tubelike snout; a strawlike sucking structure of some insects.

Prolegs: Fleshy leglike structures on the abdomen of some insect larvae.

Protozoan: A single-celled, microscopic organism with a nucleus that is neither plant nor animal.

Pulsating: Beating rhythmically.

Pupa: The transition stage between larvae and adult that does not feed or walk.

R

Rainforest: A tropical woodland area of evergreen trees that has heavy rainfall all year long.

Raptorial: Grasping.

Reproductive organs: The body parts that produce young.

Resilin: A rubberlike protein found in the bodies of insects.

Resin: A sticky substance produced by plants.

Rheumatism: Any disorder that causes pain and stiffness in the joints of limbs or back.

S

Scavenger: Animal that eats decaying flesh.

Sea anemone: A small sea animal with long, thin, armlike body parts called tentacles, which looks much like a flower.

Second-growth forest: Forest that grows naturally after cutting or a fire.

Seep: A spot where water has oozed to the ground surface and formed a pool.

Setae (sing. seta): Hair-like structures on the arthropod exoskeleton.

Silt: Fine, tiny specks of earth that settle out of water or fall to the bottom; also, soil material containing very fine particles of rock.

Span: The spread, or distance between two limits, such as the ends of an insect's unfolded wings.

Species: A group of animals that share many traits and can mate and produce young with one another.

Spawn: To produce or release eggs.

Sperm: The reproductive cells that are made by male animals and that fertilize the eggs of female animals.

Spiracles: Breathing holes on the bodies of many arthropods.

Stationary: Unmoving, fixed in position.

Subphyla (sing. subphylum): The major subdivisions of a phylum.

Subtropics: Regions that border on the tropics.

Suture: A thread, wire, or something similar used to close a wound.

T

Telson: The end segment of the body of an arthropod.

Temperate: Mild; used in reference to climate.

Tentacles: Long, thin, armlike body parts used for touching and grasping.

Territorial: Protective of a living or breeding area.

Thigmotactic: Describing animals that must maintain contact with a solid surface, usually by hiding in cracks and crevices.

Thorax: Midsection of an arthropod's body.

Tidal pool: A pool of water that remains after an ocean tide has risen and fallen.

Toxin: A poison produced by a plant or animal.

Trachea: Tubes that transport air throughout the body of most arthropods.

Transparent: See-through, clear.

Tropical: Referring to a climate with an average annual temperature more than 68°F (20°C).

V

Vaccine: Inactive, or dead, germs of a disease that are administered to human beings to help protect against the disease.

Venom: Poison.

Viviparity: Act of producing live offspring inside the body.

Vulnerable: Facing a high risk of extinction in the wild.

W

Wetland: Land that is covered with shallow water or that has very wet soil.

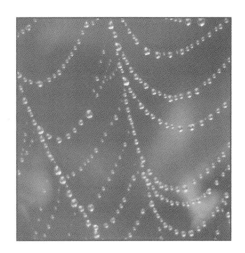

Getting to Know Insects and Spiders

WHAT ARE INSECTS AND SPIDERS?

Insects, spiders, and their relatives are all arthropods (ar-thro-pawds), or animals with a hard outer skeleton and several pairs of jointed limbs. Arthropods form the largest group of animals on Earth. They are found almost everywhere, from the deepest ocean trenches to the tallest mountain peaks. There are nearly one million species of insects known, nearly half of all the different plants and animals combined. There may be as many as ten to thirty million insect species total. Even a "typical" backyard may be the home to several thousand species of insects and spiders. Estimates of species numbers vary because scientists still know so very little about them. Millions of new species await discovery, especially among insects and mites on land and crustaceans in the ocean.

It is estimated that for every human being alive today, there are as many as two hundred million individual insects. Just the total weight of all the ants in the world, all nine thousand different kinds, is twelve times greater than the weight of all the humans on the planet. Despite their amazing numbers and the fact that they are found virtually everywhere, insects and other arthropods are still very alien to us, as if they were beings from another planet. They move on six or more legs, stare with un-blinking eyes, breathe without noses, and have hard skinless bodies made up of rings and plates, yet there is something strangely familiar about them, too. Arthropods have to do all the things people do to survive, such as find food, defend themselves from their enemies, and reproduce. They also rely on their finely tuned senses to see, touch, hear, smell, and taste the world around them.

Because of their numbers and the fact that they eat almost everything that is plant, fungus, or animal, arthropods have a huge impact on all the species sharing their habitats. They pollinate flowers, disperse seeds, recycle dead organisms, and bury animal waste. Plant-feeding species provide a natural pruning service that keeps plant growth and populations in check, while flesh-eaters control the populations of other animals. They, in return, are an important food source for fishes, reptiles, amphibians, birds, mammals, and other arthropods.

Many different kinds of scientists study the lives of insects, spiders, and their relatives. Entomologists (EHN-tih-MA-luh-jists) examine the lives of insects, while arachnologists (uh-rak-NA-luh-jists) look at spiders and their relatives. Myriapodologists (mi-RI-ah-po-DAL-luh-jists) focus their attentions on millipedes, centipedes, and their kin. Invertebrate zoologists (in-VER-teh-breht zu-AH-luh-jists)and some marine biologists study marine crustaceans, sea spiders, and horseshoe crabs. It is the work of all these scientists that has provided the information found on these pages.

OLDER THAN DINOSAURS

Arthropods were swimming in lakes, crawling on land, and flying through the air long before dinosaurs. In fact, millipedes are one of the oldest land animals on Earth and have been around for about four hundred million years. Insects are more than 380 million years old. Scientists know this by studying their fossils (FAH-suhls), or remains of animals that lived long ago, usually found set into rock or earth. Scientists who study fossils are called paleontologists (PAY-li-un-TA-luh-jists). Paleontologists study fossils to understand how life has developed and changed over time. The location and chemical makeup of fossils helps paleontologists to determine their age. By studying fossils scientists know that some groups of organisms, such as horseshoe crabs, millipedes, silverfish, and cockroaches, have changed very little over millions of years. The process of organisms changing over time is called evolution (EH-vuh-LU-shun). Organisms must adapt in form and behavior to survive in an environment that is also changing. Studying fossils not only reveals clues about the evolution of these ancient animals but also gives a glimpse of the environments in which they lived.

How to become a fossil

For arthropods, the process of fossilization (FAH-suhl-ih-ZAY-shun) begins when footprints, bodies, or body parts are quickly covered in mud or sand made up of fine particles. The finer the particles, the greater the detail preserved in the fossil. Under just the right circumstances, the mud and sand will be compressed, or squeezed, as more mud and sand settle on the remains, until it becomes rock. This process takes millions of years. Fossils are only impressions of the ancient animals. Their tissues are replaced, molecule by molecule, with surrounding minerals. In time, the remains of the arthropod are transformed physically and chemically and resemble the surrounding rock.

Some of the most detailed remains of ancient arthropods are preserved in hardened tree sap called amber (AM-bur). Amber comes from the sticky sap, or resin (REH-zin), of trees. Trees produce resin to heal wounds and to defend against insect borers. Insects, spiders, and other organisms became trapped and

Some of the most detailed remains of ancient arthropods are preserved in hardened tree sap called amber. (JLM Visuals. Reproduced by permission.)

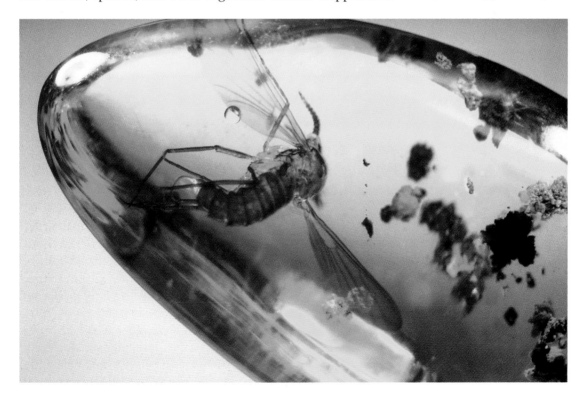

completely encased in the sticky stuff. The resin quickly hardened and eventually fell to the ground, where it was buried by decomposing plants and soil. Storms washed the hardened resin into low-lying areas that were eventually covered by the ocean. These ancient sea bottoms eventually changed into layers of limestone and sandstone that are now filled with scattered bits and chunks of fossilized resin, or amber. Over millions of years, as new mountains and islands formed, the sea bottoms were lifted above sea level, exposing pieces of amber with the ancient remains of arthropods. The oldest known insect fossils in amber are about one hundred twenty million years old.

Only a tiny fraction of all the arthropods that ever lived during ancient times were preserved as fossils. The remains of species living on land were less likely to be preserved than those living in freshwater and marine habitats. Fossilization in stone or amber depends on animals dying in the right place, at the right time, and under the right circumstances. The odds of this all happening are extremely low. Even today arthropods are quickly eaten by other animals or decompose and break up within hours or days of their deaths.

Flights of fancy

Insects are one of only four groups of animals (with pterosaurs, birds, and bats) to have achieved true flight and were the first to take to the air. The power of flight gives many insects the opportunity to find food and mates over wide areas. Flying insects also have the ability to avoid being eaten by other animals and to colonize new and suitable habitats. Birds, bats, and pterosaurs all evolved wings from their forelimbs, or front legs, but insects did not have to give up a pair of legs to fly. So where did insect wings come from?

Based on the study of fossils, the first winged insects appeared between three hundred fifty and three hundred million years ago. Their wings may have evolved from flexible structures that were first used as gills for breathing underwater. Or they may have developed from stiff projections growing out of their midsection, or thorax, and eventually evolved into more flexible, winglike structures. But why did the first insect wings evolve? Did the oldest winged insects use them for gliding through their habitat, or did they use them as solar panels to collect heat to warm their bodies? The discovery of even older fossils of winged insects may help to unravel the mystery.

DRESSED FOR SUCCESS

One way to measure the success of any group of animals is to look at biodiversity (BI-o-dih-VUHR-seh-tee), or the variety of species in a particular place. Another way is to count the numbers of individuals of a particular species. By either measure, arthropods are the most successful group of animals on Earth. The physical features that make them so successful are the size and structure of their bodies. Most arthropods range in length from 0.04 to 0.4 inches (1 to 10 millimeters). This allows them to live in numerous small habitats where larger animals cannot hope to make a living. Furthermore, their bodies are wrapped in a hard, protective, external covering called the exoskeleton (EHK-so-SKEH-leh-tin). Small and armored, arthropods are perfectly suited for living and reproducing on land or in the water.

A suit of armor

The exoskeleton works both as skin and skeleton. It protects the animal from harm as it swims, crawls, burrows, or flies through the habitat, and it provides a means of support for the muscles and internal organs inside. The exoskeleton is made up of several layers that are composed mostly of chitin (KYE-tehn), a complex material that is made of fibers and combines with a protein to make the exoskeleton light, tough, and flexible, just like fiberglass. The surface of the exoskeleton is covered with small pits, spines, and hairlike structures called setae (SIH-tee). Some setae are sensitive to touch and sometimes help to protect the body from injury. In most insects and spiders, a waxy layer covering the exoskeleton helps to maintain the moisture levels inside the body. Millipedes, centipedes, and crustaceans do not have this protection.

The exoskeleton is divided into two or three body regions. Each region is made up of a series of armored plates that are sometimes closely joined together to increase strength or distinctly segmented to maintain flexibility. The appendages (mouthparts, antennae, legs) are jointed, or divided into segments to increase their flexibility. In fact, the name arthropod means "jointed foot." All plates and segments are joined together by a thin, flexible membrane of pure chitin.

The mouthparts of arthropods are made up of two to four pairs of appendages. These appendages come in a variety of forms and are used as lips, jaws, and fangs. Insect jaws may

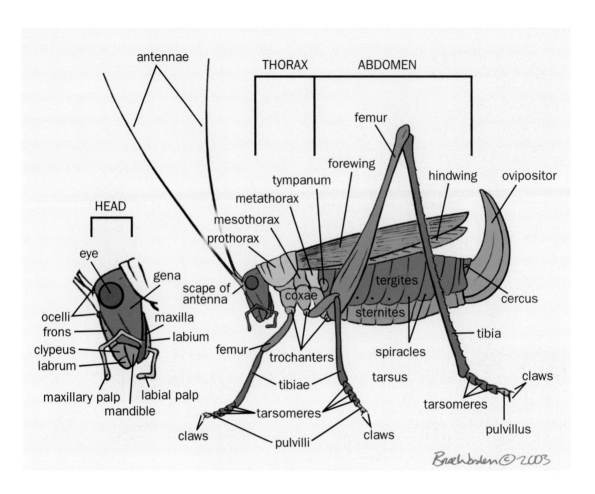

antennae

THORAX   ABDOMEN

femur

forewing

tympanum

hindwing   ovipositor

HEAD

metathorax

mesothorax

prothorax

eye

gena

scape of
antenna

coxae

tergites

cercus

ocelli
frons

maxilla

sternites

clypeus

labium

tibia

labrum

femur

trochanters

spiracles

maxillary palp   labial palp

tibiae

tarsus

claws

mandible

tarsomeres

tarsomeres

claws

pulvilli

claws

pulvillus

Brehborden © 2003

A lateral view showing the
major features of an insect.
(Illustration by Bruce Worden.
Reproduced by permission.)

form piercing-sucking or lapping mouthparts for drinking plant
or animal fluids.

The eyes, if present, are either compound or simple. Compound eyes are made up of several to tens of thousands of individual lenses and are used for seeing images. Some species, as well as all larval insects or young, have only simple eyes, which have just one lens for each eye. Simple eyes are used primarily to distinguish light and dark. One or two pairs of antennae (an-TEH-nee), or sense organs, are covered with setae that are especially sensitive to touch and often have special pits for detecting certain odors.

Adults have three or more pairs of jointed legs and, in many insects, one or two pairs of wings. The legs come in a variety of shapes and are used for running, jumping, climbing, digging, swimming, and grasping prey. The abdomen contains the in-

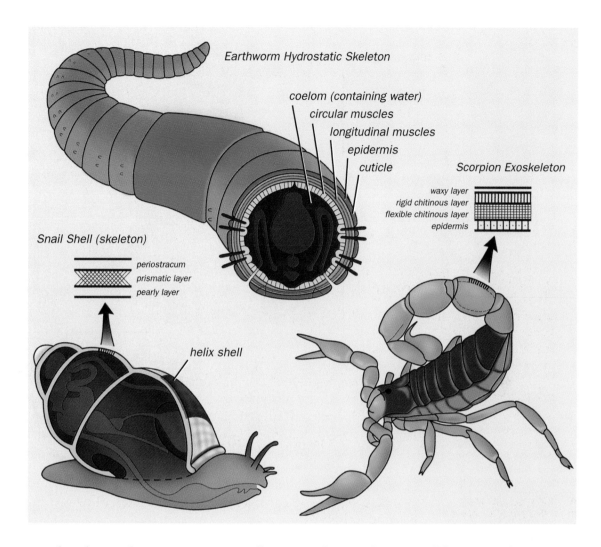

Earthworm Hydrostatic Skeleton

coelom (containing water)
circular muscles
longitudinal muscles
epidermis
cuticle

Scorpion Exoskeleton

waxy layer
rigid chitinous layer
flexible chitinous layer
epidermis

Snail Shell (skeleton)

periostracum
prismatic layer
pearly layer

helix shell

ternal and reproductive organs, as well as special appendages used for defense (as in scorpions), steering (in horseshoe crabs), or spinning silk (as in spiders). The abdomen is distinctly segmented in most arthropods but not in ticks, mites, and nearly all spiders.

Different types of skeletons: external (snail), hydrostatic (earthworm), and jointed (scorpion). (Illustration by Kristen Workman. Reproduced by permission.)

A PEEK INSIDE

Inside arthropod bodies are incredibly powerful muscles that make mouthparts chew, antennae wiggle, legs dig, and wings fly. The nervous system helps to coordinate these and other movements. The brain is located inside the head. Trailing behind the brain is a nerve chord that runs along the entire length

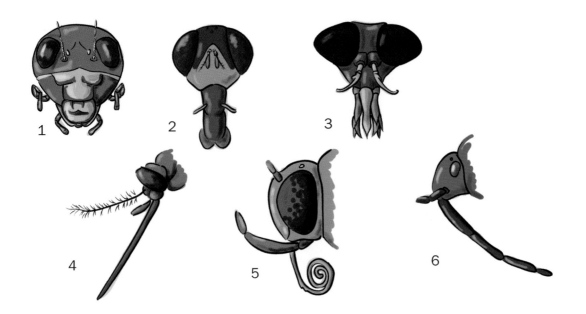

Insects have different mouth parts for feeding. 1. Cricket (chewing); 2. House fly (mopping); 3. Horse fly (piercing and sucking); 4. Mosquito (piercing and sucking); 5. Moth (sucking); 6. Froghopper (piercing and sucking). (Illustration by Ryan Burkhalter. Reproduced by permission.)

of the arthropod's underside. Along the nerve chord are bundles of nerves called ganglia (GANG-lee-uh) that help control the various parts of the body. A pair of ganglia controls each pair of appendages. All abdominal segments have a pair of ganglia except in millipedes, where each segment has two pairs. Most body segments of millipedes are actually two segments joined as one. This is also why millipedes have two pairs of legs on most of their body segments.

The blood of fishes, amphibians, reptiles, birds, and mammals circulates inside arteries and veins. This is called a closed circulatory system. But arthropods have an open circulatory system. They have a tube that runs along their backs. A series of pumps, or hearts, inside the abdomen, or body trunk, pumps the blood forward in the tube. Eventually, it spills out behind the head into various body cavities. The blood usually does not carry oxygen, but it does carry nutrients and chemicals called hormones (HOR-moans) that help the body to function. All the tissues and organs are bathed in blood. The blood eventually moves back to the abdomen where it enters the tube through tiny holes located between the hearts.

Arthropods do not have lungs. The respiratory, or breathing, system of most species living on land is made up of a series of holes and tubes. Oxygen enters the body through a series of

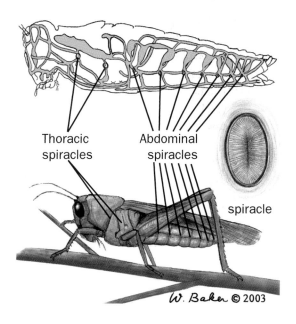

Insect respiratory system. Oxygen and carbon dioxide move through a system of tubes (trachea) that branch to all parts of the body. Air enters via the spiracles on the insects' bodies. (Illustration by Wendy Baker. Reproduced by permission.)

Thoracic spiracles

Abdominal spiracles

spiracle

W. Baker © 2003

holes along the sides of the body called spiracles (SPIH-reh-kuls). Each spiracle is attached to a network of tubes, or trachea (TRAY-key-uh). The trachea carry oxygen throughout the body. Carbon dioxide, a waste product of living tissues, is expelled out of the body through the same system. Some spiders have a tracheal system, but most use book lungs. Book lungs are made up of folded tissue inside the abdomen that resembles the pages of a book. Aquatic insects either trap a bubble of air over their spiracles or use gills or gill-like structures. A very thin layer of exoskeleton covers the gills, allowing dissolved oxygen in the water to pass through and enter the tracheal system. Some species have no respiratory system at all. Instead, oxygen in the water simply seeps in all over their bodies.

GETTING ORGANIZED

Animals are classified into various groups on the basis of having similar features. Sharing these similar features suggests that they share a common ancestor or history. The more features they share, the closer the relationship. Arthropods are grouped in the Phylum Arthropoda (AR-thruh-PO-duh) because they all have the following special features: exoskeletons, segmented bodies, pairs of jointed appendages, open circulatory systems, and a ventral nerve cord that runs down the underside of the animal. Arthropods are further divided into three smaller groups, or subphyla (sub-FAI-leh).

The subphylum Cheliceriformes includes sea spiders, horseshoe crabs, scorpions, spiders, ticks, mites, and their relatives. Their bodies are divided into two major regions, the forebody, sometimes called the cephalothorax (SEH-fe-lo-THO-raeks), and abdomen. The forebody has six pairs of appendages, including the pinchers or grasping arms, claw-like pedipalps (PEH-dih-paelps), and eight walking legs. They never have antennae. The reproductive organs are located at the front or rear of the abdomen. The abdomen sometimes has a tail-like structure that is used as a rudder (horseshoe crabs), a defensive weapon (scorpions), as a sensory organ (whip scorpions), or a silk-producing organ (spiders and mites). There are about sixty-one thousand species, most of which live on land.

The Uniramia includes arthropods with only one pair of antennae and legs that are not branched at their bases. Insects and their relatives have bodies that are divided into three major regions: the head, thorax, and abdomen. The head has five pairs of appendages, including the mouthparts and one pair of antennae. Adults have three pairs of legs and sometimes one or two pairs of wings. Their reproductive organs are located toward the rear of the abdomen.

Centipedes, millipedes, and their relatives have bodies that are divided into two major regions. The head is followed by a long trunk-like body. The head has four pairs of appendages, including the mouthparts and one pair of antennae. Adults have one or two pairs of legs on most body segments. Depending on the species the adults have eleven to 382 pairs of legs. Their reproductive organs are located at the end of the body or just behind the head. There are about 818,000 species of insects, millipedes, centipedes, and their relatives that live on land or in freshwater habitats.

The Crustacea include crabs, lobsters, crayfish, shrimp, barnacles, beach hoppers, pillbugs, and their relatives. Their bodies are divided into two major regions: the head, which is usually covered by a broad shield, or carapace (KARE-a-pays), and the body trunk. The head has five pairs of appendages, including the mouthparts and two pairs of antennae. The appendages of crustaceans are usually branched at their bases. The abdomen may also have paired appendages underneath. The reproductive organs are usually found on the midsection or near the front of the abdomen. There are about sixty-seven thousand species, most of which live in the ocean.

Classifications help scientists sort and identify species, as well as organize and locate information about them. But the system of classification is not carved in stone. As understanding of these animals continues to improve, classifications will also change. Groups will be combined, divided, added, or discarded. This constant state of change is sometimes frustrating, but the goal is to have a classification that reflects the true relationships of all organisms based on their evolutionary history.

TRANSFORMATIONS

Arthropods grow by breaking out of their rigid exoskeletons. Most species molt, or shed their exoskeletons, only as larvae (LAR-vee). Larvae are immature animals that are not able to reproduce. However, crustaceans, arachnids, some insects, and other arthropods will continue to grow and molt throughout their adult lives. Each stage between molts is called an instar (IHN-star). The number of instars varies among species, ranging from three to more than twenty times in insects. The number of larval molts remains the same for each species. With each molt a soft pale body escapes from its old exoskeleton through a special escape hatch. After a few hours, days, or weeks the new exoskeleton darkens and hardens. This process of change and growth is called metamorphosis (MEH-teh-MORE-feh-sihs).

There are four basic types of metamorphosis. Some millipedes and centipedes, as well relatives of insects known as proturans, develop by anamorphosis (ANN-eh-MORE-feh-sihs). Their larvae hatch from eggs with fewer body segments than they will have as adults. Additional segments and legs are added as they molt. When wingless diplurans, springtails, silverfish, and bristletails molt, the only noticeable change is that they are larger. They molt many times as larvae and will continue to molt after they reach adulthood. Grasshoppers, true bugs, dragonflies, and some other winged insects develop by gradual metamorphosis. The larvae strongly resemble the adults when they hatch, but they lack developed wings and reproductive organs. These insects stop molting once they reach the adult stage. Beetles, butterflies, moths, flies, fleas, ants, bees, wasps, and others develop by complete metamorphosis. They have four very distinct stages: egg, larva, pupa, and adult. They do not continue to grow or molt once they reach adulthood.

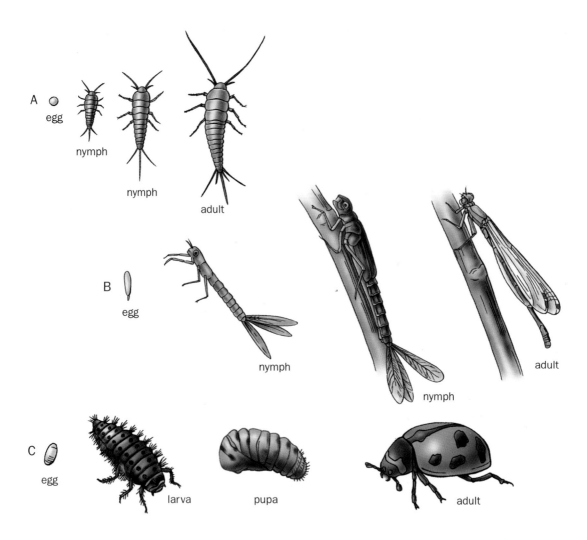

Insect metamorphosis:
A. Ametabolous development;
B. Incomplete metamorphosis;
C. Complete metamorphosis.
(Illustration by Patricia Ferrer.
Reproduced by permission.)

Spiders and other arachnids lay their eggs in a protective sac. The eggs hatch into helpless prelarvae that are unable to move. Their legs are not fully developed, and their bodies show traces of segmentation not visible in the adults. The prelarvae molt into larvae, which still show traces of segmentation on the abdomen but have legs that are more fully developed. The larvae molt into nymphs (nihmfs), or spiderlings. The very active spiderlings leave the egg sac and resemble small versions of the adults. Many arachnids continue to molt after they reach adulthood.

BEHAVIOR

Arthropods engage in all kinds of behaviors that help them to survive and reproduce. They not only have to find food, but they also need to avoid their enemies, find and select mates, and secure a future for their young.

Feeding behavior

Ecologists (ih-KA-luh-jists), scientists who study where and how organisms live, sometimes divide arthropods into different groups based on what they eat. Herbivores (URH-bih-vorz) eat plants, and carnivores (KAR-nih-vorz) eat animal flesh, while omnivores (AM-nih-vorz) eat both plants and animals. Another way to look at the feeding ecology of arthropods is by viewing them as generalists or specialists. For example, generalist herbivores eat all kinds of plants, but specialists feed on only one kind of plant or a small group of closely related species. Parasitoids (PAE-re-SIH-toyds) live and feed inside the bodies of certain kinds of animals (hosts) and eventually kill them. Parasites are also specialists, attacking only certain animal hosts but seldom killing them.

Suitable foods are found by sight, smell, touch, and taste. Herbivores chew or suck fluids from all parts of plants, including roots, trunks, stems, buds, leaves, flowers, fruits, and seeds. Some species even bleed leaves of their sticky or toxic resins before eating them. Many collect a variety of plant materials and store them as food, while others simply use them as mulch for growing their own food. Some predators (PREH-duh-ters) actively hunt their prey, while others sit and wait to ambush them. Spiders build webs that are specifically designed to trap insects and other arthropods. Omnivores are opportunists and eat any-

Centipedes are strictly carnivores and actively hunt for small animals, usually insects. Occasionally larger centipedes will catch and kill a small mammal, such as a young mouse. (Arthur V. Evans. Reproduced by permission.)

thing they find, even scavenging dead plants and animals. Some even feed on the waste products of other animals.

Defense

Insects, spiders, and other arthropods rely on many different strategies to defend themselves against predators. For example, large horned beetles avoid being eaten simply by being large and horned. Some orb-weaving spiders have hard spiny bodies that would make them an unwelcome mouthful even to the hungriest of predators. Millipedes coil up their bodies to protect their delicate heads, legs, and undersides, exposing only a series of hard plates along their backs. Others whip or kick spiny antennae and legs at their attackers. Tarantulas and other spiders rear up, flash their fangs, and adopt threatening poses. If this fails to work, many tarantulas will brush a cloud of painfully itchy hairs off their bodies into the faces of predators. While many arthropods bite, run, jump, burrow, swim, or fly to escape, others simply remain still or fall to the ground to get out of sight. Some rely on the protection of other well-defended species, such as ants.

Many insects and arachnids scavenge dead animals. This female scorpionfly and a mite are picking over the remains of a cricket. (Arthur V. Evans. Reproduced by permission.

Others startle would-be predators by suddenly flashing bright colors or eye spots. Mantids strike out with their spiny front legs to display their bright colors. The hind wings of some grasshoppers and stick insects are also brightly patterned, but they usually remain hidden under the forewings. Moths suddenly spread their plainly patterned forewings to reveal hind wings marked with large "eyes" or bright contrasting bands of color. Centipedes and caterpillars have "false heads" that either direct attacks away from sensitive parts of their bodies or simply confuse predators hoping to make a sneak attack.

Many insects and spiders use camouflage to stay out of sight, blending in with backgrounds of living or dead leaves. (Arthur V. Evans. Reproduced by permission.)

Many insects and spiders use camouflage to stay out of sight, blending in with backgrounds of living or dead leaves. Stick insects, grasshoppers, katydids, and mantids may go a step further by actually having bodies shaped like sticks, stones, leaves, or flowers. Arthropods that conceal themselves by looking like another object, living or dead, are called cryptic (KRIP-tik). They even act like the objects they mimic by remaining very still, although stick and leaf mimics sometimes gently sway back and forth, as if they were in a gentle breeze. Some spiders and caterpillars avoid detection by looking like something unappetizing, such as bird droppings.

Biting, stinging, bad tasting, and foul smelling arthropods are often brightly marked or distinctively colored as a warning to potential predators. The colors, patterns, and body shapes of harmful species, especially ants, bees, and wasps, frequently serve as models for other species that do not bite or sting. Species that resemble each other in color or behavior are called mimics.

The mating game

In some species, males are rare or unknown. The females lay unfertilized eggs that usually develop into more females. This process is called parthenogenesis (PAR-thuh-no-JEH-nuh-sihs). But most arthropods reproduce by mating. Males usually mate as many times as possible, but females mate only once, just a few times, or many times, depending on the species. In some species males and females gather at a food resource, such as a patch of flowers, sapping limbs, decomposing bodies, or piles of dung.

Some males claim these resources as territories and engage in battles with other males to win the favor of a nearby female.

Many males and females find one another by releasing pheromones (FEH-re-moans), chemicals that are especially attractive to members of the opposite sex of the same species. Others use flashing lights or sounds to attract one another. Once they get together, many species engage in courtship behaviors that help them to establish each other's suitability for mating. Courtship may involve biting, grappling, touching, leg waving, wing flapping, flashing mouthparts, and vibrating bodies.

In species that live on land, the male usually grasps the female with his legs or jaws and deposits sperm or a sperm packet directly into her body. These packets not only contain sperm but also provide nutrition for the female so she can produce bigger and better eggs. The act of mating may be brief or last several hours. To prevent the female from mating with other males, some males will remain with their mate until she lays her eggs. In some species, such as honeybees and many spiders, males leave part or all of their reproductive organs in the female's body to block mating attempts by other males.

Other groups of arthropods do not mate directly. For example, male spiders must first transfer their sperm to special containers on their pedipalps before they are ready to mate. They use the pedipalps to put the sperm directly into the female's reproductive organs. Male horseshoe crabs climb on the back of the females and release their sperm onto her eggs as she lays them in the sand. Silverfish males deposit a drop of sperm on the ground and then guide the female over it so she can pick it up with her reproductive organs. Male millipedes, centipedes, scorpions, and other arachnids put their sperm packets on the ground. Then they engage in a variety of courtship behaviors to guide the females over the packets. In some arthropods the females must find these packets without the help of males.

Parental care

Parental care is rare among arthropods. In most species it consists only of a female laying her eggs in places where they will not be eaten or destroyed, preferably near food that is suitable for the young. However, in a few species, the female keeps

Most species lay their eggs somewhere in their habitat. Some prepare special chambers for their eggs. (Arthur V. Evans. Reproduced by permission.)

the eggs inside her body until they hatch or are "born." The eggs are nourished by their own yolks. This type of development is called ovovivipary (O-vo-vai-VIH-pe-ree). Vivipary (vai-VIH-pe-ree) occurs in some flies and parasitic true bugs. The females produce only one or a few eggs at a time and keep them inside their bodies. The eggs are nourished by the mother's body, and the larvae are born alive.

Most species lay their eggs somewhere in their habitat, either singly or in batches. Some species have special egg-laying tubes called ovipositors (O-vih-PA-zih-terz) that place their eggs out of harm's way deep in the soil or wood or inside plant or animal tissues. Others have special glands that allow them to glue their eggs to surfaces or surround them in protective cases. Some species prepare special chambers for their eggs, provide them with all the food the larvae will need to develop, and then leave. Females of a few species guard the eggs until they hatch. Some will even remain with the young for a short period, but the greatest level of parental care is seen in the social insects.

Social behavior

True social behavior is defined by overlapping generations of the same species living and working together to raise their young. They also cooperate in gathering food and defending,

repairing, and expanding the nest. Insects are the only truly social arthropods. Social insects include all termites and ants but only some bees and wasps. They live in colonies with up to one million individuals. The tasks within each colony are divided among distinctly different forms or castes. The castes include workers, soldiers, and reproductives (queens and males).

Workers form the majority of the colony. They care for the young and the queen and perform all other tasks in the nest. They divide the labor among themselves on the basis of age or size. Some ants and termites also have a soldier caste. Soldiers are usually larger than the workers and sometimes equipped with powerful jaws to drive away intruders. Both workers and soldiers are sterile and cannot reproduce. The workers and soldiers of ants, bees, and wasps are always sterile females, but in termites they are male or female.

The reproductive caste consists of queens and males. Each colony has at least one queen, and she is usually the mother of the entire colony. She may live many years, laying millions of eggs in her lifetime. Males are short-lived and usually die after mating with the queen. However, termite kings usually stay with the queen long after they mate.

Social insects include all termites and ants but only some bees and wasps. (Arthur V. Evans. Reproduced by permission.)

Colony members communicate with pheromones to identify nest mates, recruit other members of the colony to find food or defend the nest, and to coordinate other activities. For example, honeybee queens use a pheromone called queen substance to hold the colony together. Workers pick up the pheromone as they lick and groom the queen. As they feed one another, they pass it along to other workers in the colony. The queen substance "tells" the workers to feed and care for the queen and her eggs and lets all the members of the colony know that she is alive and well. Every worker in the colony will know if their queen has died within a day, even though only a few workers will have actually had contact with the body.

Other arthropods occasionally gather in groups to feed, mate, or temporarily guard their young, but they are not truly social. There are about 40 species of spiders that live in groups in large webs and feed together. A huntsman spider, *Delena cancerides*, lives under bark in groups of up to three hundred individuals. These groups consist mainly of young spiders with just a few adults. They work together to attack and kill insect prey, as well as defend their shelter against spiders from other colonies.

DANCES WITH PLANTS

Arthropods, especially insects, have had a long and close relationship with flowering plants that dates back between 135 and sixty-five million years ago. From the plant's point of view this relationship is both negative and positive. A negative example is their relationship with herbivorous insects. As herbivores, insects have strongly influenced the evolution of flowering plants. Over millions of years, plants have evolved several ways of defending themselves against insects. Many have developed bad-tasting chemicals, or toxins (TAK-sihns), that discourage herbivorous insects from eating their stems and leaves. Those plants that survived insect attacks were able to pass along their characteristics to the next generation through their seeds. At the same time, the defensive strategies of plants have influenced the evolution of insects. They have evolved systems within their bodies that breakdown these toxins into harmless chemicals so they can continue to eat the plant. Those insects that were able to get enough food were able to pass their characteristics on to the next generation through their eggs. Over time, plants and insects continued to change, or evolve, into new species as they attempt to overcome the attacks and defenses of the other. The mutual influence that plants and insects have over each other's evolution continues today and is called coevolution (ko-EH-vuh-LU-shun).

From a plant's point of view, pollination is an example of a positive interaction with insects. Plants produce flowers with nectar and more pollen than they need to reproduce to attract insects. Flowers are like brightly colored, sweet-smelling road signs that encourage insect pollinators to stop and visit. These pollinators either accidentally or purposefully collect pollen from the flower. Many flowers depend on bees, flies, beetles, and thrips to carry their pollen from one flower to another so their seeds will develop. Some species of orchids rely on specific insects to pollinate them. In fact, the flowers of some species mimic female wasps. Male wasps pollinate the flowers as they attempt to "mate" with the flower. This very special type of interaction between a plant and an insect is another example of coevolution.

BENEFICIAL INSECTS AND SPIDERS

People depend on insects to pollinate their crops, ensuring that they have plenty of food, fiber, and other useful products. Honeybees are not only valued for their pollination services but also for their honey and wax. Silk from the cocoons of the silk moth, *Bombyx mori*, has been harvested for centuries. Each caterpillar must eat 125 pounds (56.7 kilograms) of mulberry leaves before it can spin a cocoon. About seventeen hundred cocoons are required to make one dress. China and Japan are the world's largest producers of silk.

Beekeeping and silkworm culture were the first forms of insect farming, but today many other insects are raised and sold for use as research animals, fish bait, and pet food. Others are used to combat weeds and insect pests. Butterflies and other tropical insects are raised and shipped alive to insect zoos and butterfly houses around the world. Money earned by butterfly farmers in Central and South America, Malaysia, and Papua New Guinea is used to support families, to maintain the farm, and to preserve or improve butterfly habitats.

Grasshoppers, termites, beetles, caterpillars, and crustaceans are important sources of food for humans and are even considered delicacies in many parts of the world. They are an excellent source of fat and protein. Western European culture has largely ignored insects as food but considers lobster, crab, and shrimp as delicacies.

Every species of arthropod is a flying, walking, or swimming pharmacy filled with potentially useful medicines and other chemical compounds. For example, venoms from insect stings are used to treat patients with rheumatism (RU-me-TIH-zem), a disease that affects the joints. The venom helps to increase blood flow to the diseased joints and stops the pain.

Arthropods also provide an early warning system for detecting changes in the environment caused by habitat destruction, pollution, and other environmental disturbances. Aquatic insects and arthropods living in the ocean are especially sensitive to even the smallest changes in water temperature and chemistry. The presence or absence of a particular species may demonstrate that a particular habitat is polluted as a result of illegal dumping, pesticides from nearby agricultural fields, or chemical waste from mining operations.

INSECTS AND SPIDERS AS SYMBOLS

People around the world have used insects as symbols to explain how the world began. There is a tribe in South America that believes a beetle created the world and, from the grains of sand left over, made men and women. In the American Southwest the Hopis believed that the world began through the activities of Spider Woman, the Earth Goddess. The sacred scarab beetle appeared in wall paintings and carvings and played an important role in the religious lives of the early Egyptians. Early Christians used insects as symbols of evil and wickedness, but eastern cultures, especially in China and Japan, often used them to signify good luck. The ancient Greeks used insects and spiders in their plays and fables about good and evil.

INSECTS AND SPIDERS IN ARTS AND CRAFTS AND IN LITERATURE

Images of insects have appeared on 6,000-year-old cave paintings, as well as on the walls of ancient Egyptian tombs. The Egyptians wore sacred scarab carvings and other insect ornaments. The ancient Greeks used insect images on jewelry and coins. Insects were also used to adorn decorative boxes, bowls, and writing sets in the Middle Ages. The hard and tough bodies of beetles have long been used to make pendants and earrings. Today, boxed collections of large tropical species are sold to tourists as decorative pieces.

Ants, bees, fleas, flies, grasshoppers, spiders, and scorpions are frequently mentioned in the Bible. Images of arthropods were once used to decorate the brightly painted borders of other important religious books and papers. They have influenced language with such words as lousy, nitpicker, grubby, and beetle-browed. Beetles have also inspired the names of a world-famous rock group and a well-known German automobile.

INSECTS AND SPIDERS AS PESTS

Insects are humanity's greatest competitors and cause huge economic losses when they feed on timber, stored foods, pastures, and crops. Termites and other insects infest and weaken wood used to build homes, businesses, floors, cabinets, and furniture. The larvae of clothes moths and carpet beetles destroy woolen clothing, rugs, and hides. Mites, moths, beetles, and other insects invade homes and infest stored foods and destroy books and other paper products. Crops lost to insect damage cause enormous economic hardship and may lead to starvation and death among hundreds or thousands of people. One-third to one-half of all food grown worldwide is lost to damage caused by insects and mites, not only by devouring the foliage but also by infecting plants with diseases.

Arthropods not only eat people's belongings, they also attack human bodies. The bites of blood-feeding mosquitoes, flies, fleas, lice, and ticks are not only irritating, they are also responsible for spreading diseases that can infect and kill people, pets, and farm animals. Over the centuries more people have died from diseases carried by arthropods than any other reason. Even today, more people die from malaria and yellow fever, diseases transmitted by mosquitoes, than from HIV/AIDS, cancer, accidents, and wars. Spiders, millipedes, centipedes, and other arthropods are not often pests but are considered nuisances when they enter homes. The venomous bites of some spiders and centipedes may be painful but are seldom life-threatening for healthy adults.

These and other pests are effectively controlled by integrated pest management, or IPM. IPM includes plowing fields to kill pests in the ground, rotating crops so that they will not have anything to eat, or planting other crops nearby that will give their enemies a place to live and prosper. Whenever possible, natural enemies are used to combat pests instead of pesticides. The use of predators, parasitoids, and diseases is called biological control. Spiders might be considered biological controls in some fields, but most species tend to eat anything they can catch, not just the pest. IPM depends on accurate identification of the pest and a thorough knowledge of its life history so that control efforts can be directed at the pest's most vulnerable life stages. However, if not used wisely, any pest control method may harm other species or their habitats.

CONSERVATION

Habitat destruction is the number one threat to all insects, spiders, and their relatives. Pollution, pesticides, land development, logging, fires, cattle grazing, and violent storms are just some of the events that damage or destroy their habitats. Introduced, or exotic, plants and animals can also have devastating effects. They compete with native arthropods for food and space. Native arthropods are usually capable of dealing with organisms that they have evolved with over millions of years, but they are often defenseless against exotic predators and diseases.

Loss of habitat and competition with exotic species affect the availability of food, mates, and egg-laying and nesting sites. The reduction or loss of any one of these resources can make a species vulnerable to extinction (ehk-STINGK-shun). Extinct species have completely died out and will never again appear on Earth. Arthropods that are widely distributed or feed on a variety of plants or animals are less likely to become extinct, but those living in small fragile habitats with specialized feeding habits are more likely to become extinct when their habitats are disturbed or destroyed. The fossil record shows that extinction is a natural process. Yet today, the loss of thousands of species of plants and animals each year, mostly arthropods, is not the result of natural events but is a direct result of human activities.

Scientists, politicians, and concerned citizens around the world have joined together to establish laws that protect arthropods and their habitats. The United States Fish and Wildlife Service helps to protect species threatened with extinction. They list seventy-seven species of arthropods as Threatened or Endangered, including forty-four insects (mostly butterflies), twelve arachnids, and twenty-one crustaceans. Some countries set aside land as preserves specifically to protect arthropods and their habitats.

The World Conservation Union (IUCN) publishes a list of species threatened by extinction. It places species in the categories Extinct, Extinct in the Wild, Critically Endangered, Endangered, Vulnerable, Near Threatened, Data Deficient, or Least Concern. In 2003 the list included 1,252 species of insects, spiders, and other arthropods. The sad fact is that scientists will probably never know just how many arthropod species are threatened with extinction and need protection. For example, tropical rainforest and coral reef habitats are disappearing so quickly that scientists have little or no time to collect and study their arthropod species before they are lost forever. Humanity's health and well-being depend on preserving all life, not just species that are big, pretty, furry, or feathered. Maybe you can be one of the scientists of the future that helps to save an insect or spider from becoming extinct.

FOR MORE INFORMATION

Books:

Brusca, R. C., and G. J. Brusca. *Invertebrates. Second edition.* Sunderland, MA: Sinauer Associates, Inc., 2003.

Craig, S. F., D. A. Thoney, and N. Schlager, editors. *Grzimek's Animal Life Encyclopedia*. Second Edition. Volume 2: *Protostomes*. Farmington, MI: Thomson Gale, 2003.

Eisner, T. *For Love of Insects*. Cambridge, MA: Harvard University Press, 2003.

Evans, A. V., R. W. Garrison, and N. Schlager, editors. *Grzimek's Animal Life Encyclopedia*. Second Edition. Volume 3: *Insects*. Farmington, MI: Thomson Gale, 2003.

Imes, R. *The Practical Entomologist*. New York: Simon & Schuster Inc., 1991.

Kritsky, G., and R. Cherry. *Insect Mythology*. San Jose, CA: Writers Club Press, 2000.

Menzel, P. *Man Eating Bugs. The Art and Science of Eating Bugs*. Berkeley, CA: Ten Speed Press, 1998.

O'Toole, C. *Alien Empire*. London: BBC Books, 1995.

Poinar, G., and R. Poinar. *The Quest for Life in Amber*. Reading, MA: Addison-Wesley Publishing Company, 1994.

Preston-Mafham, R., and K. Preston-Mafham. *The Encyclopedia of Land Invertebrate Behaviour*. Cambridge, MA: The MIT Press, 1993.

Tavoloacci, J., editor. *Insects and Spiders of the World*. New York: Marshall Cavendish, 2003.

Periodicals:

Evans, A. V. "Arthropods on Parade." *Critters USA 2000 Annual* 5 (2000): 67–75.

Hogue, C. L. "Cultural Entomology." *Annual Review of Entomology* 32 (1987): 181–199.

Web sites:

"Arthropoda." http://paleo.cortland.edu/tutorial/Arthropods/arthropods.htm (accessed on November 19, 2004).

"Directory of Entomological Societies." http://www.sciref.org/links/EntDept/index.htm (accessed on November 19, 2004).

"Directory of Entomology Departments and Institutes." http://www.sciref.org/links/EntSoc/intro.htm (accessed on November 19, 2004).

"Introduction to the Arthropods." http://www.ucmp.berkeley.edu/arthropoda/arthropoda.html (accessed on November 19, 2004).

"Information on Arachnids." The American Entomological Society. http://www.americanarachnology.org/AAS_information .html (accessed on November 19, 2004).

"Insects in Human Culture." Cultural Entomology. http://www .insects.org/ced/ (accessed on November 19, 2004).

"Insects on WWW." http://www.isis.vt.edu/~fanjun/text/Links .html (accessed on November 19, 2004).

"Phylum Arthropoda." http://animaldiversity.ummz.umich.edu/ site/accounts/information/Arthropoda.html (accessed on November 19, 2004).

Videos:

Alien Empire. New York: Time Life Videos, 1995.

WEBSPINNERS
Embioptera

Class: Insecta
Order: Embioptera
Number of families: 8 families

PHYSICAL CHARACTERISTICS

Webspinners are small to medium insects, ranging from 0.06 to 0.78 inches (1.5 to 20 millimeters) in length. They have long, narrow bodies that are usually brown or black in color. Their distinctive head has chewing mouthparts that are directed forward. The antennae (an-TEH-nee), or sense organs, are long and threadlike. They have compound eyes, with each eye having multiple lenses, but no simple eyes, each with a single lens.

The legs are short and thick. Both adults and larvae (LAR-vee), or the developing young form of the animal, are easily distinguished from other insects by their enlarged front feet. These feet contain about one hundred silk glands. The glands are used to spin silk into a network of narrow, hollow tubes, or galleries, that make up the webspinner's home. Their legs are built in such a way that they can move forward and backward with equal agility and speed. Both winged and wingless males may occur in the same species, but the larvae and females are always wingless. All four of the male's wings are similar in size and shape. In flight the wings stiffen through increased blood pressure within special chambers inside each wing. At rest the chambers deflate and the wings lay flat over the body. They are capable of bending or crumpling at any point without damage and are easily bent forward to allow for easy backward movement through the narrow galleries.

The abdomen appears ten-segmented. The eleventh segment is small and difficult to see. The abdomen ends in a pair of short, fingerlike projections bristling with tiny hairs. These

phylum
class
subclass
● **order**
monotypic order
suborder
family

structures function like antennae and help to guide their backward movement within the galleries.

GEOGRAPHIC RANGE

There are about three hundred species of webspinners known worldwide, but it has been estimated that there may be as many as two thousand. There are thirteen species found across the southern United States. Webspinners are found on all continents, except Antarctica. Most species live in tropical or subtropical climates. There are usually very few or no species living on remote islands. Some species have spread to several continents through overseas trade.

HABITAT

Webspinners build their silk galleries on exposed bark or rock surfaces in humid habitats or underneath bark, stones, or leaf litter. Others live in crevices (KREH-vuh-ses) or cracks in bark, soil, rocks, or termite mounds. Galleries are also found on hanging moss in mountain rainforests.

DIET

Larval and adult female webspinners feed mostly on vegetable matter, including moss, lichens (LIE-kuhns), dead leaves, and old bark. Adult males do not feed.

BEHAVIOR AND REPRODUCTION

Webspinners spend most of their lives inside their silk galleries. The galleries maintain a moist environment, provide clear routes to food sources, and serve as shelters from predators (PREH-duh-ters), or animals that hunt other animals for food. The galleries are slightly wider than the webspinners to allow the sensory hairs covering their bodies to remain in constant contact with the walls. Some species add bits of vegetable materials and their own waste to the outside gallery walls to provide additional camouflage and protection. Both larvae and adults are capable of spinning silk, and the galleries are continuously expanded over or into new food supplies. Webspinners live in groups with one or more adult females and their young. When threatened, they will retreat backwards into the silken tubes or, on occasion, pretend to be dead.

On warm afternoons or after the first rains following the dry season, winged males take to the air in search of mates. Mating takes place within the safety of the gallery. Males use their mouthparts to hold the female's head while mating. Because of their lack of mobility wingless or reduced-winged males often mate with their sisters. Males die soon afterward, and the females lay a single layer of eggs in a batch in the gallery. In some species, the females are able to reproduce by parthenogenesis (PAR-thuh-no-JEH-nuh-sihs), a process where the young develop from unfertilized eggs. Females guard their eggs and young. In some species, females coat their eggs with their own waste and chewed up bits of vegetable material, while others move the eggs about inside the galleries. The young strongly resemble the adults and develop gradually through a series of molts, or shedding of their exoskeleton, or hard outer covering. Wing pads develop only in the male larvae of winged species.

WEBSPINNERS AND PEOPLE

Because most species are very secretive, spending most of their lives in silk galleries, webspinners are hardly noticed by humans. They are never considered pests because they feed on dead vegetable matter.

CONSERVATION STATUS

No webspinner is listed as endangered or threatened.

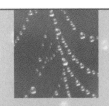

DR. WEBSPINNER

For more than 60 years, Dr. Edward S. Ross, Curator Emeritus at the California Academy of Sciences in San Francisco, has devoted his life to the study of webspinners. He has traveled thousands of miles on every continent that webspinners call home. Over the years he has collected more than 300,000 specimens, representing about 1,000 species. Of these, approximately 750 are new to science. Dr. Ross has maintained hundreds of living colonies of webspinners in his laboratory to study and photograph their behavior.

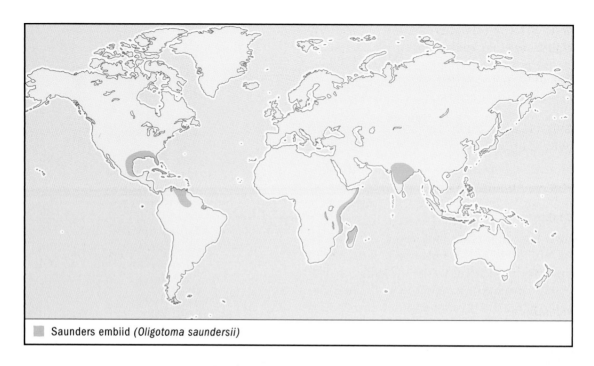

Saunders embiid (*Oligotoma saundersii*)

SAUNDERS EMBIID
Oligotoma saundersii

Physical characteristics: Adults measure 0.35 to 0.5 inches (8.9 to 12.7 millimeters) in length. Males have toothed jaws and reddish brown bodies, while the females are chocolate brown.

Geographic range: This species is native to north central India but is now widespread throughout the tropical regions of the world, as well as parts of the southern United States and Southeast Asia.

Habitat: This species is commonly found on trunks of rainforest trees, as well as on royal palms in gardens and parks.

Diet: They eat lichens (LIE-kuhns) or mosses and algae (AL-jee), tiny plantlike organisms, growing on the bark of tree trunks.

Behavior and reproduction: This species lives in colonies made up primarily of mothers and their offspring. The females guard the eggs. Gallery surfaces are almost completely camouflaged with webspinner waste or finely chewed pieces of wood and bark. Winged males are commonly attracted to lights.

Saunders embiids and people: This species does not impact humans or their activities.

Conservation status: This species is not endangered or threatened ■

FOR MORE INFORMATION

Books:

Ross, E. S. "Embiidina (Embioptera, Webspinners)." In *Encyclopedia of Insects*, edited by V. H. Resh and R. T. Cardé. San Diego: Academic Press/Elsevier Science, 2003.

Periodicals:

Edgerly, J. S. "Maternal Behavior of a Webspinner (Order Embiidina)." *Ecological Entomology* 12 (1987): 1–11.

Valentine, B. D. "Grooming Behavior in Embioptera and Zoraptera (Insecta)." *Ohio Journal of Science* 86 (1986): 150–152.

Web sites:

"Embioptera." Department of Entomology, North Carolina State University. http://www.cals.ncsu.edu/course/ent425/copendium/webspi~1.html (accessed on September 27, 2004).

"Embioptera." *Ecowatch.* http://www.ento.csiro.au/Ecowatch/Insects_Invertebrates/embioptera.htm (accessed on September 27, 2004).

This species lives in colonies made up primarily of mothers and their offspring. The females (like that pictured here) guard the eggs. (Illustration by John Megahan. Reproduced by permission.)

order

PHYSICAL CHARACTERISTICS

Angel insects are small, ranging from 0.08 to 0.16 inches (2 to 4 millimeters) in length. They are long, somewhat flattened brown or black insects resembling termites. Their distinctive and triangular heads have chewing mouthparts with toothed jaws that are directed downward. The antennae (an-TEH-nee), or sense organs, have nine beadlike segments. All three segments of the thorax, or midsection, are distinctive.

Both males and females of each species have winged and wingless forms. Wingless angel insects are the most common form. They are pale and blind. Winged forms are darker and have compound eyes, or eyes with many lenses, and three simple eyes, or eyes with only one lens each. Winged females are usually more common than winged males. When present, the wings are long, broad, and have very few veins. The hind wings are shorter than the forewings and have fewer veins. At rest they fold their four wings flat over their backs. Like termites, they shed their wings easily, leaving four small stubs behind.

The front and middle legs of angel insects are similar to one another. The thighs of the back legs are slightly enlarged and have a row of thick spines underneath. The feet have two segments and are tipped with a pair of claws. The abdomen of all angle insects is broadly attached to the thorax, giving them a thick-waisted appearance. The short abdomen is oval in shape and ten-segmented. The tip has a pair of projections, each made up of a single segment. Each of these projections has a single, long bristle.

The larvae (LAR-vee), or young form of the animal that must change in form before becoming adults, are pale creamy brown and resemble wingless adults. Unlike the adults, the larvae have eight-segmented antennae. There are two different kinds of larvae that develop into winged or wingless adults.

GEOGRAPHIC RANGE

There are thirty-three species of angel insects worldwide. Angel insects are found on all continents, except Australia and Antarctica. Most species live in the New World tropics, but other species are known from North America, Southeast Asia, Africa, or the Pacific islands. Three species are found in the United States, including Hawaii.

HABITAT

Angel insects are found in warm, moist habitats, usually under the bark of dead, rotten logs. In the eastern United States, they also have been found in piles of sawdust in lumber mills. They are sometimes found with termites. Winged individuals are sometimes attracted to lights at night.

DIET

They feed on various parts of funguses or scavenge small, dead worms, insects, and mites. In captivity they will eat crushed yeast, rat chow, and sometimes each other.

BEHAVIOR AND REPRODUCTION

Angel insects live in groups that are probably founded by a single female. They may have a well-defined social structure. Larger, older males dominate these colonies. They will either avoid other males or engage in head butting, grappling, chasing, and kicking. Angel insects spend a great deal of time grooming themselves and each other.

Winged angel insects are carried over wide distances by wind currents. This explains the presence of some species on isolated islands out in the ocean. After finding a suitable habitat, winged individuals seek the shelter of a rotten log and soon shed their wings. Adults with wing stumps are frequently found in young colonies.

Zorapterans usually reproduce by mating, but males are sometimes very rare. Females of a Panamanian species usually reproduce by parthenogenesis (PAR-thuh-no-JEH-nuh-sihs), a

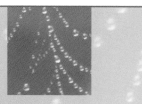

process where the young develop from unfertilized eggs. However, they will also mate with males on those occasions when they meet. Males are larger than females and sometimes fight each other before they can mate with nearby females. Females may mate every few days, either with the same male or with a variety of partners.

In another Central American species, males do not dominate the colonies. During courtship the male presents the female with a drop of liquid produced from a gland on his head. Males and females touch each other with their antennae before mating. Mating is brief but may occur several times, one right after the other.

Angel insects guard their eggs and cover them with chewed bits of food. Eggs take several weeks to hatch. The larvae closely resemble the adults but lack wings and are not capable of reproduction. They develop gradually and molt, or shed their exoskeletons or hard outer coverings, four or five times before reaching adulthood. Adults live for about three months.

ANGEL INSECTS AND PEOPLE

Angel insects do not impact people or their activities.

CONSERVATION STATUS

No species of angel insects are endangered or threatened. The entire order is poorly known and many species are known only from single individuals. There has been some concern expressed for the Hawaiian species because of the loss of habitat. Unfortunately, there are no estimates of the population size of this or any other species, and it is impossible to say whether or not their populations are shrinking or growing in size.

Hubbard's angel insect *(Zorotypus hubbardi)*

HUBBARD'S ANGEL INSECT
Zorotypus hubbardi

Physical characteristics: This species resembles a leggy, medium to dark brown termite. They are small, ranging in size from 0.10 to 0.11 inches (2.6 to 2.9 millimeters) in length.

Geographic range: This species is found in the Eastern United States, from Pennsylvania and Maryland, south to Florida, and west to Iowa and Texas. Its wide distribution in North America is thought to be, at least partially, the result of accidental introductions by humans.

Habitat: They are found under the bark of moist logs and old sawdust piles in lumber mills.

Diet: They eat bits of funguses and scavenge pieces of dead small insects and mites.

Behavior and reproduction: They live in colonies numbering 15 to 120 individuals. Some colonies may live for several years.

This species reproduces either by mating or by parthenogenesis.

Hubbard's angel insects and people: This species is small, secretive, and seldom if ever noticed by people.

Conservation status: This species is not endangered or threatened. ∎

FOR MORE INFORMATION

Books:

Tavolacci, J., ed. *Insects and Spiders of the World.* Volume 10: *Wandering spider-Zorapteran.* New York: Marshall Cavendish, 2003.

Periodicals:

Gurney, A. B. "A Synopsis of the Order Zoraptera, with Notes on the Biology of *Zorotypus hubbardi* Caudell." *Proceedings of the Entomological Society of Washington* 40 (1938): 57–87.

Valentine, B. D. "Grooming Behavior in Embioptera and Zoraptera (Insecta)." *Ohio Journal of Science* 86, no. 4 (1986): 150–152.

Web sites:

Zoraptera. http://www.cals.ncsu.edu/course/ent425/compendium/zorapt.html (accessed on October 4, 2004).

The Zoraptera Data Base. http://www.famu.org/zoraptera/links.html (accessed on October 4, 2004).

order

phylum

class

subclass

● **order**

monotypic order

suborder

family

PHYSICAL CHARACTERISTICS

Most psocids (SO-sids) are small, ranging from 0.04 to 0.4 inches (1 to 10 millimeters) in length. They are usually brownish or whitish with black markings, but some tropical species are brightly colored with distinctive markings. The large and distinctive head has small to bulging compound eyes, with each eye made up of multiple lenses. The antennae (an-TEH-nee), or sense organs, are long and threadlike. The chewing mouthparts are directed downward and include parts that are sharp and pointed. The front of the head is usually swollen to make room inside for special muscles that control the part of the mouth known as the sucking pump. The thorax or midsection, especially the first segment, is usually narrower than the head or abdomen. Most adult psocids have four wings that are fully developed and are held like a roof over the body when at rest. Some species have wings that are reduced in size or absent altogether. The legs are usually slender, but in some species the back legs are swollen to help with jumping or crawling backward. The relatively large abdomen is eleven-segmented.

GEOGRAPHIC RANGE

Psocids are found on all continents, including Antarctica. There are 4,408 species of psocids worldwide, mostly in the tropics. About 260 species occur in the United States and Canada.

HABITAT

Psocids live in a wide variety of habitats on land. In spite of the common names that include the word "louse," these insects do not live on other animals. They are most common on dead or living leaves, on stone or bark surfaces, and in leaf litter. Some species prefer living in caves; others are known to bore into wood. A few species of psocids are common in homes and buildings, especially where food is stored.

DIET

Psocids eat lichen (LIE-kuhn) or mosses, funguses, and other bits of plant and animal tissues. They will even feed on the skin flakes of humans and their animals. Some species scavenge dead insects or eat their eggs.

BEHAVIOR AND REPRODUCTION

Most psocids spend their time living alone. However, the larvae (LAR-vee), or young of an animal that must change form before becoming adults, of some species gather together to form colonies. Some species produce silk to make nests of various shapes and sizes. These nests may have one to many individuals living inside. Sound production in adult psocids is widely known and is thought to be a part of their courtship behavior.

Most psocids reproduce by mating, with males transferring sperm or sperm packets directly into the reproductive organs of the female. However, reproduction by parthenogenesis (PAR-thuh-no-JEH-nuh-sihs), the development of young from unfertilized eggs, is widespread. Parthenogenetic species produce only females. Eggs are laid singly or in groups. They are placed in the open, covered with silk webbing or with psocid waste material. A few species are viviparous (VAI-vih-pe-rus), or give live birth. The larvae hatch from eggs using a specialized egg-burster. The egg-burster is a bladelike or sawlike structure on the head that cuts through the eggshell as the young larva rocks back and forth inside. The larvae closely resemble the adults but lack wings and are unable to reproduce. They usually molt, or shed their exoskeletons or hard outer coverings, four or five times in four to six weeks before reaching adulthood. Some species molt only three or four times.

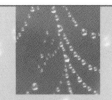

BOOKISH BOOK LICE

Warm, damp homes, offices, and other buildings are perfect habitats for book lice. They forage for food in cellars, furniture stuffing, and inside food storage areas. Sometimes they will even eat the glue behind peeling wallpaper. They are particularly fond of libraries, nibbling the glue used in book bindings as well as the funguses that grow on the pages of books. Their feeding activities can cause great damage to old and rare books and papers.

PSOCIDS AND PEOPLE

Most psocids live in the wild and are seldom, if ever, noticed by humans. However, species common in homes are often considered household pests. They can reproduce rapidly under warm, humid conditions and will become serious pests in foods stored in cupboards and pantries. These species are known to cause sneezing, coughing, itching, and rashes, as well as asthma attacks in sensitive people.

CONSERVATION STATUS

No species of psocids is endangered or threatened. Still, many species, especially those living only on single islands or in caves, could easily become threatened by habitat destruction due to bad weather or human activities.

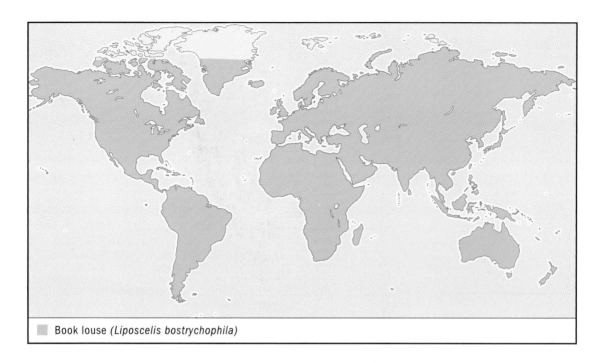

Book louse (*Liposcelis bostrychophila*)

BOOK LOUSE
Liposcelis bostrychophila

Physical characteristics: Book lice are small, about 0.04 inches (1 millimeter) in length. They are wingless, somewhat flattened, and are pale brown in color. Each compound eye is made up of seven lenses.

Geographic range: They are found on all continents.

Habitat: Book lice are commonly found in homes and businesses where foods are stored. They also occur in the wild in the nests of birds and other animals.

Diet: They eat funguses and other bits of plant and animal materials.

Behavior and reproduction: Different populations vary in size, color, egg production, and tolerance to insecticides.

Reproduction is by parthenogenesis only. Eggs are laid singly or in small batches and covered with a powdery dust. The larvae molt four times before reaching adulthood.

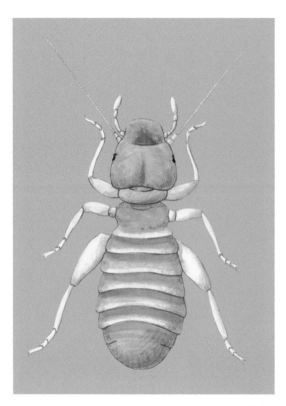

Book lice are considered a nuisance when they infest stored foods and libraries. Their presence in the home may also set off allergy and asthma attacks. (Illustration by Barbara Duperron. Reproduced by permission.)

Book lice and people: Book lice are considered a nuisance when they infest stored foods and libraries. Their presence in the home may also set off allergy and asthma attacks.

Conservation status: This species is not endangered or threatened. ∎

FOR MORE INFORMATION

Books:

Mockford, E. L. "North American Psocoptera." In *Flora & Fauna Handbook*, No. 10. Gainesville, FL: Sandhill Crane Press, 1993.

Tavolacci, J., editor. *Insects and Spiders of the World.* Volume 2: *Beetle-Carpet Beetle.* New York: Marshall Cavendish, 2003.

Web sites:

Psocids as Pests. http://www.kcl.ac.uk/ip/bryanturner/other/indexpsocids.html (accessed on October 5, 2004).

"Psocoptera. Book lice." Ecowatch. http://www.ento.csiro.au/Ecowatch/Insects_Invertebrates/psocoptera.htm (accessed on October 5, 2004)

Psocoptera. Psocids, barklice, booklice. http://www.cals.ncsu.edu/course/ent425/compendium/psocop1.html (accessed on October 5, 2004).

order
CHAPTER

PHYSICAL CHARACTERISTICS

Lice are small, flattened, wingless insects measuring 0.01 to 0.4 inches (0.3 to 11 millimeters) in length. Females are typically larger than males. Many species are pale whitish or yellowish, while other species are brown or black. Some species have color patterns that help them to blend in with the fur or feathers of the animal on which they live. Their heads are broad and blunt to narrow with a snout. They have short antennae (an-TEH-nee), or sense organs, with only three to five segments, and no simple eyes. Compound eyes, eyes with multiple lenses, are either very small or absent. The mouthparts are directed forward. Chewing lice have well-developed jaws that either open from side to side or up and down. In most sucking lice the jaws are entirely absent, although some species have greatly reduced jaws inside their heads. The abdomen has eight to ten segments, depending on the species.

The flattened bodies are perfect for moving in the narrow spaces between feathers and fur, and the short, strong legs have one or two claws that help them to cling. The legs of most sucking lice have a single claw that clamps onto hair shafts. This reduces their chances of being removed when the animal cleans and grooms itself.

GEOGRAPHIC RANGE

Chewing and sucking lice are found on all continents, including Antarctica. The distribution of lice is roughly similar to that of the birds and mammals on which they live. However, their distribution within the host population is not uniform. They are usually quite patchy or concentrated in some areas. There are 4,927 species of lice worldwide, with about 780 species in the United States and Canada.

HABITAT

Chewing and sucking lice are ectoparasites (EHK-teh-PAE-rih-saits), organisms that live on the outside of their host organism. All species spend their entire lives on the body of the host animal. They require the constant temperature and moisture of this habitat to feed and reproduce. Most species of lice are found only on a single kind of host or on small groups of closely related species.

More than 4,300 species of chewing lice have been found on 3,910 different kinds of animals, including 3,508 species of birds and 402 species of mammals. All orders and most families of birds have chewing lice. Five hundred and forty-three species of sucking lice have been found on 812 species of mammals. Mammals that do not have lice include bats, whales, dolphins, dugongs, manatees, pangolins, echidnas, and platypuses.

Although the host body would seem to be a uniform habitat, it is actually a series of smaller habitats that differ slightly in terms of temperature and moisture. For example, the different parts of a bird's body, such as the head, back, wings, and rump, are completely different habitats from the viewpoint of a louse. These different habitats might allow several species of lice with slightly different temperature and humidity requirements to live on the same host animal without having to compete with one another directly for food and space. Some species occupy more than one part of the body at different times in their lives. For example, a species of lice live inside the throat pouches of pelicans and cormorants where they feed on blood. However, they must return to the head feathers to lay their eggs.

DIET

The sucking lice feed exclusively on the blood of mammals. They use their mouthparts to pierce the skin of their host and suck up blood from the small blood vessels located near the skin surface. Chewing lice use their biting mouthparts to feed on feathers, hair, bits of skin, dried blood, and other skin secretions.

BEHAVIOR AND REPRODUCTION

Most louse species remain attached to their host for their entire lives. Their populations vary greatly in size and are strongly influenced by the condition and health of their hosts. For example, birds with damaged bills or feet may have more lice because they are unable to preen or clean themselves efficiently. Some lice escape preening by wedging themselves between feather barbs or by living at the bases of fluffy feathers on the bird's abdomen. They will bite into the feathers with their mouthparts and lock their jaws in place. Some species go to the extreme of actually living inside the quills of wing feathers to escape preening by their shorebird hosts. The dead, dried bodies of lice are found firmly attached to bird and mammal skins in museum collections, sometime hundreds of years after the collection and death of their host.

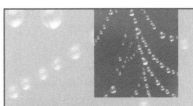

ENDANGERED SPECIES ARE LOUSY TOO!

The extinction of a bird or mammal species leads directly to the extinction of many of their parasites. Nearly 370 species of birds and mammals are listed by the IUCN as Extinct in the Wild or Critically Endangered. At least fifty species of lice share their fate, yet none appear on any list. By 1990 at least eight species of lice had already followed their host birds and mammals to extinction.

Direct physical contact between hosts is usually the best way for lice to disperse within a host species population. Host animals also pick up new lice by sharing nests and nest materials with other infested animals. One of the most unusual and rare methods of louse dispersal is by means of phoresy (FOR-uh-see), or hitchhiking. These lice attach themselves to the abdomens of certain flies and hitch a ride to the next host.

For most species of lice, it is known that there are both males and females and they reproduce primarily by mating. A few species reproduce by parthenogenesis (PAR-thuh-no-JEH-nuh-sihs), a process where the young develop from unfertilized eggs. Females glue their whitish eggs, also known as nits, to parts of feathers or hair shafts. Human body lice will sometimes attach eggs to clothing fibers that stick from the garment like hairs. Eggs usually take four to ten days to hatch depending on species and temperature. The larvae (LAR-vee), or young of an animal that must change form before becoming adults, closely resemble the adults but are incapable of reproducing. They develop gradually through a series of molts, shedding their exoskeletons or hard outer coverings four times before reaching adulthood. Adult lice live for about a month. Human body lice will lay 50 to 150 eggs in their lifetime.

CHEWING AND SUCKING LICE AND PEOPLE

The human body and head louse carries and spreads bacteria that cause the diseases louse-borne typhus, trench fever, and louse-borne relapsing fever. Louse infestations commonly occur among the homeless, or persons in refugee camps and other crowded conditions that result from war and natural disasters. Head lice are common among school children around the world. They are passed from one host to the next through infested clothing. Pubic lice, also known as "crabs," are normally spread through very close, personal contact by grownups.

Lice also infest domesticated mammals and poultry. Infested animals and louse control cost farmers and breeders hundreds of millions of dollars every year in lost production and the purchase of expensive chemical controls. For example, infested chickens will lay fewer eggs, resulting in less money earned by poultry farmers. Chemical pesticides are commonly used to kill lice on poultry and livestock. However, there are concerns over the safety of using these chemicals on large numbers of animals on a regular basis. There is also evidence that some lice are becoming resistant to pesticides. Louse resistance to pesticides was noted by the fact that fewer and fewer lice are killed with each application of the same amount of chemical.

CONSERVATION STATUS

Only one species of louse is listed by the World Conservation Union (IUCN). The pygmy hog louse is listed as Endangered or facing a very high risk of extinction in the wild. Its host, the pygmy hog of India, is also listed as Endangered.

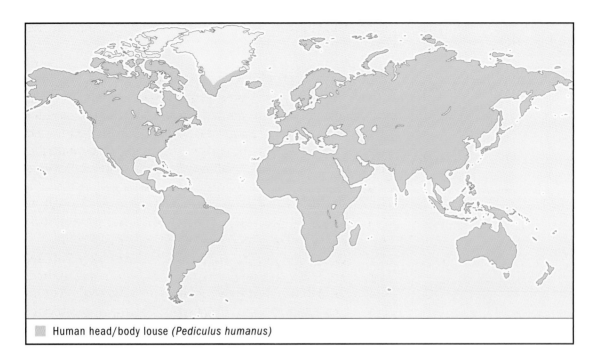

Human head/body louse (*Pediculus humanus*)

HUMAN HEAD/BODY LOUSE
Pediculus humanus

Physical characteristics: The body of this louse is gray, longer than wide, and measures 0.078 to 0.12 inches (2 to 3 millimeters) in length. The head has distinctive dark eyes. Their abdomens lack distinct bumps. The head louse is usually 20 percent smaller than the body louse.

Geographic range: This species is found worldwide. It is an ectoparasite of humans but is also found on gibbons and New World monkeys.

Habitat: Two forms exist. Head lice are found on the human scalp. Body lice prefer clothing and the human chest and stomach.

Diet: Both head and body lice feed on blood.

Behavior and reproduction: Head lice feed regularly every few hours, while body lice feed only once or twice per day when the host

is resting. Both forms are capable of adapting to the different ecological conditions on the human scalp, body, or clothing. They carry several important human diseases.

Head lice attach their eggs to the base of hair shafts. Body lice glue their eggs to hairlike fibers of clothing worn by the host. Eggs hatch in five to seven days. The larvae reach adulthood in ten to twelve days.

Human head/body lice and people: This species, also known as cooties or gray backs, was called "mechanized dandruff" by American soldiers during World War II. The body louse spread epidemic typhus that resulted in the death of hundreds of millions of people up to the early 1900s. Since World War II, large outbreaks of this disease have occurred in Africa, mostly in Burundi, Ethiopia, and Rwanda. The head louse can be common in children. Up to one out of five students are infested in some primary schools in parts of Australia, the United Kingdom, and the United States. Head lice are not normally known to transmit disease.

Conservation status: This species is not endangered or threatened. However, populations found on small, isolated human tribes and non-human hosts are probably threatened with extinction due to declining host populations and habitat loss. ■

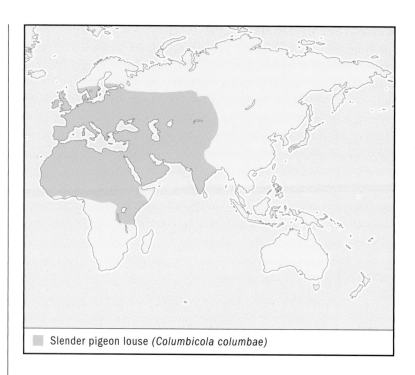

Slender pigeon louse (*Columbicola columbae*)

SLENDER PIGEON LOUSE
Columbicola columbae

Physical characteristics: The slender pigeon louse is a long, slender louse with two bladelike hairs near the front of its head. The threadlike antennae are five-segmented. They measure 0.078 to 0.12 inches (2 to 3 millimeters) in length.

Geographic range: This louse is only found on four species of pigeons, including the widely distributed rock dove or city pigeon. Rock doves (and their ectoparasites) live with humans and have been introduced throughout the world. The distribution of the slender pigeon louse is thought to match that of the rock dove.

Habitat: They are found only among the feathers on the upper and lower sides of the wings of pigeons.

Diet: Slender pigeon lice eat the fluffy parts of the feathers.

Behavior and reproduction: The slender body of this louse allows it to move in between the feather barbs. They grab the edges of feather barbs with their jaws to avoid the preening activities of the host.

Females attach their eggs on the underside of the wing feathers near the pigeon's body. They hatch in three to five days at 98.6°F (37°C).

Slender pigeon lice and people: They are used as research animals by scientists studying how animals change over time and how they interact with parasites.

Conservation status: This species is not endangered or threatened. However, populations present on the Pale-backed Pigeon from Central Asia and the Middle East should be considered vulnerable, or at high risk of extinction in the wild. ■

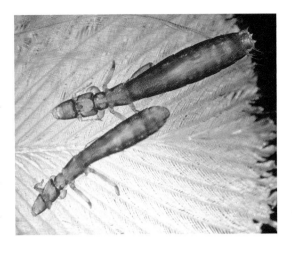

The slender pigeon louse is only found on four species of pigeons, including the widely distributed rock dove or city pigeon. (Kim Taylor/Bruce Coleman Inc. Reproduced by permission.)

FOR MORE INFORMATION

Books:

Kim, K. C., H. D. Pratt, and C. J. Stojanovich. *The Sucking Lice of North America.* University Park: Pennsylvania State University Press, 1986.

Periodicals:

Conniff, R. "Body Beasts." *National Geographic* 194, no. 6 (December 1998): 102–115.

Price, M. A., and O. H. Graham. "Chewing and Sucking Lice as Parasites of Mammals and Birds." *USDA Agricultural Research Service Technical Bulletin* 1849 (1997): 1–309.

Web sites:

National Pediculosis Association. http://www.headlice.org (accessed on October 6, 2004).

Phthiraptera Central. http://www.phthiraptera.org (accessed on October 6, 2004).

Phthiraptera. Lice. http://www.ento.csiro.au/Ecowatch/Insects_Invertebrates/phthiraptera.htm (accessed on October 6, 2004).

Class: Insecta

Order: Hemiptera

Number of families: About 140
families

order

phylum

class

subclass

● **order**

monotypic order

suborder

family

PHYSICAL CHARACTERISTICS

The hemiptera are divided into four smaller groups based on their physical features. These groups include aphids, mealybugs, and scale insects; cicadas and hoppers; moss bugs; and true bugs. The relationships of whiteflies are uncertain, and they are sometimes included with aphids or hoppers.

Hemipterans are extremely variable in form, ranging from long, slender, and sticklike, to short and round, to very flat. The bodies of female scale insects are completely covered by a waxy shield. They don't even look like insects. Still other species are partially or completely covered in protective secretions of white wax that resemble dust, cotton, or feathers. The wax hides their bodies from predators and helps to seal in moisture. Hemipterans range in size from 0.03 to 4.3 inches (0.8 to 110 millimeters) in length. Their bodies come in a wide variety of bright or dull colors and patterns, and some species are virtually clear or colorless.

They have strawlike mouthparts for piercing plant or animal tissues and sucking out plant sap or body fluids. The mouthparts of most true bugs are long and flexible and are usually brought forward while feeding. The short, bristlelike mouthparts of all other hemipterans are permanently pointed backward toward the front pair of legs. In fact, the mouthparts of aphids, whiteflies, scales, and their relatives are actually attached between the front pair of legs. The antennae (an-TEH-nee), or sense organs, of all true bugs living on land are long and easy to see, but those of aquatic species and other hemipterans are usually short and bristlelike. Compound eyes, or eyes with multiple lenses, are usually present in most hemipterans; some species also have simple eyes, or eyes with only one lens.

Most adult hemipterans have four wings, but some species are wingless. The forewings of true bugs are thick and leathery at the base, but thin and membranelike toward the tip. The wings of true bugs are also folded flat over the back to form an 'X' pattern. The forewings of other hemipterans are entirely clear and membranelike or colored and slightly thickened. In many of these species, such as aphids and cicadas, all four wings have the same texture. Their wings are usually folded like a roof over the body with a single line running down the back. The legs of most hemipterans are especially fitted, or adapted for walking, running, jumping, swimming, or skating on water, grasping prey, or digging. In some species, such as scale insects and whitefly larvae (LAR-vee), the legs are greatly reduced in size or entirely absent.

The larvae of true bugs, or young of animals that must change form before becoming adults, are usually similar in appearance to the adults but are smaller and lack fully developed wings. However, the larvae of some hemipterans are very different from the adults. For example, adult whiteflies are slender with long legs, but their larvae are broad, flat, and lack legs.

GEOGRAPHIC RANGE

The hemiptera are found on all continents except Antarctica. They are even found on remote islands in the middle of the ocean. And they are the only insects that live on the surface of the ocean. There are about 82,000 species of hemiptera worldwide, with about 12,000 species in the United States and Canada.

HABITAT

Hemipterans live in nearly all kinds of aquatic and terrestrial habitats, from the seashore to high mountain peaks. Aquatic species live in fresh and brackish waters. They swim through the open water, crawl over the bottom or on plants, or skate across the surface. Sea skaters are the only truly marine insects and live their entire lives among mats of floating algae (AL-jee) on the surface of the ocean. Most hemipterans are terrestrial and are found on all parts of living plants. Some species live under the bark of dead trees. Others are found along the shores of ponds, lakes, streams, and rivers. Some species occur only in caves, spider webs, or animal nests, including those of other insects.

DIET

Most true bugs and other hemipterans suck fluids from leaves, stems, bark, flowers, seeds, and fruit, as well as algae and funguses. Other true bugs prey on living insects, spiders, slugs, snails, fish, frogs, and tadpoles. Some species prefer to feed on recently dead or dying insects. Some hemipterans, such as male scale insects, do not feed at all as adults. A few species such as bed bugs are parasites (PAE-rih-saits) on birds and mammals. Parasites live on another organism, or host, from which they obtain their food. The host is harmed but usually not killed by the parasite.

BEHAVIOR AND REPRODUCTION

Most hemipterans are active during the day. They spend most of their time feeding on plants, hunting for prey, and searching for mates and sites to lay their eggs. Some species, either as larvae or adults, gather in large, temporary feeding groups. Many species, especially true bugs, defend themselves with special glands that release bad-smelling and bad-tasting chemicals that repel their enemies. The glands open underneath or on the sides of the thorax, or midsection, of adults and on the back of the abdomen of the larvae. The smell released by these glands has given at least one group the common name "stink" bugs.

Aquatic bugs trap layers of air over parts of their bodies or capture a bubble underneath their wings so they can breathe under water. Water scorpions have long breathing tubes on the tip of their abdomen that they use like a snorkel to breath underwater. The exoskeletons, or hard outer coverings, of some aquatic hemipteran larvae are so thin that they can draw oxygen into their bodies directly from the water.

Courtship is usually brief and involves flashing legs, wings, and antennae that are brightly colored or distinctly hairy. Some species produce sounds. Male and sometimes female cicadas vibrate special plates on the sides of their bodies to produce buzzes and clicks that are attractive to potential mates. Some hoppers vibrate their bodies to send signals that travel through stems. Male water striders use their front feet to send ripples over the surface of the water to stake out territories and attract mates. Many species produce pheromones, special chemicals that are used to attract members of the opposite sex as mates.

Males usually deposit sperm directly into the female's reproductive organs. During mating the male may ride on the back of the female, or the pair will become joined at the tips of their abdomens. They may remain together only briefly or for several hours. Terrestrial species usually mate on the surfaces of plants, rocks, logs, or on the ground. Water bugs mate above or below the water surface. Under water they will perch on rocks, logs, or floating plants.

Nearly all species of true bugs must mate in order to reproduce. However, some mealy bugs and scale insects reproduce by parthenogenesis (PAR-thuh-no-JEH-nuh-sihs), a process where the young develop from unfertilized eggs. Nearly all aphids reproduce by switching back and forth between mating and parthenogenesis. In spring and fall, winged males and females mate to produce eggs that hatch into wingless females. These females reproduce by parthenogenesis, giving live birth to more wingless females. At the end of summer the wingless females lay eggs that hatch into winged males and females. Some scale insects are hermaphrodites (her-MAE-fro-daits). Hermaphrodites are individual animals that have both male and female reproductive organs. This means that any two individuals, not just a male and female, can get together to mate to produce offspring.

Eggs may be laid singly or in batches on or near suitable sources of food. Parasitic bat bugs and aphids reproducing by parthenogenesis do not lay eggs and give live birth. The adults of only a few species care for their eggs or young or both. Male giant water bugs remain close to egg clusters in order to guard them. In some species of terrestrial true bugs either the males or females will stand directly over the eggs until they hatch. The larvae of true bugs and many other hemipterans usually resemble the adults but lack fully developed wings and the ability to reproduce. They develop gradually by molting, or shedding their exoskeletons, five times before reaching adulthood. Their life cycles may take just a few weeks or more than seventeen years to complete.

WHAT'S BUGGING YOU?

The word "bug" comes from the Middle English word *bugge*, meaning spirit or ghost. Some people use the term "bug" to describe almost any kind of insect. But ladybugs and lightningbugs are actually beetles. And pillbugs and sowbugs are not insects at all but crustaceans related to shrimp and lobsters. Entomologists, scientists who study insects, use the name "true bug" to distinguish a specific group of hemiptera from all insects and other animals.

HEMIPTERANS AND PEOPLE

Hemipterans are used as food for both people and their pets. In parts of Mexico, humans eat egg masses of water boatmen that are fried or dried in the sun. Giant water bugs in India are cooked in syrup and are sold as an expensive treat. Female cicadas full of eggs are eaten in many countries throughout Asia. Stink bugs and their eggs are also dried and sprinkled on food like pepper.

A reddish-purple dye known as carmine comes from a scale insect that feeds on the juices of cactus. This dye is used to color fabrics and as a food coloring. The bodies of a related insect, the lac scale, are used to make shellac.

A few species of true bugs are reared by the millions and released in agricultural fields. They are used instead of pesticides to control crop pests. For example, predatory stink bugs will attack caterpillars that eat soybean plants.

Cicadas have been used to symbolize life after death in the Far East. Jade carvings of these were once put into the mouths of dead princes and other important people. Today the Chinese keep cicadas in cages to hear them sing. They also make and fly kites that look like cicadas.

Several species of hemiptera are important crop pests. They damage leaves, stems, and fruits. Some species also spread plant fungus and viruses. In South America, blood-feeding species attack humans and other wild and domestic animals, spreading Chagas disease.

CONSERVATION STATUS

Five species of hemiptera are listed by the World Conservation Union (IUCN). Two are listed as Extinct, or no longer living. Three species of cicadas are listed as Near Threatened, or likely to qualify for a threatened category in the near future. Like most other organisms, hemipteran populations are threatened by a variety of things that cause habitat loss and destruction, such as logging, development, pollution, overuse of insecticides, and the introduction of exotic species.

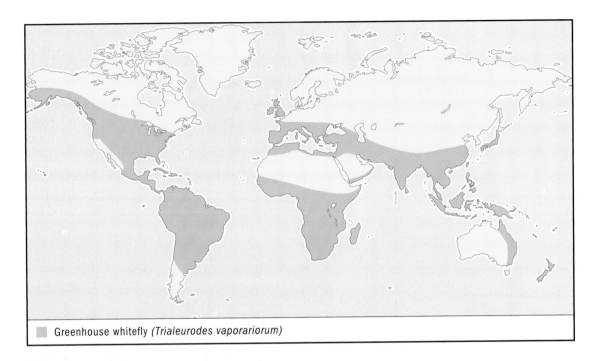

Greenhouse whitefly (*Trialeurodes vaporariorum*)

GREENHOUSE WHITEFLY
Trialeurodes vaporariorum

Physical characteristics: Greenhouse whiteflies are small insects measuring 0.06 inches (1.5 millimeters) in length. Males and females are similar in size and appearance and winged. The yellowish to pale brown body and wings are coated with a powdery white wax. Larvae are flat and yellowish.

Geographic range: They are found on all continents except Antarctica.

Habitat: They are usually found on twigs and the undersides of leaves on a wide variety of tropical plants. They are also widespread on cultivated plants in greenhouses.

Diet: Greenhouse whiteflies feed on plant sap.

Behavior and reproduction: After hatching, the larvae wander for several hours before finding a feeding site on the underside of a leaf.

After piercing the leaf with their mouthparts the larvae will remain at that same spot until they reach adulthood. The exoskeleton of the last (fourth) larval stage becomes a protective case where the winged adult develops. Both adults and larvae feed in groups. The adults move about and feed at different sites and will quickly fly if disturbed.

Males and females mate all year long. The yellow eggs are attached to the leaf surface in curved rows.

Greenhouse whiteflies and people: This species is a serious pest in greenhouses. When feeding in large numbers they can weaken a plant by draining its sap. Adults and larvae produce a sticky waste product called honeydew. Sooty mold develops on the honeydew. Cultivated plants covered with black, fuzzy mold do not sell, resulting in growers losing money.

Conservation status: This species is not endangered or threatened. ■

The greenhouse whitefly is a serious pest in greenhouses. When feeding in large numbers, they can weaken a plant by draining its sap. (Illustration by Amanda Humphrey. Reproduced by permission.)

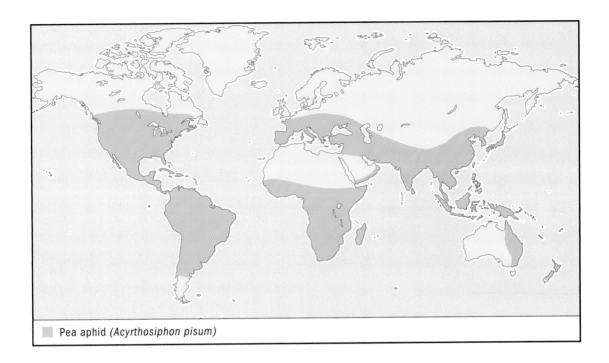

Pea aphid (*Acyrthosiphon pisum*)

PEA APHID
Acyrthosiphon pisum

Physical characteristics: Pea aphids are small, green, insects (either with or without wings) measuring 0.08 to 0.16 inches (2 to 4 millimeters) in length. They have red eyes and threadlike antennae as long as the body. The legs are also long and slender. Wings, if present, are clear. Projections on the abdomen are long and slender. The larvae resemble small, wingless adults.

Geographic range: They are found on all continents except Antarctica.

Habitat: Pea aphids live on their food plants. They are especially fond of plants related to peas, such as alfalfa, beans, clovers, peas, and other crops.

Diet: Adults and larvae suck sap from leaves, stems, and flowers.

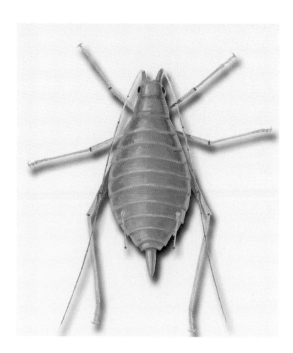

Behavior and reproduction: Females survive through the winter on food plants. Winged males and females appear in spring. Adults and larvae feed in dense patches on plants.

The species reproduces by parthenogenesis all year long in warmer climates. In some areas they alternate between mating and parthenogenesis.

Pea aphids and people: This species can become a pest of alfalfa crops but is usually effectively controlled by using the parasitoid (PAE-re-sih-toyd) wasp. The larvae of parasitoids feed inside the body of the host, eventually killing it.

Conservation status: This species is not endangered or threatened. ■

Pea aphids live on food plants. They are especially fond of peas and other plants related to peas, such as alfalfa, beans, clover, and other crops. (Illustration by John Megahan. Reproduced by permission.)

Seventeen-year cicada (*Magicicada septendecim*)

SEVENTEEN-YEAR CICADA
Magicicada septendecim

Physical characteristics: The seventeen-year cicada (sih-KE-duh) has a plump body, dull dark brown to shiny black in color, with reddish eyes, legs, and wing veins. They measure 1.37 to 1.57 inches (35 to 40 millimeters) in length. The underside of the abdomen has broad orange bands. The antennae are very short and hairlike. Legs are short and adapted for walking. At rest, the clear wings are folded rooflike and extend beyond the abdomen. The underground larvae are nearly colorless.

Geographic range: They are found in the eastern United States, east of the Great Plains.

Habitat: They live in a canopy of deciduous trees in temperate forests and rainforests.

Diet: Cicadas suck plant sap. Adults feed from twigs, while larvae attack roots.

Behavior and reproduction: Adults are active during the day from late May through early July. Males chirp loudly to attract both males and females. Larvae feed underground, feeding on the same root for long periods of time. As they grow larger they move to thicker and thicker roots. When they are ready to become adults, they dig a tunnel upward. They emerge from the soil and crawl up a tree or fence to molt for the last time. Each population reaches adulthood about the same time, every seventeen years. However, different populations called broods will reach maturity on a different cycle.

Males call to attract females. Mating occurs on stems with the male and female connected by the tips of their abdomens. Females embed their eggs in plant stems. The larvae hatch, drop to the ground, and search for a suitably sized root to feed. The larvae resemble the adults but lack wings, have strong front legs adapted for digging, and are incapable of reproducing. They molt, or shed their exoskeletons, five times over a seventeen-year period to reach adulthood. The adults live four to six weeks.

Seventeen-year cicada and people: The appearance of thousands of cicadas every seventeen years has fascinated naturalists and scientists for more than three hundred years. If abundant in nurseries and orchards, larval feeding can be harmful to trees. Adult females in large numbers can also damage twigs by the egg-laying activities. The sound of thousands of male cicadas singing at once is annoying to many people.

Conservation status: This species is listed by the World Conservation Union (IUCN) as Near Threatened, or likely to qualify for a threatened category in the near future. They are not under immediate threat of extinction, but many populations are threatened by the removal of large numbers of trees from their habitats. ■

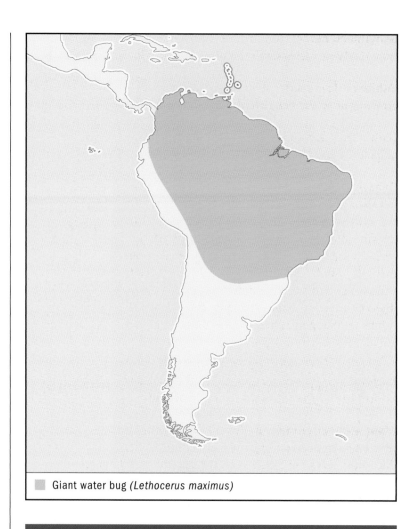

Giant water bug (*Lethocerus maximus*)

GIANT WATER BUG
Lethocerus maximus

Physical characteristics: The giant water bug is the largest true bug in the world, with adults reaching 4.5 inches (115 millimeters) in length. The body is uniformly pale to dark grayish brown. The forelegs are large, powerful, and adapted for grasping prey. The middle and hind legs are flattened for swimming. Males and females are similar in both size and appearance. The larvae resemble the adults but are smaller and lack fully developed wings.

Geographic range: Giant water bugs are found from the West Indies south to northern Argentina.

Habitat: This species lives on submerged plants growing along the margins of pools and lakes.

Diet: They eat aquatic insects, fish, frogs, and tadpoles.

Behavior and reproduction: Giant water bugs kill their prey with digestive saliva that turns the victim's tissues into liquid. The fluid is then sucked up with short, beaklike mouthparts. They will successfully capture and kill prey that is larger than they are. Adults breathe by capturing air under their wings. Larvae rely on patches of short hairs underneath their bodies to trap a layer of air. Adults fly to different bodies of water at night and are often attracted to lights.

Clusters of dozens of eggs are laid on twigs above the water surface and are guarded by the male until they hatch. The larvae disperse at hatching.

Giant water bugs and people: Giant water bugs prey on young fish and may seriously reduce production at fish farms. Bites are very painful but infrequent.

Conservation status: This species is not endangered or threatened. ■

Giant water bugs kill their prey with digestive saliva that turns the victim's tissues into liquid. The fluid is then sucked up with short, beaklike mouthparts. They will successfully capture and kill prey that is larger than they are. (Illustration by Katie Nealis. Reproduced by permission.)

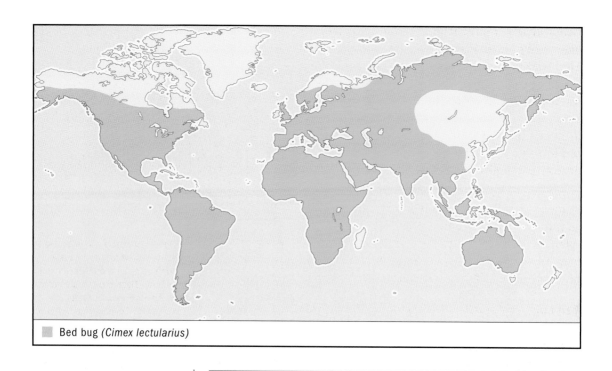

Bed bug (*Cimex lectularius*)

BED BUG
Cimex lectularius

Physical characteristics: A bed bug has a body that is rusty brown to dull red, flat, oval to round when not fed, and much fatter and longer after a meal. They measure 0.16 to 0.19 inches (4 to 5 millimeters) in length. The mouthparts are short and beaklike. The antennae have four segments. The front segment of the thorax or midsection is expanded so that it surrounds the back of the head. The legs and wings of these flightless insects are short. The larvae resemble small adults.

Geographic range: Bed bugs are found on all continents, except Antarctica. They are rare or absent in large areas of Asia.

Habitat: They prefer to live in human dwellings and usually find shelter in the narrow spaces found in bedrooms, bed frames, and mattresses, or under wallpaper.

Diet: They feed on human blood but will also attack chickens, dogs, and bats.

Behavior and reproduction: Adults and larvae hide during the day and emerge at night to feed. They walk across bedding and clothing to look for sleeping people. When they find a human host they use their mouthparts to pierce the skin and suck blood from the wound. They will suck up four to five times their body weight. In cold climates they can live without food for more than a year but are unable to reproduce during this time.

Males and females mate while they are hidden in their shelters. Males use their reproductive organs to puncture the female's abdomen and place sperm in her body cavity. The sperm eventually finds its way into the female's reproductive organs. Eggs are attached to any surface on or near beds. The larvae start feeding as soon as they hatch.

Cimex lectularius prefer to live in human dwellings and usually find shelter in the narrow spaces found in bedrooms, bed frames, and mattresses, or under wallpaper. They feed on human blood but will also attack chickens, dogs, and bats. (©Sinclair Stammers/Photo Researchers, Inc. Reproduced by permission.)

Bed bugs and people: Bed bugs have been considered pests since the time of ancient Egypt and classical Greece. Their populations expand rapidly among humans living in crowded conditions. Bed bug bites are painless, but their saliva does cause itching. They can spread some parasites with their bites.

Conservation status: This species is not endangered or threatened. ■

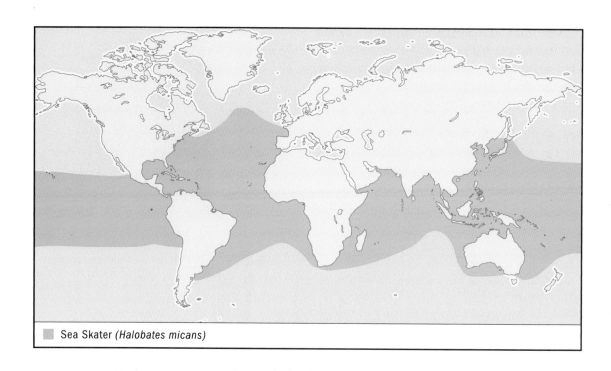

Sea Skater (*Halobates micans*)

SEA SKATER
Halobates micans

Physical characteristics: The sea skater has a short, thick body, with a very short abdomen. They measure about 0.16 to 0.18 inches (4.0 to 4.6 millimeters) in length. The dull brown to black body is covered with a coat of small, silvery hairs. The head has a pair of yellow marks.

Geographic range: They are found between the latitudes 40° north and 40° south, with most species living on warm, tropical waters.

Habitat: Sea skaters live among mats of floating algae on the surface of the ocean.

Diet: Adults and larvae feed on tiny crustaceans, small fish, and floating jellyfish. Crustaceans have a soft segmented body covered by a hard shell.

Behavior and reproduction: Sea skaters move quickly on the ocean surface to find food and mates.

Males and females mate on the ocean surface. Eggs are laid in great numbers and are attached to any floating object, including feathers, seaweed, wood, or the bodies of cuttlefish. The larvae molt five times before reaching adulthood.

Sea skaters and people: Sea skaters do not affect people or their activities.

Conservation status: This species is not endangered or threatened. ■

Male and female sea skaters mate on the ocean surface. Eggs are laid in great numbers and are attached to any floating object, including feathers, seaweed, wood, or the bodies of cuttlefish. (Illustration by Emily Damstra. Reproduced by permission.)

Backswimmer (*Notonecta sellata*)

BACKSWIMMER
Notonecta sellata

Physical characteristics: The backswimmer's body is widest at the middle. The head is rounded, while the abdomen narrows at the tip. They measure 0.31 to 0.35 inches (8 to 9 millimeters) in length. Their bodies usually have dark blue and white markings, but some individuals are colorless. The mouthparts are short and cone-shaped. The front and middle legs are short. The hind legs are long, fringed with hairs, and are held away from the body and used like boat oars. The larvae closely resemble the adults but are smaller and lack wings.

Geographic range: They are found in the lowlands of southern South America from central Bolivia, Paraguay, and southern Brazil to northern Argentina, east of the Andes.

Habitat: This species prefers to live in cloudy water in shallow ponds and pools with few plants. It is often found in temporary rain pools.

Diet: They feed on all kinds of small insects and crustaceans living near the water surface.

Behavior and reproduction: Backswimmers slowly swim upside down near the water surface, searching for prey, but can move quickly when threatened. They seize prey and hold it with the front and middle legs. Winged adults escape drying ponds by flying away. They are often attracted to lights at night.

Mating takes place near the surface of the water. Eggs are glued individually to submerged twigs and algae. The larvae molt five times before reaching adulthood.

Backswimmers and people: Backswimmers may harm small fish, but they may also control mosquito larvae.

Conservation status: This species is not endangered or threatened. ■

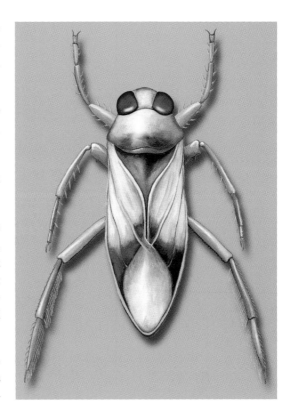

Backswimmers slowly swim upside down near the water surface, searching for prey, but can move quickly when threatened. They seize prey and hold it with the front and middle legs. (Illustration by Emily Damstra. Reproduced by permission.)

FOR MORE INFORMATION

Books:

McGavin, G. C. *Bugs of the World.* London: Blandford, 1999.

Schuh, R. T., and J. A. Slater. *True Bugs of the World (Hemiptera: Heteroptera): Classification and Natural History.* Ithaca, NY: Cornell University Press, 1995.

Tavolacci, J., ed. *Insects and Spiders of the World.* Volume 2: *Beetle-Carpet Beetle.* Vol. 3: *Carrion Beetle-Earwig.* New York: Marshall Cavendish, 2003.

Periodicals:

Evans, A. V. "Dogdays Are Here Again." *Fauna* (July-August 2001): 58–66.

Web sites:

"Hemiptera. Bugs, Aphids, Cicadas." Ecowatch. http://www.ento.csiro.au/Ecowatch/Hemiptera/Hemiptera.htm (accessed on October 8, 2004).

Order: Homoptera. http://insectzoo.msstate.edu/Students/homoptera.html (accessed on October 8, 2004).

Periodical Cicada Page. http://insects.ummz.lsa.umich.edu/fauna/Michigan_Cicadas/Periodical/Index.html (accessed on October 8, 2004).

Scale Net. http://www.sel.barc.usda.gov/scalenet/scalenet.htm (accessed on October 8, 2004).

"True Bugs. Heteroptera." BioKids Critter Catalog. http://www.biokids.umich.edu/critters/information/Heteroptera.html (accessed on October 8, 2004).

Videos:

Bug City. Aquatic Insects. Wynnewood, PA: Schlessinger Media, 1998.

Class: Insecta

Order: Thysanoptera

Number of families: 9 families

order

CHAPTER

PHYSICAL CHARACTERISTICS

The common name "thrips" refers to a single insect or many individuals. It comes from Latin and Greek words that mean "woodworm," a reference to the fact that many species live on dead branches. Thrips are long, slender, flat insects measuring 0.02 to 0.6 inches (0.5 to 15 millimeters) in length. Depending on the species, males are either larger or smaller than females. They are usually black in color, but many species range from whitish to yellow. Other species are black, red, and white. Both adult and larval thrips are unique among insects in that they have only the left jaw in their head. The body absorbs the right jaw while the thrips is still developing in the egg. The remaining left and right mouthparts form a sucking tube with a single channel inside. Both food and saliva flow through this channel. The compound eyes are well developed, but may have as few as ten lenses in some wingless species. Winged species have three simple eyes located between the compound eyes, but they are absent in thrips that are wingless as adults. The antennae (an-TEH-nee), or sense organs, are short and have four to nine segments.

Winged adults have four slender wings that lie side by side flat over the back when at rest. The wings have few, if any, veins and are fringed with long, hairlike structures. Their legs are all similar to one another in appearance. The feet have one or two segments and lack claws. Instead each foot has a sticky, inflatable, pouchlike sac. In some species, the ten-segmented abdomen is tipped with an ovipositor, or egg-laying tube.

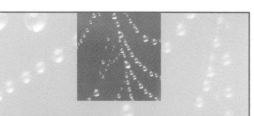

GEOGRAPHIC RANGE

Thrips are found on every continent except Antarctica. There are about 5,500 species known worldwide, with approximately seven hundred species in the United States and Canada.

HABITAT

Nearly half of all thrips species live on dead branches or in leaf litter. The remaining species are evenly divided between living on green leaves or on flowers. Leaf feeders often produce galls (gawls), abnormal swellings on plants. These unusual plant growths provide thrips with both food and shelter. Many species live inside leaves curled or deformed by their feeding activities, or inside bundles of leaves they attach together by glue or silk. Many flower-feeding species prefer grasses. A few species are found on mosses. Pest species eat a wide range of plants in a variety of habitats, but most thrips prefer just a few plants in specific habitats. Most species are found in tropical forests, but the largest populations are found in open habitats, such as mountain meadows.

DIET

The feeding habits of most thrips are unknown. Most species eat funguses. Others feed on leaves or flowers and pollen. Some species prey on small insects and spiders.

BEHAVIOR AND REPRODUCTION

Thrips are thigmotactic (THIG-mo-TAK-tik), animals that always seek the security of confined and narrow spaces. Both larvae (LAR-vee) and adults live together. The larvae are young of the animal that must change form before becoming adults. Males of fungus-feeding species will defend a single female or groups of females they have mated with as well as the egg masses they produce. These males will compete with one another for females by flicking their abdomens at one another or by attempting to stab each other to death with spines on their legs. In other species, males form groups, or leks (lehks), that attract females that are ready to mate.

Eggs usually hatch in just a few days. In species that reproduce by mating, males develop from unfertilized eggs. Some species reproduce by parthenogenesis (PAR-thuh-no-JEH-nuh-sihs), a process where the larvae also develop from unfertilized eggs. However, these eggs always develop into females.

The development of thrips is unique. Each larval stage ends with the molt, or shedding of the exoskeleton, or hard outer covering. The first two larval stages are active and feed for 2 to 5 days. In winged species, neither of these larvae shows any sign of wing development on the outside of the body. The larval stages are followed by two or three pupal (PYU-pul) stages. The pupa (PYU-pah) is the stage of insect development when the transition between larva and adult becomes obvious. The pupa cannot walk and does not feed. In thrips, the antennae are very small, and the developing wings can clearly be seen on the outside of the pupa. Depending on species, the pupae are sometimes found on leaves, but most species pupate on bark or in leaf litter.

Thrips found on flowers usually produce only one generation per year, but most species reproduce whenever conditions are good. Pest species usually reproduce all the time, with a new generation developing every few weeks.

THRIPS AND PEOPLE

Thrips are seldom noticed except when they become pests on garden and crop plants. Their feeding activities damage leaves, flowers, and fruit. However, they cause the most damage by spreading plant diseases. Although generally considered pests, less than ten percent of all known species are known to damage or infect crops.

When their populations reach high numbers, some thrips may bite humans by probing the skin with their mouthparts. Their thigmotactic behavior has resulted in thrips setting off smoke detectors as they enter these devices to seek shelter during mass flights in late summer.

CONSERVATION STATUS

No thrips are endangered or threatened. Their survival depends on the conservation of their food plants and habitats. Developed and agricultural habitats have few or no native species of thrips.

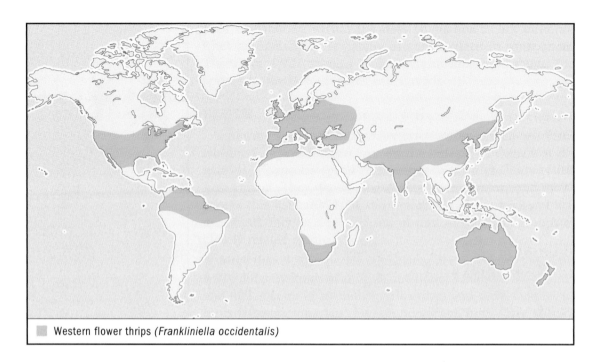

■ Western flower thrips (*Frankliniella occidentalis*)

WESTERN FLOWER THRIPS
Frankliniella occidentalis

Physical characteristics: Western flower thrips are yellow to dark brown and measure about 0.04 inches (1 millimeter) in length.

Geographic range: Originally from the western United States, they now live throughout the temperate parts of North and South America, Europe, Africa, Asia, Australia, and New Zealand.

Habitat: They live on the flowers and leaves of many different kinds of plants.

Diet: They eat pollen as well as new flower and leaf tissues. They will occasionally prey on mites.

Behavior and reproduction: Western flower thrips fly up to one hundred yards at a time when their food plants are disturbed. Their distribution across oceans, however, is a result of hitchhiking on plants sold around the world. Males will compete with other males for territory on a leaf, but only when the population density of thrips is low.

Thrips reproduce by mating, with males developing from unfertilized eggs.

Western flower thrips and people: The western flower thrip is one of the most important pests in the world. Their feeding activities cause serious damage to flower crops, tomatoes, capsicums and cucumbers, as well as stone fruits and table grapes. They also infect many plants with disease as they feed.

Conservation status: This species is considered a pest. It is not listed as endangered or threatened. ■

FOR MORE INFORMATION

Books:

Lewis, T., ed. *Thrips as Crop Pests.* Wallingford, U.K.: CAB International, 1997.

Tavolacci, J., ed. *Insects and Spiders of the World.* Volume 9: *Stonefly-Velvet worm.* New York: Marshall Cavendish, 2003.

Web sites:

Thrips. Thysanoptera. http://www.biokids.umich.edu/critters/information/Thysanoptera.html (accessed on October 11, 2004).

"Thysanoptera. Thrips." Ecowatch. http://www.ento.csiro.au/Ecowatch/Thysanoptera.htm (accessed on October 11, 2004).

CD-ROM:

Moritz, G., D. C. Morris, and L. A. Mound. *Thrips ID: Pest Thrips of the World.* Melbourne: CSIRO Publishing, 2001.

Western flower thrips fly up to one hundred yards at a time when their food plants are disturbed. Their distribution across oceans, however, is a result of hitchhiking on plants sold around the world. (Illustration by John Megahan. Reproduced by permission.)

DOBSONFLIES, FISHFLIES, AND
ALDERFLIES
Megaloptera

Class: Insecta

Order: Megaloptera

Number of families: 2 families

order

CHAPTER

phylum

class

subclass

● **order**

monotypic order

suborder

family

PHYSICAL CHARACTERISTICS

Adult alderflies measure 0.4 to 0.6 inches (10 to15 millimeters) in length, while dobsonflies and fishflies are 0.6 to 2.4 inches (40 to 75 millimeters). They are soft-bodied insects and are black, brown, or yellowish orange to dark green. The head is broad and flat and has chewing mouthparts that are directed forward. The antennae (an-TEH-nee), or sense organs, are long, feathery (fishflies), threadlike (dobsonflies), or beadlike (alderflies). Their compound eyes, or eyes with multiple lenses, are large. Only the dobsonflies and fishflies have simple eyes, or eyes with only one lens. The four wings of alderflies are held like a roof over the body when at rest, but those of dobsonflies and fishflies are kept flat. Megalopteran wings are membranelike and have a complex network of veins that is not branched at the edges of the wings. The hind wings are broader than the forewings and are folded fanlike underneath them. The abdomen is ten-segmented and does not have any projections at the tip.

The larvae (LAR-vee), or young of animals, do not resemble the adults. Larvae of alderflies reach a maximum length of 1 inch (25 millimeters), while those of dobsonflies (known as hellgrammites) and fishflies measure 1.2 to 2.9 inches (30 to 65 millimeters). Their bodies are long and flat. The head is flat and has short antennae. The chewing mouthparts are directed forward. A hard, shieldlike plate covers each of the three segments of the thorax, or midsection. The first segment of the thorax is almost square in shape. The abdomen has seven or eight long slender abdominal gills on each side. The gills absorb oxygen from the water, allowing the larvae to breathe. In alderflies, the abdomen ends in a single, threadlike projection, but in dobsonflies and fishflies it ends in a pair of leglike structures, each with two hooklike claws.

GEOGRAPHIC RANGE

Megalopterans live in North, Central, and South America, South Africa, Madagascar, and parts of Asia and Australia. Most species are found outside of the tropics. There are about 300 species of megalopterans worldwide, 43 of which are found in the United States and Canada.

HABITAT

Aquatic larvae live in standing or flowing waters, including streams, spring seeps, rivers, lakes, ponds, and swamps. Some species burrow in soft mud or sand, while others hide in crevices or under stones or bark. Adults are found on vegetation beside aquatic habitats.

DIET

The larvae actively hunt a wide variety of small aquatic insect larvae, crustaceans, clams, and worms. Adult alderflies may feed on flowers, while female dobsonflies and some fishflies take in plant sap or other fluids. Male dobsonflies do not eat.

BEHAVIOR AND REPRODUCTION

The adults are short-lived and are seldom seen in large numbers. Alderflies are active during the warmest parts of the day and sometimes fly for very short distances. Most dobsonflies and fishflies are active at night and are attracted to lights. Their flight is slow and awkward, but they are capable of covering long distances.

Some alderflies and dobsonflies locate their mates with pheromones (FEH-re-moans), or special chemicals that attract males as mates. Male dobsonflies have very long jaws, which they use to battle other males over females. Males place their jaws over the wings of the female for a short time before mating. Megalopterans usually mate on plants near the water.

The life cycle of megalopterans includes four very distinct stages: egg, larva, pupa, and adult. Females attach layered masses of two hundred to three thousand eggs on objects that hang over the water. They usually select mostly shady sites that are pro-

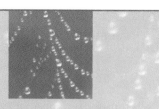

tected from direct sun during the hottest time of day. The larvae drop into the water after hatching. They will molt, or shed their exoskeletons or hard outer coverings, ten to twelve times over a one- to five-year period before reaching the pupal stage. Mature larvae leave the water and pupate in a chamber dug in the soil or leaf litter near the shore. Adults usually emerge in late spring to midsummer and live for only a week or two.

The legs, wings, antennae, and mouthparts of all megalopteran pupae are distinct. These appendages are not attached along their entire length to the body. The pupae are also not enclosed in a cocoon.

MEGALOPTERANS AND PEOPLE

The larvae of some species are important trout food and are used as fish bait. In the Japanese tradition, the dried larvae of some dobsonflies are thought to be a cure for children's emotional problems.

CONSERVATION STATUS

No megalopterans are listed as endangered or threatened, but like all species that live only in small geographic areas, their populations are vulnerable to logging, pollution, and other human activities, as well as to natural events that lower water quality.

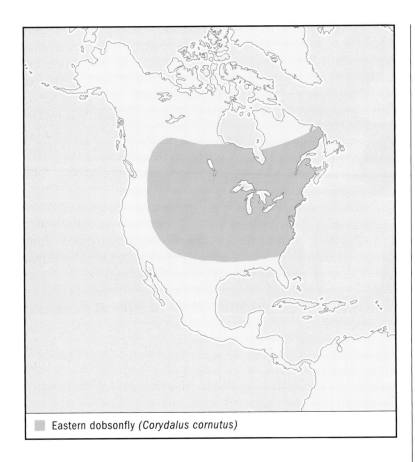

Eastern dobsonfly *(Corydalus cornutus)*

EASTERN DOBSONFLY
Corydalus cornutus

Physical characteristics: Adults measure up to 2 inches (50 millimeters) in length, with wingspans up to 5.5 inches (140 millimeters). The larvae, known as hellgrammites, are 2.6 inches (65 millimeters) long. The head is almost circular, and the first section of the thorax is slightly narrower than the head. The wings are see-through gray with dark veins and white spots. The jaws of the male are half as long as the body. They are curved and pointed at the tips and held crossing each other. The jaws of the female are shorter.

Geographic range: Eastern dobsonflies live east of the Rocky Mountains in the United States and Canada.

The male eastern dobsonfly uses its big jaw as a weapon against other males when battling over females. (©Ken Thomas/Photo Researchers, Inc. Reproduced by permission.)

Habitat: The hellgrammites live in fast-flowing streams. The adults are found resting on streamside vegetation.

Diet: The hellgrammites eat small insect larvae, crustaceans, clams, and worms. Adult females drink various fluids, but the males do not drink or eat.

Behavior and reproduction: Adults are active at night during the summer and are sometimes attracted to lights. They are seldom seen during the day, spending most of their time hidden under leaves high up in trees. The larvae usually crawl on the bottom of the stream. Sometimes they move like a snake, swimming forward and backward in the water.

Males use their big jaws as weapons against other males over females. Courtship behavior is limited but does include fluttering of the wings. Females lay one hundred to one thousand eggs in round masses on rocks, branches, and other objects close to the water. Each mass is coated with a chalky, whitish substance. The larvae drop into the water or crawl to the nearby stream. They take two to three years to reach the pupal stage. Mature larvae crawl out of the water to dig their pupal chambers beneath logs and rocks along the shore.

Eastern dobsonflies and people: Fishermen use hellgrammites as bait for trout, largemouth bass, catfish, and other fishes. Eastern dobsonflies also help control populations of aquatic pest insects such as the Asian tiger mosquito.

Conservation status: This species is not listed as endangered or threatened. ■

FOR MORE INFORMATION

Books:

Evans, E. D., and H. H. Neunzig. "Megaloptera and Aquatic Neuroptera." In *An Introduction to Aquatic Insects of North America*, edited by R. W. Merritt and K. W. Cummins. 3rd edition. Dubuque, IA: Kendall/Hunt Publishing Company, 1996.

McCafferty, W. P. *Aquatic Entomology: The Fisherman's and Ecologist's Illustrated Guide to Insects and Their Relatives.* Boston: Jones and Bartless Publishers, 1981.

Tavolacci, J., ed. *Insects and Spiders of the World.* Volume 1: *Africanized Bee-Bee Fly.* Volume 3: *Carrion Beetle-Earwig.* New York: Marshall Cavendish, 2003.

Web sites:

"Dobsonflies." Critter case files. http://www.uky.edu/Agriculture/CritterFiles/casefile/insects/dobsonflies/dobsonflies.htm (accessed on October 17, 2004).

Eastern dobsonfly. http://www.fcps.k12.va.us/StratfordLandingES/Ecology/mpages/dobsonfly.htm (accessed on October 17, 2004).

Megaloptera. Alderflies, dobsonflies. http://www.ento.csiro.au/Ecowatch/Insects_Invertebrates/megaloptera.htm (accessed on October 17, 2004).

"Megaloptera. Alderflies, dobsonflies, fishflies." Tree of Life. http://tolweb.org/tree?group=Megaloptera&contgroup=Endopterygota (accessed on October 17, 2004).

order

PHYSICAL CHARACTERISTICS

Adult snakeflies have slender bodies that range from 0.20 to 0.79 inches (5 to 20 millimeters) in length. The head is flat and has chewing mouthparts that are directed forward. The antennae (an-TEH-nee), or sense organs, are long and threadlike. Some species also have three simple eyes, or eyes with one lens, in between the large compound eyes, or eyes with multiple lenses. The first section of the three-segmented thorax, or midsection, is long and slender. The four wings are similar to one another in size and shape. They are clear, with a network of dark veins, and are held like a roof over the body when at rest. Each wing has a distinct yellow, white, or black spot on the leading edge near the tip. All six legs are similar in appearance and are adapted or built for walking. The abdomen is ten-segmented. The abdomen of the female is tipped with a long egg-laying tube, called an ovipositor, while the abdomen of the male ends with the reproductive organs. These organs sometimes have very complicated shapes.

The larvae (LAR-vee), or young of an animal, are long and flat. The head has chewing mouthparts that are directed forward, short antennae, and four to seven simple eyes on each side. The head and the first segment of the thorax are hard, while the rest of the thorax and abdomen are soft. The abdomen is ten-segmented.

GEOGRAPHIC RANGE

Snakeflies are found in North America, Eurasia, and parts of North Africa. In North America they are found only in the southern United States and extend south to southern Mexico.

Their range in Eurasia includes nearly all forested regions. In the Old World, their distributions range as far south as the mountainous regions of Morocco, northern Algeria, northern Tunisia, Israel, Syria, northern Iraq, northern Iran, northern Pakistan, northern India, Bhutan, Myanmar, northern Thailand, and Taiwan. There are 206 species of snakeflies worldwide, 21 of which occur in the United States and Canada.

HABITAT

Snakeflies prefer habitats where there is a winter period and lots of woody shrubs. They are found from sea level up to more than 9,840 feet (3,000 meters). Adults are found resting on vegetation. The larvae live under the bark of trees or shrubs or in the top layer of soil. The larvae of a few species are found in rock crevices.

DIET

Both larval and adult snakeflies eat soft-bodied insects and spiders. Some adults are known to eat pollen.

BEHAVIOR AND REPRODUCTION

Snakeflies are active during the day and spend most of their time cleaning themselves. They use their front legs like a comb over their head and pull their antennae through their leg segments. The legs are then pulled to their mouthparts for cleaning. As adults, snakeflies are weak flyers and are not able to move very far from where they grew up as larvae. Like most animals that hunt other animals for food, adult snakeflies live alone and come together only to mate. Courtship in some species involves movements of the antennae, wings, and abdomens. The male places sperm directly into the reproductive organs of the female. Mating lasts up to three hours.

The life cycle of snakeflies includes four very distinct stages: egg, larva, pupa, and adult. The eggs are laid in the crevices (KREH-vuh-ses) of tree bark or under leaf litter. The eggs may take just a few days or up to three weeks to hatch. Snakefly larvae do not resemble the adults at all. The larval stage usually

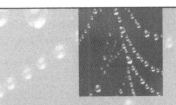

WHY NOT PUT SNAKEFLIES TO WORK?

Both adult and larval snakeflies are potentially valuable predators. After all, the adults eat soft-bodied arthropods, like aphids that are considered crop pests. There have been several attempts to use snakeflies as biological controls. Biological controls are natural enemies of pests that can be used instead of pesticides or poisons. Unfortunately, snakeflies are picky eaters and their long development stages prevent them from being effective predators of pests that only live short-term in agricultural fields.

lasts one to three years. During this time they will molt, or shed their exoskeletons or hard outer coverings, ten to fifteen times or more before reaching the pupal stage. The pupa is the stage that separates the larva from the adult. The pupal stage may last up to ten months. In most insects with a pupal stage, the pupae move very little. However, the pupae of snakeflies are incredibly active and resemble adults with short wing pads.

SNAKEFLIES AND PEOPLE

Images of snakeflies were carved on wood blocks that were then used to print their likenesses as illustrations in books as early as the seventeenth century. However, scientists did not begin to study them until 1735.

CONSERVATION STATUS

No snakeflies are listed as endangered or threatened. Many species might be threatened by extinction someday due to habitat destruction. This is because they are found only in very small geographic areas.

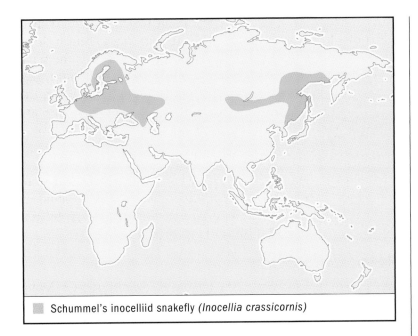

Schummel's inocelliid snakefly (*Inocellia crassicornis*)

SCHUMMEL'S INOCELLIID SNAKEFLY
Inocellia crassicornis

Physical characteristics: The males of this small to medium-sized insect including wings measure 0.31 to 0.43 inches (8 to 11 millimeters), while females are 0.41 to 0.59 inches (10.5 to 15.0 millimeters). The wing spots are dark brown. The head lacks simple eyes.

Geographic range: This species is found from central and northern Europe to eastern Asia.

Habitat: This species lives in pine, in forests up to elevations of 3,280 feet (1,000 meters). The larvae are found underneath the bark of cone-bearing trees, especially pines.

Diet: The larvae eat soft-bodied arthropods, such as insects and spiders. It is not known what the adults eat, but their diets probably include pollen.

Behavior and reproduction: Very little is known about their behavior, other than the fact that they are very clumsy flyers. The life

The males of this small to medium-sized insect, including wings, measure 0.31 to 0.43 inches (8 to 11 millimeters). (Illustration by Bruce Worden Reproduced by permission.)

cycle, from egg to adult, usually takes about two to three years.

Schummel's inocelliid snakeflies and people: This species is not known to impact people or their activities.

Conservation status: This species is not listed as endangered or threatened. It is rare, but it does not appear to be threatened with extinction. ■

FOR MORE INFORMATION

Books:

Tauber, Catherine A. "Order Raphidioptera." In *Immature Insects*, edited by Frederick W. Stehr. 2 vols. Dubuque, IA: Kendull/Hunt Publishing Company, 1991.

Tavolacci, J., ed. *Insects and Spiders of the World*. Volume 8: *Scorpionfly-Stinkbug*. New York: Marshall Cavendish, 2003.

Periodicals:

Acker, Thomas S. "Courtship and Mating Behavior in *Agulla* species (Neuroptera: Raphidiidae)." *Annals of the Entomological Society of America* 59 (1966): 1–6.

Web sites:

"Rhaphidioptera. Snakeflies." Tree of Life Web Project. http://tolweb.org/tree?group=Raphidioptera&contgroup=Endopterygota (accessed on October 12, 2004).

ANTLIONS, LACEWINGS, AND RELATIVES
Neuroptera

Class: Insecta
Order: Neuroptera
Number of families: 17 families

PHYSICAL CHARACTERISTICS

Adult neuropterans (new-ROP-te-ruhns) are long, slender, soft-bodied insects measuring up to 0.12 to 3.15 inches (3 to 80 millimeters) in length with wingspans up to 5.63 inches (143 millimeters). The head is distinct with well-developed compound eyes, or eyes with multiple lenses. In owlflies, each compound eye is divided into an upper and lower section. Simple eyes, or eyes with only one lens, are found only in the moth lacewings. The chewing mouthparts are directed downward or forward. The antennae (an-TEH-nee), or sense organs, are long and thick, threadlike, feathery, or swollen at the tips. The thorax, or midsection, is divided into three segments. The first segment is shorter than the last two wing-bearing segments. In most species the four clear wings are long, narrow, and held like a roof over the body when at rest. The wings are reduced in size or absent in a few species. In most species the wings all have a lacey network of finely branched veins. The forewings may or may not be similar in size or shape to the hind wings. For example, the hind wings of spoonwing lacewings are very slender and shaped like long-handled spoons, while the forewings are shorter and normal in shape. The legs are long and slender. The legs of antlions and owlflies are spiny with well-developed claws for capturing insect prey on the wing. Mantidflies use the front legs for grasping insect prey. The abdomen is long and slender.

The larvae (LAR-vee), or young of an animal, do not resemble the adults at all and are wingless. Their bodies are usually flat and tapered at both ends; only rarely are they thick and

phylum

class

subclass

● **order**

monotypic order

suborder

family

grublike. Their heads are flat with mouthparts directed forward. The jaws are long and may be toothed or smooth. Some spongilla fly larvae have jaws that are longer than their bodies. The jaws are used for stabbing prey and sucking out their body fluids and tissues. Like most insects with chewing mouthparts, neuropterans have two sets of jaws that lock together to form a hollow tube that works as both a syringe and a soda straw. The larvae pump digestive chemicals through the tube into their victims and suck out their liquefied internal organs. They are equipped with only five to seven eyespots on each side of the head, and their eyesight is very poor. The antennae are long or short.

The thorax is usually short and wide, but on the larvae of spoonwing lacewings the first segment of the thorax is long and necklike. The legs are long in climbing species such as green lacewings. In antlions and owlflies, the legs are short and strong for digging. The legs are greatly reduced in mantidflies that feed on spider egg sacs. The abdomen is long or egg-shaped. Both thorax and abdomen may be covered with fleshy projections and bristly hairlike structures.

GEOGRAPHIC RANGE

Neuropterans live on all continents except Antarctica. There are about six thousand species of neuropterans worldwide, with four hundred found in the United States and Canada.

HABITAT

Adults are often found on vegetation. The larvae are usually more specific in their selection of habitats, preferring certain soil types, freshwater habitats, or other locations that guarantee the availability of certain kinds of prey. The larvae of antlions and spoonwing lacewings prefer sandy habitats mostly in drier regions. Those of green and brown lacewings are found only on shrubs and trees. Larval dustywings also prefer trees and shrubs and are usually quite specific about the species of plant. Others prefer freshwater streams or hunt under rocks or in leaf litter along the shore. The larvae of moth lacewings are grublike and live among the roots of plants.

DIET

Most adult and larval neuropterans are predators (PREH-duh-ters) that will hunt for and eat anything they can catch, especially insects. However, the larvae of some species specialize and eat only certain kinds of animals, such as freshwater sponges or spider eggs. For example, the larvae of most mantidflies eat only spider eggs. A few species are not predators at all and eat sap from the roots of trees and shrubs. Many adults are omnivores and will eat both plant and animal tissues, including soft-bodied insects, honeydew, and pollen. However, spoonwing lacewings and green lacewings eat only pollen and nectar from flowers. Antlions, owlflies, and mantidflies are strictly predators, although antlions will occasionally scavenge freshly dead insects.

BEHAVIOR AND REPRODUCTION

Many adult neuropterans are active at dusk or in the evening and are attracted to lights. During the day they remain inactive and hidden among vegetation. Some species rely on camouflage to avoid detection by predators. Some brown and green lacewings will pretend to be dead when threatened. Others produce a bad odor to discourage predators. Some mantidflies not only mimic the color and appearance of paper wasps but will also adopt their movements and postures when disturbed.

Larvae engage in a variety of behaviors to capture prey. The larvae of owlflies are "sit-and-wait" predators, ambushing hapless prey as they walk into their open jaws. Some antlions hide at the bottom of cone-shaped pits they construct to trap crawling insects. Green lacewings, brown lacewings, and dustywings actively hunt for prey, as do larvae living in freshwater habitats. Spongilla flies eat only freshwater sponges and moss animals and use their incredibly long and slender jaws to pierce individual cells. Some species living along the shore use their long jaws to probe wet sand and mud for fly larvae. Pleasing and silky lacewings hunt in crevices and under bark for arthropods (AR-thruh-pads), or animals with hard outer skeletons and several pairs of jointed limbs, such as insects and spiders. The first and third stages of beaded lacewing larvae burrow in the soil in search of termites, while the second state is inactive and does not feed.

The larvae of mantidflies feed in spider egg sacs or in the nests of social wasps. Immediately after hatching, the larvae that prey on spider eggs actively seek a suitable host spider and climb up on its body. Eventually the larvae enter the egg sac to feed. The second and third larval stages look very different from the first stage and have very large, bloated abdomens. Scientists think that these larvae might produce chemicals that slow down

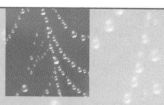

WAY TO GO!

The insect digestive system has three sections: the foregut, midgut, and hindgut. Larvae of this order are unique in that the midgut is not connected to the hindgut. As they feed, their waste is stored in the midgut. They cannot rid their body of waste until they reach adulthood and gain a fully formed digestive system. A lifetime of waste is released as a single pellet as they emerge from the pupa.

the development of the spider eggs to give them plenty of time to feed. Mantidfly larvae are specialists and attack only a single species or several closely related species of spiders.

Only two groups of neuropteran larvae are not predators. Moth lacewings eat sap from the roots of trees and shrubs as they burrow through the soil. It is not known what the larvae of giant lacewings eat, but their mouthparts are blunt and unsuitable for stabbing insect prey.

Many neuropterans use chemicals to communicate with potential mates during courtship. Males have special organs on their abdomen or wings that produce pheromones, chemicals that are attractive to females. Green lacewing males use sound to attract mates, vibrating their abdomens to communicate with females.

Males and females must mate to produce eggs that will develop into larvae. Males deposit sperm directly into the reproductive organs of the female. Mating is either brief or lasts up to several hours. Mating usually occurs when a male and female meet, but swarms of mating moth lacewings have been observed in Australia and the United States.

The life cycle of neuropterans includes four very distinct stages: egg, larva, pupa, and adult. Eggs are laid one at a time or in batches on rocks, bark, or in crevices of bark. Some species of green lacewings, mantidflies, and split-footed lacewings lay a single egg on top of a silk stalk. This keeps them out of the reach of hungry predators, especially other lacewing larvae. There is little or no parental care of the eggs. The larvae look nothing like the adults and do not live in the same habitat. The larvae usually molt, or shed their exoskeletons or hard outer coverings, three times over several months or years before transforming into a pupa. The pupa is formed inside a silk cocoon. Neuropteran larvae produce silk with special organs inside their abdomen. These same organs work like kidneys in other insects, filtering out waste in the blood. The legs and wings of the pupa are not completely attached to the body and the abdomen is capable of some movement.

NEUROPTERANS AND PEOPLE

The larvae of both green and brown lacewings are known as aphidlions, and they prey on pests in a variety of garden, greenhouse, and agricultural situations. They are sold to gardeners and farmers as eggs. The adults are also reared by the thousands and released among various crops to control insect and mite pests.

CONSERVATION STATUS

No species of neuroptera are endangered or threatened. Since many species are known to be from very small geographical areas, they are especially vulnerable to habitat destruction due to human activities. Several countries, states, and provinces list species of neuroptera that are considered rare or possibly threatened with extinction.

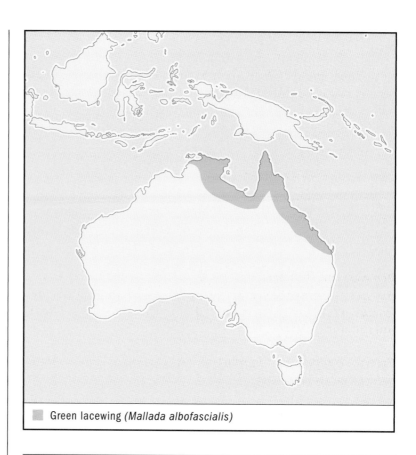

Green lacewing (*Mallada albofascialis*)

GREEN LACEWING
Mallada albofascialis

Physical characteristics: This species is one of the small lacewings. The light to dark green body is long and slender, with broad wings. The head and first segment of the thorax have red patches. The face has a distinctive white area above the mouth. The larvae are long and have special hairs on their backs. The hairs are used for holding debris that helps to camouflage the larvae.

Geographic range: Green lacewings are found in the Northern Territory and in coastal Queensland, Australia.

Habitat: They live in forested areas.

Diet: Adults eat honeydew and flower nectar. The larvae eat soft-bodied arthropods, especially mealybugs.

Adult green lacewings eat honeydew and flower nectar. The larvae eat soft-bodied arthropods, especially mealybugs. (Illustration by Barbara Duperron. Reproduced by permission.)

Behavior and reproduction: Little is known about the behavior of this species. The larvae climb trees and shrubs to hunt for food. Adult females lay single eggs on the tips of silk stalks. The eggs are laid in batches of ten to fifteen.

Green lacewings and people: This species does not impact people or their activities.

Conservation status: This species is not listed as endangered or threatened. ∎

Moth lacewing (*Megalithone tillyardi*)

MOTH LACEWING
Megalithone tillyardi

Physical characteristics: The moth lacewing is a relatively large, robust insect that resembles a moth. The body and wings are dull brown. The body is covered with numerous long hairs. The wings are folded like a roof over the body. The larva are grublike.

Geographic range: Moth lacewings are found in Southeastern Queensland and in northern New South Wales, Australia.

Habitat: This species is found at higher elevations, often on sandy soils. Larvae burrow through soil.

Diet: It is not known what the adults eat, if they eat at all. The larvae feed on plant sap through the roots of trees.

Behavior and reproduction: Adults emerge in large numbers and gather in large mating swarms made up of many more males than females. This swarming behavior may last as long as three weeks.

The females emerge from the pupa with their reproductive organs blocked with a plug. The plug is apparently removed by the act of mating.

Moth lacewings and people: Swarms of these insects sound like a hailstorm when they hit the metal roofs of houses. Their swarms can be a nuisance when they enter homes, which happens rarely.

Conservation status: Moth lacewings are not listed as endangered or threatened. As with most organisms, habitat destruction seems to be the greatest threat. However, the vulnerability of this species is difficult to determine because the larvae are hidden in the ground, and swarms of adults do not appear very often. ■

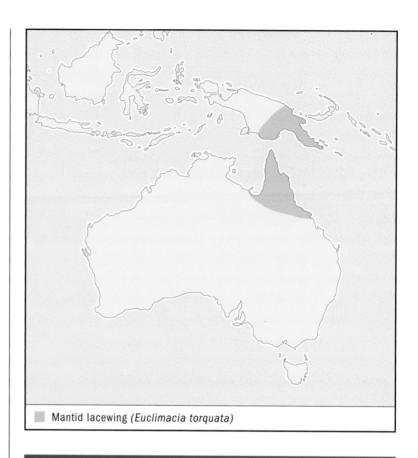

Mantid lacewing (*Euclimacia torquata*)

MANTID LACEWING
Euclimacia torquata

Physical characteristics: The mantid lacewing is a medium-size lacewing. The body is robust with narrow wings that are darkened along their leading edges. This species is wasplike in appearance and is brightly marked with black, yellow, and orange. The front legs are used for grasping insect prey. The larvae are unknown.

Geographic range: The species is found in Queensland, Australia, and in Papua, New Guinea.

Habitat: This species lives in forested areas.

Diet: Adults eat any insects they can catch. The larvae probably eat spider eggs of a particular spider or group of closely related spider species.

Behavior and reproduction: Adults protect themselves by looking and behaving like paper wasps. Nothing is known about their reproductive behavior.

Mantid lacewings and people: This species does not impact people or their activities.

Conservation status: This species is not listed as endangered or threatened. ■

This species is wasplike in appearance and is brightly marked with black, yellow, and orange. The front legs are used for grasping insect prey. (Illustration by Barbara Duperron. Reproduced by permission.)

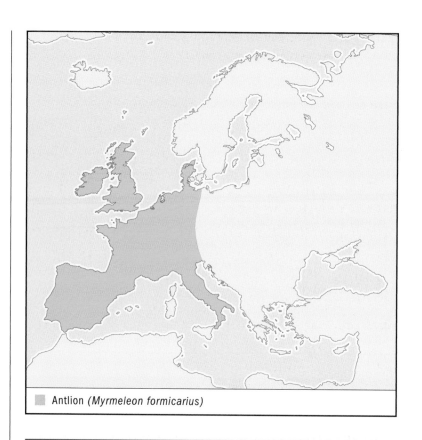

Antlion (*Myrmeleon formicarius*)

ANTLION
Myrmeleon formicarius

Physical characteristics: Antlions are very long and slender insects. The head and thorax are short and thick, while the abdomen is very long and slender. The body is brown with tan markings. The antennae are thickened, especially at the tips. The wings are long, narrow, and transparent with brown, black, and white spots. The larvae are robust and egg-shaped with large curved jaws. Their body is built or adapted for burrowing backward through sandy soil.

Geographic range: Antlions are found in Western Europe.

Habitat: Antlions live in a wide variety of habitats, especially grasslands and sandy deserts.

Diet: Adults capture all kinds of flying insects on the wing. The larvae seize any small insects that fall into their pits.

Behavior and reproduction: Adults are active at night and rest on foliage during the day. The long body and brown color helps them to blend in as they lie perfectly still and flat on a twig or branch. The larvae dig cone-shaped pits in loose, sandy soil. They rapidly flick sand out of the pit with their flat heads. They hide at the bottom of the pit with only their jaws exposed. When a suitable prey falls into the pit, the larva will quickly impale it with its jaws and inject it with paralyzing venom. It will then pull the prey down into the sand. They will abandon their pits and quickly burrow deep in the sand when threatened by anything larger than a small prey animal.

Adult females lay their eggs in sandy soil. The larvae burrow through the soil until they find a suitable place to dig a pit. They prefer sandy areas under rocky overhangs or in caves. By choosing these protected sites, the larvae avoid rain that will ruin their pits or cause them to drown. When fully grown, the larva spins a spherical cocoon made of silk coated with particles of sand.

Antlions and people: Antlion larvae, or "doodlebugs," have fascinated humans for centuries. They are featured in folktales, especially in the chants and charms of European children. The charms specifically refer to their cone-shaped pits and backward movements.

Conservation status: This species is not listed as endangered or threatened. ■

Adult antlions are active at night and rest on foliage during the day. Their long bodies and brown color help them to blend in as they lie perfectly still and flat on a twig or branch. (Illustration by Barbara Duperron. Reproduced by permission.)

Spoonwing lacewing (*Nemoptera sinuata*)

SPOONWING LACEWING
Nemoptera sinuata

Physical characteristics: Spoonwing lacewings are large to medium-size insects measuring approximately .63 inches (16 millimeters) in length, with a wingspan up to 2.16 inches (55 millimeters). The body is long and thick, with relatively broad, rounded forewings. The hind wings are particularly long and slender and are narrower at the base than they are at the tips. The wings are marked with irregular yellow and black bands. At rest the forewings are held over the body, while the hind wings project toward the rear. The larvae are broad and egg-shaped, with short necks and short jaws.

Geographic range: Spoonwing lacewings live throughout Europe and in parts of North Africa along the Mediterranean Sea.

Habitat: They live in forests and open grasslands.

Adult spoonwing lacewings feed at flowers on pollen and nectar. The larvae bury themselves in sand and remain inactive for long periods. (Illustration by Barbara Duperron. Reproduced by permission.)

Diet: Adults feed at flowers on pollen and nectar. The larvae bury themselves in sand and remain inactive for long periods. They actively hunt for prey on the surface of the soil. When an insect approaches, the larvae detect their movement through vibrations in the soil. The larvae approach potential prey slowly and attack, stabbing it with their sharp jaws. They will occasionally eat other spoonwing lacewings.

Behavior and reproduction: Adults are active during the day in late spring. Females lay their eggs in sand. Probably one generation is produced every year.

Spoonwing lacewings and people: This species is not known to impact humans or their activities.

Conservation status: This species is not listed as endangered or threatened. ■

FOR MORE INFORMATION

Books:

"Neuroptera (Lacewings)." In *The Insects of Australia*, edited by CSRIO. 2nd edition. Vol. 1. Carlton, Australia: Melbourne University Press, 1991.

Tavolacci, J., ed. *Insects and Spiders of the World.* Volume 1: *Africanized Bee-Bee Fly.* Volume 5: *Harvester Ant-Leaf-cutting Ant.* Volume 8: *Scorpionfly-Stinkbug.* New York: Marshall Cavendish, 2003.

Web sites:

The Antlion. http://kaweahoaks.com/html/antlion.htm (accessed on October 13, 2004).

"Green lacewings. Chrysopidae." BioKids. http://www.biokids.umich.edu/critters/information/Chrysopidae.html (accessed on October 13, 2004).

"Neuroptera. Lacewings, antlions." Ecowatch. http://www.ento.csiro.au/Ecowatch/Insects_Invertebrates/neuroptera.htm (accessed on October 13, 2004).

Neuroweb. http://neuroptera.com/main.html (accessed on October 13, 2004).

BEETLES AND WEEVILS
Coleoptera

Class: Insecta
Order: Coleoptera
Number of families: 166 families

PHYSICAL CHARACTERISTICS

Beetles are the largest order in the animal kingdom, with approximately 350,000 species known worldwide. Beetles come in a wide variety of body shapes and sizes. They range in length from 0.02 to 6.7 inches (0.55 to 170 millimeters) and are long or round, cylinder-shaped or flat, slender or heavy-bodied. Their bodies are usually very hard and rigid, but some groups, such as fireflies, soldier beetles, and net-winged beetles, typically have bodies that are soft and flexible. Although many species of beetles are plain black or brown, others have amazing metallic or shimmering colors and patterns. These colors are created by chemicals inside their exoskeletons, or hard outer coverings, or by the physical structure of the surface of the exoskeleton itself. Additional structures on the surface of the exoskeleton also influence color, such as surface texture, waxy coatings, scales, and other hairlike coverings. The colors and coatings of beetles help them to recognize one another and to protect themselves from extreme temperatures, water loss, and predators (PREH-duh-ters) that hunt them for food.

The head has chewing mouthparts that are directed forward or downward. Their jaws are used for cutting or grinding plant and animal tissues or for straining small particles from liquids. However, wrinkled beetles are unable to use their jaws for chewing. Instead, they use their other finger-like mouthparts to handle their food. The mouthparts of some net-winged beetles and weevils are place on the tip of a snout, which makes it easier for them to feed on flowers and seeds.

phylum
class
subclass
● **order**
monotypic order
suborder
family

Beetle antennae (an-TEH-nee), or sense organs, are equipped with very sensitive receptors that help them find food, water, mates, and egg-laying sites. Antennae also help them to determine temperature or detect approaching enemies by sensing changes in air currents. Some ground beetles and rove beetles have special structures on their front legs that are used regularly to clean the antennae to maintain their sensitivity. The antennae are usually shorter than the body but are often much longer in some longhorns and brentid weevils. Males may have elaborate antennal structures that increase the surface area for special chemical receptors that are sensitive to pheromones (FEH-re-moans) released by females of the same species. Pheromones are very special airborne chemicals that help potential mates find one another, sometimes over large distances. The antennae are threadlike, beadlike, elbowed or bent, sawtoothed, comblike, feathery, swollen at the tips or clubshaped, or have some segments flat or platelike.

The compound eyes, or eyes with multiple lenses, are usually well developed and may be partially or completely divided into two parts. For example, the eyes of whirligigs are completely divided. They live on the surface of water. The upper portions of the eyes are used for seeing in the air, while the portions in the water are specialized for seeing under water. Simple eyes, or eyes with only a single lens, are rarely found in beetles but are present in most hide beetles and some rove beetles, as well as a few other groups.

Some beetles, usually males, have horns on their heads, jaws, or the first section of their thorax, or midsection. In the male Hercules beetle, the head and thoracic horns work together to form a powerful pinching device. Other beetles have horns on their legs or wing covers. The size of horns varies within the same species and is influenced by adult body size and conditions that influence larval development. These include diet, temperatures, and moisture. Heredity (hih-REH-dih-ti), the physical traits passed from parent to offspring through genes, also plays an important role in horn development.

Most beetles have two pairs of wings. The hard or leathery forewings are called elytra (el-EE-tra). The elytra cover the last two segments of the thorax, the second pair of wings, and some or all of the abdomen. The elytra not only protect beetles from predators and parasites (PAE-rih-saits), or animals that live on another organism from which they obtain food; the elytra also keep beetles from getting scuffed up as they burrow through the soil and rotten wood. The air space between the elytra and the abdomen in desert species helps to insulate their body from sudden changes in temperature. This same space also gives some aquatic beetles a place to store air so they can breathe under water. The second pair of wings are also called flight wings. They do most of the work in flying beetles, while the elytra are used to help them keep their balance. Desert-dwelling darkling beetles and weevils are often unable to fly because their elytra are permanently joined together and they lack fully developed flight wings. However, this arrangement helps them to conserve moisture.

The legs of beetles are used for burrowing, swimming, crawling, or running. Males of the harlequin beetle, the long-armed chafer, and several large weevils have very long front legs that are probably used for mating defense. Desert darkling beetles living in the Kalahari Desert have long, thin legs that lift them as high as possible above the hot sands. Aquatic beetles have flat and fringed legs and use them like paddles as they swim through water. Their feet are tipped with one or two claws and are sometimes equipped with sticky or brushy pads that help them walk on plants and other surfaces. Some male diving beetles have front feet that work like suction cups to help them hold on to a female as they mate underwater.

The abdomen is usually hidden underneath the elytra, but in rove, clown, and many sap beetles, the elytra are short, leaving some or most of the abdomen exposed. The tip of the abdomen sometimes has small structures that are for egg-laying and mating. The tip of the abdomen is very flexible in some beetles. For example, whirligig beetles use their abdomen to help steer themselves on the surface of the water. In ground beetles the flexible abdominal tip is used as a defensive weapon to aim harmful chemicals at their attackers.

Beetle larvae (LAR-vee), or the young of an animal that must go through certain changes in form before becoming adults, usually do not look like the adults. They are grublike with short legs or wormlike with legs reduced in size or entirely absent. Some predatory species are flat with long legs. The distinct head has chewing mouthparts that are adapted for crushing, grinding, or tearing food. Predatory species may have sucking mouthparts for drinking liquified tissues of their prey. The antennae are small and sometimes difficult to see. They have zero to six simple eyes on either side of the head. The thorax has three distinct sections. The first section may be covered with a broad, dark plate. The legs have six or fewer segments, if they are present at all. The soft abdomen is usually divided into ten segments, but some species have only eight or nine. It is sometimes covered with wartlike or other fleshy structures that help give them traction while moving through soil or rotten wood. The next to last segment may have a pair of projections that are sometimes pincherlike.

The features of adult beetles are clearly visible in the pupae, or insects at the life stage between larvae and adults. Some pupae have their legs and developing wings tightly pressed against the body and cannot move them. In other species these structures are not firmly attached to the body and are flexible and capable of limited movement. In some species the abdomen is capable of some movement. The seams between the movable abdominal segments may have small pinchers on both sides called "gin-traps." The pupa snaps these pinchers together to protect itself from small predators and parasitic mites.

GEOGRAPHIC RANGE

Beetles are found on every continent except Antarctica. They are also found on most islands. Most species prefer certain kinds of soils, climates, and foods and live only in a particular geographical region. A few beetle species have been distributed well beyond their natural distribution through human activity, either accidentally or on purpose. About twenty-five thousand species are known in the United States and Canada.

HABITAT

Beetles live in nearly every terrestrial and freshwater habitat on the Earth, but they are not found in the ocean, on polar ice caps, or on some of the tallest mountain peaks. They live everywhere, from coastal sand dunes to wind-swept rocky fields at 10,000 feet (3,050 meters) above sea level. Most species are found in humid tropical forests. Others inhabit cold mountain streams, parched deserts, standing and flowing freshwater habitats, or deep, dark caverns. They hide under stones and bark, or burrow through the soil and wood. They live in fungus, roots, trunks, branches, stems, leaves, flowers, and fruit. Some beetles spend most of their lives in rotting plants and on dead animals. Beetles are also found in the nests of birds, reptiles, mammals, and social insects. They also live in spaces between sand grains at the seashore, adjacent dunes, and along watercourses. A few species are parasites on the bodies of beavers and other rodents.

DIET

Equipped with chewing mouthparts, beetles are capable of eating almost any organism, living or dead, including funguses, plants, and animals, especially other insects. They also eat animal waste. Numerous fungus feeders attack mushrooms and their relatives, while others eat molds and yeasts mixed with plant sap. Plant-feeding beetles eat leaves, flowers, pollen, nectar, fruits, and seeds. Many species feed inside plant tissues and bore through all parts of plants. Wood-boring beetles are unable to digest wood and must rely on bacteria, yeasts, and funguses living in their digestive systems to break it down. A few species eat the skin, dried blood, and other skin secretions of rodents. Carrion and burying beetles, hide beetles, and others scavenge dead animal tissue. Skin beetles prefer to eat feathers, fur, horns, and hooves. Dung beetles bury large amounts of animal waste for use as food for their larvae. They use their membrane-like jaws to strain out bits of undigested food, bacteria, yeasts, and molds from the waste as food for themselves. Some dung beetles prefer to eat dead animals, funguses, fruit, dead millipedes, or the slime tracks of snails.

Carnivorous beetle larvae feed mainly on liquids and produce digestive chemicals that turn their prey into "soup." This kind of digestion also occurs in some adult ground and rove beetles.

BEHAVIOR AND REPRODUCTION

Some plant-feeding beetles will nibble only the edges of leaves, while others will eat everything. Japanese beetles skeletonize leaves by eating all the soft tissue and leaving behind a network of leaf veins. Species feeding on plants with poisonous or sticky sap must first bleed the leaf of these harmful fluids. Before feeding they will bite the veins supplying the sap to the leaf to cut off the supply of sap and bleed the tissues they are about to eat.

Many predatory species will eat anything they can catch and usually choose to live in habitats where there is plenty of prey. Ground and tiger beetles capture their prey on the run, killing and tearing them into smaller chunks with large and powerful mouthparts. They attack a broad range of beetles, other insects, and invertebrates (in-VER-teh-brehts), or animals without backbones, although some prey only on snails. Many rove and clown beetles hunt for food among the nooks and crannies of leaf litter or in decaying plants or dead animals.

Other species are quite particular about what they eat and have very specialized behaviors for locating their prey. The larvae of fireflies feed only on snails and track down prey by following their slime trails. Checkered and bark-gnawing beetles eat bark beetles. They probably follow the scent of bark beetle pheromones to find them under bark. Ant-loving scarabs eat ant larvae and the nest by following the smell of ant pheromones back to the nest. Whirligig beetles identify prey by using waves across the surface of the water generated by struggling insects.

Aquatic beetles must regularly capture new supplies of fresh air to remain under water. Water scavengers do this by breaking through the surface headfirst. Using their antennae to break through the water surface, they draw a layer of air over their body and store it on the lower surface of their abdomen. Predatory diving beetles break through the surface with the tip of their abdomens to trap an air bubble under their elytra. When the oxygen supply of the bubble is nearly exhausted, the beetle must return to the surface for more air.

Beetles defend themselves from predators with a variety of structures, behaviors, and chemicals. For example, many large scarabs, stag beetles, and longhorns avoid being eaten by simply being too large or frightening in appearance. Sharp horns and big, powerful jaws protect others. Beetles with flat bodies will retreat into tight spaces to get out of reach of predators. Shiny, metallic colors and bold patterns make some species look less beetle-like so they are overlooked by predators. Many weevils and other beetles are plain in color or have blotchy patches of browns, blacks, and grays that make them almost invisible on a background of tree bark. Some beetles are protected because they look or behave as, or mimic, stinging wasps, bees, or ants. The chemical weapons of beetles are produced by special glands or taken directly from their food. These foul-smelling and bad-tasting chemicals are released as sprays from the tip of the abdomen, or dribbled out of leg joints. Bombardier beetles spray a burning, stinging fluid from their abdomens with surprising accuracy. Ladybugs, blister and soldier beetles store defensive chemicals in their blood and release them through their leg joints when attacked. Beetles that feed on toxic milkweeds sometimes use its chemical defenses as their own by storing the plant's chemicals in their own tissues.

Beetles communicate with each other using physical, visual, or chemical means, usually to find a mate. Many species use sound to locate one another. Bess beetles, longhorns, and bark beetles rub parts of their bodies together to make a squeaking sound. Male death-watch beetles bang their heads against the sides of their wooden tunnels to attract females. South African tok-tokkies drum their abdomens against soil and rocks to attract mates.

The best known form of visual communication among beetles is bioluminescence (BI-oh-LU-mih-NEH-sens), or light produced by living organisms. Fireflies produce flashes of light with special tissues in their abdomens to locate and attract mates. The speed and length of each flash is caused by a controlled chemical reaction. Each species has it own light-flashing pattern. The number and speed of the flashes help males and females of the same species to recognize one another. Males typically fly at night, flashing their lights until they see a female respond with her own signal. Upon locating a female, he continues flashing and flies toward the female's signal.

Most beetles depend on chemical communication, or pheromones, to find distant mates or those hidden nearby among tangles of vegetation. Females usually produce pheromones to attract males. Large numbers of males and females may gather in mating swarms, or leks (lehks), to improve their chances of finding a mate. Some beetles find mates at food sources, such as dead animals, animal waste, sap flows, or flowers. Others gather around open patches of ground, rocky outcrops, or lone sign posts. Horned males stake out sapping wounds on a tree or some other food source and wait for the arrival of a hungry female. They use their horns to defend the site against other insects, especially other males of the same species.

Most beetles must mate to reproduce. A few species are capable of parthenogenesis (PAR-thuh-no-JEH-nuh-sihs), or the process by which larvae develop from unfertilized eggs. Courtship behavior in beetles is uncommon. Male ground, tiger, and rove beetles may grasp the female's thorax with their jaws before mating, while some male blister beetles tug on the female's antennae. In most beetles the males simply climb on the back of the female to mate. They may stay there for some time in order to keep other males from mating with her. Males usually mate with several females if they have the opportunity. Females mate just once or with many males.

The life cycle of beetles includes four very distinct stages: egg, larva, pupa, and adult. In a few species of beetles the eggs are kept in the female's body until they hatch. However, most species lay their eggs singly or in batches. Beetles living on the ground simply drop them on the dirt, scatter them in soil rich in decaying plant materials, or place them in or near piles of decaying animal bodies or waste. The eggs of plant-feeding species are placed at the base of suitable food plants, glued to stems and leaves, or placed in the crevices of bark. Others place their eggs inside leaf tissues.

The larvae look nothing like the adults and rarely live with them. They scavenge dead animals and waste, attack roots, tunnel in plant tissues, or bore through wood. The larvae usually molt, or shed their exoskeletons or hard outer coverings, three or more times over a period of weeks or years before reaching the pupal stage. Beetle pupae are usually tucked away in soil or rotten wood, under stones, or inside plant tissues. In cooler climates, most beetles spend the winter in the pupal stage. In some beetles, such as many fireflies, the adult females lack wings and look just like the larvae. But they do have compound eyes and are capable of mating and reproducing. One or more generations of beetles are produced per year, depending on species and climate. Most adults live for weeks or months, but some desert darkling beetles are known to live ten or more years.

Parental care is uncommon among beetles. Some ground beetles build small pits to lay their eggs in and guard and clean them until they hatch. The females of several species of tortoise beetles will guard their eggs and larvae until they pupate. Bess beetles tunnel in rotten wood and live in dense colonies. They make squeaking sounds to communicate with other adults and larvae. The larvae depend on the adults for food. They only eat wood that has already been chewed or digested by the adults. In Europe some female rove beetles maintain and defend their brood tunnels and provide their larvae with algae (AL-jee) to eat. Bark and ambrosia beetles grow a special fungus that is eaten by adult beetles and larvae.

The males and females of some species, such as earth-boring beetles, dung scarabs, and burying beetles, cooperate with their mates to dig nests for their eggs and supply them with animal waste or dead animals. Other insects, such as flies, ants, mites, and other beetles, also compete for these food sources. Dung beetles reduce competition by burying animal waste in underground nests. These specially built tunnels help to keep the waste moist and fresh.

Burying beetles demonstrate the most advanced parental care known in beetles. Males and females bury small, dead animals in an underground chamber and prepare them as food for their young. They chew off the feathers or hair and shape the body into a pear-shaped mass with a small pit on top. They lick the mass to coat it with special chemicals that prevent it from decomposing. The female lays her eggs on the chamber floor, and they soon hatch. Both adults nibble on the mass and spit up fluids into the pit. Females call the young to the pit to feed with a squeaking noise made by rubbing the edge of their elytra against the abdomen. Both adults remain in the chamber until the larvae pupate.

BEETLES AND PEOPLE

Beetles have long captured the imagination of people. Ancient Egyptians used the sacred scarab on walls and carvings to symbolize the Egyptian sun god Ra. Symbols of sacred scarabs were especially popular on objects associated with funerals and human burials. For thousands of years, beetles have appeared on vase paintings, porcelain statuary, precious stones, glass paintings, sculptures, jewelry, and coins. Their images were also used to illustrate important papers and books. Fireflies have long held a special fascination for the Chinese and Japanese and appear often in their art.

Throughout history, artisans have used the likenesses of beetles or parts of their bodies to create jewelry. Today, the elytra of the jewel beetle are used in necklaces, head ornaments, and earrings. In parts of Mexico and Central America, a living beetle, popularly known as the ma'kech, is decorated with brightly colored glass beads, attached to a short chain, and pinned to clothing as a reminder of an ancient legend.

A small number of beetles have become important pests of stored foods, pastures, crops, and timber. Beetles compete with humans for food by feeding on beans, peas, tomatoes, potatoes, melons, gourds, and grains. In temperate forests throughout the world, beetles generally attack trees valued as lumber.

Predatory ground beetles and ladybugs are used to control

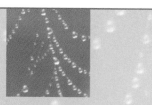

TAKE A BEETLE TO LUNCH

Some beetles are an important source of protein and fat. In the South Pacific grubs of the palm weevils are roasted and eaten with great delight. The Chinese fry large water beetles in oil or soak them in salty water. The Aborigines of Australia eat nut-flavored wood-boring grubs after roasting them like marshmallows over a fire. In the United States the larvae of the common mealworm is put inside of lollipops as a curiosity.

insect pests around the world. Several kinds of plant-feeding beetles are used to combat harmful weeds. In the 1970s the Australians began a program to import exotic dung scarabs and predatory clown beetles to control biting flies and elminate their breeding sites.

CONSERVATION STATUS

Seventy-two species of beetles are listed by the World Conservation Union (IUCN). Of these, seventeen are listed as Extinct, ten as Critically Endangered, fifteen as Endangered, twenty-seven as Vulnerable, and three as Near Threatened. Extinct means no longer living. Critically Endangered means a species is facing an extremely high risk of extinction in the wild. Endangered means the species is facing a very high risk of extinction in the wild. Vulnerable means facing a high risk of extinction in the wild, and Near Threatened means likely to qualify for a threatened category in the near future. Individual countries also list these and other species as threatened, endangered, or extinct. For example, the United States Fish and Wildlife Service lists four species as Threatened, or likely to become endangered in the foreseeable future, and twelve as Endangered, or in danger of extinction throughout all or a significant portion of range.

State and provincial governments throughout the world have also enacted laws that prohibit the collection, trading, and export of their listed species. All beetles, especially those living in small, specialized habitats, are threatened by habitat loss due to fire, development, electric lights, overgrazing, agricultural expansion, damming of rivers and streams, logging, persistent adverse weather, off-road recreational vehicles, and the introduction of exotic species.

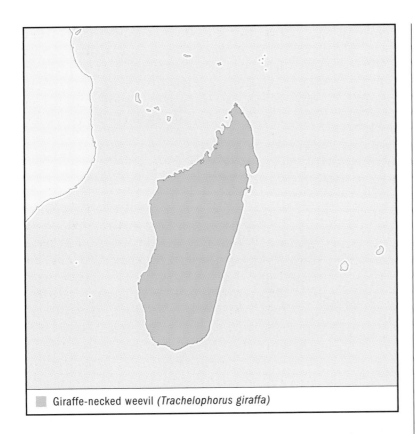

Giraffe-necked weevil (*Trachelophorus giraffa*)

GIRAFFE-NECKED WEEVIL
Trachelophorus giraffa

Physical characteristics: This species is black with red elytra. Only the male has a long "neck" and measures up to 0.98 inches (25 millimeters) in length.

Geographic range: Giraffe-necked weevils live in Madagascar.

Habitat: They live in forests.

Diet: The adults feed on the leaves of a small tree, called the giraffe beetle tree.

Behavior and reproduction: Adults rest on leaves in open areas and along roadsides. Females lay their eggs on leaves. The leaves are then rolled up into a protective tube that serves as a food source for the larvae.

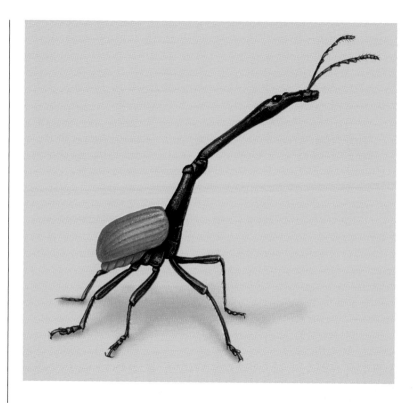

Giraffe-necked weevils and people: This species does not impact people or their activities.

Conservation status: This species is not listed as endangered or threatened. ■

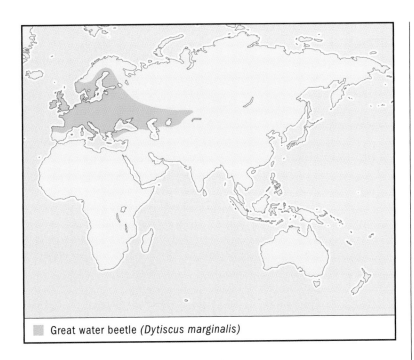

Great water beetle (*Dytiscus marginalis*)

GREAT WATER BEETLE
Dytiscus marginalis

Physical characteristics: Adults measure up to 1.4 inches (35 millimeters) in length. The midsection and elytra have pale borders. The elytra of the male are smooth, while those of the female are grooved.

Geographic range: This species is found in Europe.

Biome: Lake and pond

Habitat: Great water beetles live in standing bodies of water with muddy bottoms.

Diet: They eat other aquatic insects, clams, snails, crustaceans, and even tadpoles and small fish.

Behavior and reproduction: Great water beetles breathe underwater by breaking the water surface with the tip of the abdomen and trapping an air bubble under the elytra. Females lay their eggs singly

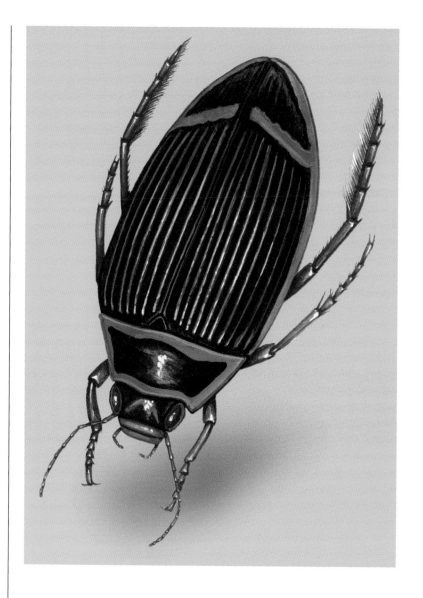

The great water beetle eats other aquatic insects, clams, snails, crustaceans, and even tadpoles and small fishes. (Illustration by Joseph E. Trumpey. Reproduced by permission.)

on the stems of aquatic plants. The larvae molt three times in thirty-five to forty days. Mature larvae pupate in damp soil next to water. There is one generation produced each year.

Great water beetles and people: This species is one of the largest and most studied of all water beetles in Europe.

Conservation status: This species is not listed as endangered or threatened. ■

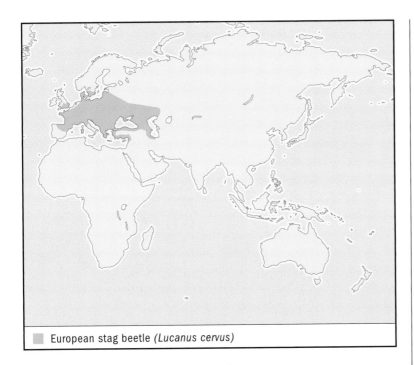

European stag beetle (*Lucanus cervus*)

EUROPEAN STAG BEETLE
Lucanus cervus

Physical characteristics: The body of a European stag beetle is dark brown or black. Males have a broad head with antler-like jaws and reach a total length of 1.4 to 2.95 inches (35 to 75 millimeters). Females have smaller heads and jaws and measure 1.2 to 1.8 inches (30 to 45 millimeters).

Geographic range: This species is found in central, southern, and western Europe; Asia Minor; and Syria.

Habitat: The European stag beetle lives in old oak forests.

Diet: The adults feed on sap, while larvae eat rotting wood.

Behavior and reproduction: Males use their big jaws against other males in battles over females. Females lay their eggs in old rotten logs and stumps. The larvae reach adulthood in three to five years. Adults

The male stag beetle shows off his large jaws that he uses against other males in battles over females.
(©Nigel Cattlin/Photo Researchers, Inc. Reproduced by permission.)

mature in fall but remain in their pupal cases until the following summer.

European stag beetles and people: This species was once thought of as a symbol of evil and bad luck.

Conservation status: This species is not listed as endangered or threatened. Still, it is legally protected in several European countries. ■

Hercules beetle (*Dynastes hercules*)

HERCULES BEETLE
Dynastes hercules

Physical characteristics: Adult males have a horn on their heads and midsections and measure 5.9 to 6.7 inches (150 to 170 millimeters) in length. The long horn on the midsection takes up to one-half of the total length. Females lack horns.

Geographic range: Hercules beetles are found in Mexico, Central America, northern South America, Guadeloupe, and the Dominican Republic.

Habitat: This species lives in humid tropical forests.

Diet: Adults eat sap and sweet fruits, while the larvae feed on rotten wood.

Behavior and reproduction: They are active at night and are often attracted to lights. Males guard feeding sites that attract hungry females. They will use their horns against other males in battles over females.

Hercules beetles and people: Some people mistakenly believe that they will become stronger and have more energy by eating the horns of the male.

Conservation status: This species is not listed as endangered or threatened. ■

Adult Hercules beetles eat sap and sweet fruits, while the larvae feed on rotten wood. (E. R. Degginger/Bruce Coleman Inc. Reproduced by permission.)

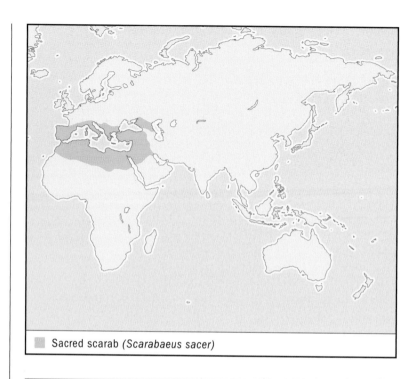

Sacred scarab (*Scarabaeus sacer*)

SACRED SCARAB
Scarabaeus sacer

Physical characteristics: The body of a sacred scarab is broad and black with a rakelike head and forelegs. They measure 0.98 to 1.2 inches (25 to 30 millimeters) in length.

Geographic range: This species is found in the Mediterranean region and central Europe.

Habitat: They live in steppe, forest-steppe, and semi-desert habitats.

Diet: Adults use their membrane-like jaws to strain fluids, molds, and other suspended particles from animal waste. The larvae eat solid waste.

Behavior and reproduction: Adult sacred scarabs fly during the day in a zig-zag pattern, following the odor of fresh animal waste. The female carves out chunks of waste with her head and legs, shapes it into a ball, and lays a single egg inside. She then stands head down and rolls the ball forward with her middle and back legs. The ball is buried and becomes the only source of food for the larva.

Sacred scarabs and people: This species recycles nutrients and destroys the breeding sites of pest flies by burying significant amounts of animal waste. Ancient Egyptians used images of the sacred scarab as a symbol of the sun god Ra. Today scarab jewelry is worn as a good luck charm.

Conservation status: This species is not listed as endangered or threatened. ■

Ancient Egyptians used images of the sacred scarab as a symbol of the sun god Ra. Today scarab jewelry is worn as a good luck charm. (Illustration by Joseph E. Trumpey. Reproduced by permission.)

American burying beetle (*Nicrophorus americanus*)

AMERICAN BURYING BEETLE
Nicrophorus americanus

Physical characteristics: Adult American burying beetles are shiny black with four wide orange spots on the elytra. The head and mid-section each have a central orange spot. The tips of the antennae are also orange. They measure 0.8 to 1.4 inches (20 to 35 millimeters) in length.

Geographic range: This species was once found throughout eastern North America. It is now found only in isolated populations in the Midwest, Rhode Island, and Massachusetts.

Habitat: American burying beetles live in woodlands, grassland prairies, forest edge, and scrubland.

Diet: Both adults and larvae feed on dead animals.

Behavior and reproduction: The adults bury small, dead animals and prepare their bodies as food for themselves and their larvae. They feed and care for the larvae and remain with them until they pupate.

American burying beetles and people: Listed as an Endangered species by the World Conservation Union (IUCN), the American burying beetle symbolizes the effect of widespread habitat modification and destruction in the eastern United States.

Conservation status: This species is listed as Endangered by the World Conservation Union (IUCN) and by the United States Fish and Wildlife Service. This means it is facing a very high risk of extinction in the wild and is in danger of extinction throughout all or a significant portion of its range. ■

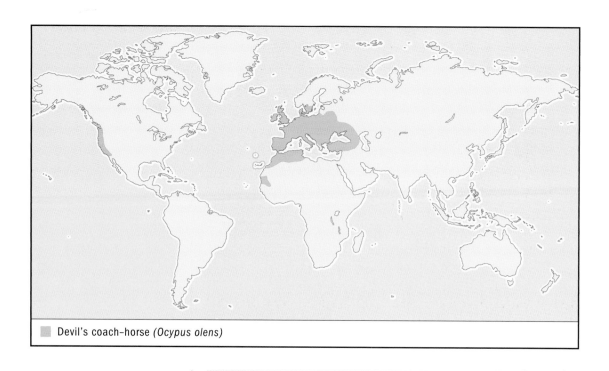

Devil's coach–horse (*Ocypus olens*)

DEVIL'S COACH-HORSE
Ocypus olens

Physical characteristics: Adult beetles are long, slender, black, and measure 0.9 to 1.3 inches (22 to 33 millimeters) in length. The body is black with short elytra exposing most of the abdominal segments.

Geographic range: This species lives in lower elevations of Europe, Russia, Turkey, North Africa, and the Canary Islands and is established in parts of North America.

Habitat: The devil's coach-horse lives in forests and gardens under stones, damp leaves, and moss, or in damp wood.

Diet: Adults and larvae prey on small, soil-dwelling arthropods, worms, slugs, and snails.

Behavior and reproduction: When threatened, the devil's coach-horse spreads its powerful jaws and bends its abdomen up over its back to spray a foul-smelling brown fluid. Nothing is known about its reproductive behavior.

When threatened, the devil's coach-horse spreads its powerful jaws and bends its abdomen up over its back to spray a foul-smelling brown fluid. (Illustration by Joseph E. Trumpey. Reproduced by permission.)

Devil's coach-horses and people: This beetle was once a symbol of evil and death.

Conservation status: This species is not listed as endangered or threatened. ■

FOR MORE INFORMATION

Books:

Evans, A. V., and C. L. Bellamy. *An Inordinate Fondness for Beetles.* Berkeley: University of California Press, 2000.

Evans, A. V., and J. N. Hogue. *Introduction to California Beetles.* Berkeley: University of California Press, 2004.

Klausnitzer, B. *Beetles.* New York: Exeter Books, 1983.

Lawrence, J. F., and E. B. Britton. *Australian Beetles.* Carlton, Australia: Melbourne University Press, 1994.

Meads, M. *Forgotten Fauna: The Rare, Endangered, and Protected Invertebrates of New Zealand.* Wellington, New Zealand: Department of Scientific and Industrial Research, 1990.

Tavolacci, J., editor. *Insects and Spiders of the World.* Volume 2: *Beetle-Carpet Beetle.* Volume 3: *Carrion Beetle-Earwig.* Volume 4: *Endangered Species-Gypsy Moth.* New York: Marshall Cavendish, 2003.

White, R. E. *A Field Guide to the Beetles of North America.* Boston: Houghton Mifflin, 1983.

Periodicals:

Cave, R. D. "Jewel Scarabs." *National Geographic* 199, no. 2 (2001): 52–61.

Chadwick, D. H. "Planet of the Beetles." *National Geographic* 193, no. 3 (1998): 1–111.

Eberhard, W. G. "Horned Beetles." *Scientific American* 242, no. 3 (1980): 166–182.

Evans, A. V. "Arizona's Sky Island Beetles." *Reptiles Magazine* 12, no. 8 (2004): 80–84.

Hadley, N. F. "Beetles Make Their Own Waxy Sunblock." *Natural History* 102, no. 8 (1993): 44–45.

Milne, L. J., and M. J. Milne. "The Social Behavior of Burying Beetles." *Scientific American* 235, no. 2 (1976): 84–89.

Web sites:

"Beetles. Coleoptera." BioKids. Critter Catalog. http://www.biokids. umich.edu/critters/information/Coleoptera.html (accessed on October 14, 2004).

"Coleoptera. Beetles, weevils." Ecowatch. http://www.ento.csiro.au/ Ecowatch/Coleoptera/Coleoptera.htm (accessed on October 14, 2004).

Coleopterists Society. http://www.coleopsoc.org (accessed on October 14, 2004).

Videos:

Bug City. Aquatic Insects. Wynnewood, PA: Schlessinger Media, 1998.

Bug City. Beetles. Wynnewood, PA: Schlessinger Media, 1998.

Bug City. Ladybugs and Fireflies. Wynnewood, PA: Schlessinger Media, 1998.

PHYSICAL CHARACTERISTICS

Adult males look like insects and measure 0.04 to 0.3 inches (1 to 7 millimeters) in length. The surfaces of their compound eyes are rough and resemble blackberries because each lens is slightly separate and clearly distinct from the surrounding lenses. Their antennae (an-TEH-nee), or sense organs, are branched and resemble tiny antlers. The mandibles, or biting mouthparts, if they have them at all, are cone-shaped and pointed downward. The first segment of the three-segmented thorax, or midsection, is short and saddle-shaped, while the last segment is much larger and houses most of the flight muscles. The front wings are twisted and knob-like. In flight they are used as balancing organs. The hind wings are clear and fan-shaped, with few supporting veins. Some of the leg segments are fused together, and the feet sometimes lack claws. The abdomen is distinctly segmented.

Most adult females strongly resemble larvae (LAR-vee), or young animals, and measure 0.08 to 1.18 inches (2 to 30 millimeters) in length. They lack wings and legs and have greatly reduced mouthparts, antennae, and eyes. The head and thorax are covered by a thick exoskeleton, or hard outer covering, and are joined together in a single body region. This part of the body sticks out from between the abdominal segments of the host's body. The abdomen is large and barely shows any traces of segmentation. The abdominal exoskeleton is very thin. The abdomen swells up like a balloon when it is filled with eggs.

The larvae have two distinct forms. Those hatching from eggs move freely in the environment and lack antennae, but have

phylum

class

subclass

● **order**

monotypic order

suborder

family

simple eyes with one lens each, mouthparts, and legs. The abdomen is tipped with two long, threadlike projections. Once they find a host they transform into a grub without legs. The pupa forms inside the hollow exoskeleton of the mature larvae. In most species male and female characteristics are clearly visible in the pupa.

GEOGRAPHIC RANGE

Twisted-wing parasites are found on all continents except Antarctica. There are about 550 species worldwide, of which 109 live in the United States and Canada.

HABITAT

Twisted-wing parasites are found in a wide variety of habitats wherever their hosts live, especially in tropical habitats. Both females and larvae are endoparasites (EN-doh-PAE-rih-saits). Endoparasites are organisms that live inside the bodies of their hosts. They invade the bodies of silverfish, cockroaches, mantids, grasshoppers, crickets and katydids, true bugs and hoppers, some flies, and ants, bees, and wasps. Males are sometimes found under stones or are attracted to lights at night.

DIET

The parasitic larvae and adult females absorb nutrients directly from the blood of their insect hosts. Free-living adult males and females do not feed.

BEHAVIOR AND REPRODUCTION

The life cycles of twisted-wing parasites are complex. Adult males move about freely in the environment, while most females live their entire lives as parasites inside the bodies of other insects. However, in one group of twisted-wing parasites the females are free-living and go about their lives outside the bodies of their host insects.

Emerging adult males use an inflatable sac on their heads to burst out of their pupal case. They have only a few hours to live and spend all their time looking for a mate. Adult females are surrounded by their old larval exoskeleton inside their host. With only their head and part of their thorax sticking out of the host's body, they release pheromones (FEH-re-moans). Pheromones are chemicals that are especially attractive to males of their own species. There is no courtship. Males deposit sperm directly into the female's body by injecting it between her head and thorax. In some species the females are able to reproduce without being fertilized by a male.

The eggs remain inside the female's body and are nourished directly by the host's blood. The hatching larvae emerge from their mother and the host to search actively for a new host on nearby vegetation. Some will hitch a ride on a wasp and settle in on an egg or larva in its nest. Others simply attack the developing larvae of other insects. Once they enter the body of their new host, the larva will molt, or shed its exoskeleton, and become a legless grub. This type of development, where the larvae alternate between active, legged forms and legless grubs is called hypermetamorphosis (HAI-purh-MEH-te-MOR-fe-sihs). Hypermetamorphosis is typical of many parasitic insects. The larvae of twisted-wing parasites molt four to seven times before reaching the pupal stage. Pupation usually takes place inside the last larval exoskeleton, with just the head and thorax sticking out from between the fourth and fifth abdominal segments of the host.

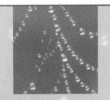

A LESSON IN ADAPTATION

Adaptations (ae-dep-TAY-shuns) include physical features or behaviors that help an organism survive and reproduce. Most female twisted-wing parasites are surrounded by food and have no need to leave their hosts. Developing wings and legs would only be a waste of energy for them. But males need plenty of mobility so they can search for females. For them, having legs and wings to get around in the environment is an absolute necessity!

TWISTED-WING PARASITES AND PEOPLE

Twisted-wing parasites are not very common, and few people ever see them. Although they do not kill their hosts, they do keep them from getting enough food and prevent them from reproducing. This means that they might be considered beneficial if their hosts happen to be considered pests.

CONSERVATION STATUS

No twisted-wing parasites are listed as endangered or threatened.

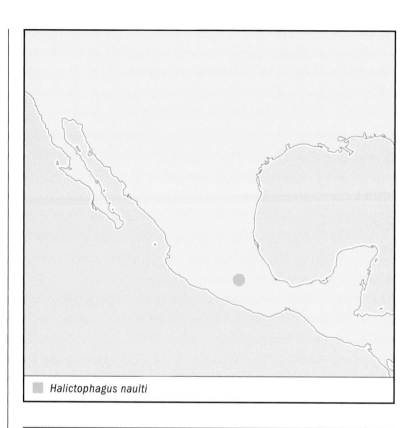

Halictophagus naulti

NO COMMON NAME
Halictophagus naulti

Physical characteristics: Adult males are about 0.04 inches (1 millimeter) in length. They have three-segmented feet and seven-segmented antennae. The females are pale yellow and brown and resemble the larvae.

Geographic range: This species is known only from the state of Morelos, Mexico.

Habitat: This species parasitizes the corn leafhopper.

Diet: The larvae and adult females are parasites that live inside the bodies of corn leafhoppers. They feed on the body fluids of their hosts. Adult males are free-living and do not eat.

Behavior and reproduction: Nothing is known about the behavior or reproduction of this species.

Halictophagus naulti and people: The corn leafhopper is the most destructive pest for corn crops in Latin America. *Halictophagus naulti* parasitizes the corn leafhopper and may prove to be useful for controlling this pest.

Conservation status: This species is not listed as endangered or threatened. ■

FOR MORE INFORMATION

Books:

Carvalho, E. L., and M. Kogan. *Order Strepsiptera. Immature Insects. Vol. 2*, ed. by F. W. Stehr. Dubuque, IA: Kendall/Hunt Publishing, 1994.

Tavolacci, J., ed. *Insects and Spiders of the World*. Vol. 9: *Stonefly-Velvet Worm*. New York: Marshall Cavendish, 2003.

Periodicals:

Kathirithamby, J. "Review of the Order Strepsiptera." *Systematic Entomology* 14 (1989): 41–92.

Web sites:

Strepsiptera. http://www.strepsiptera.uni-rostock.de/e/strepsiptera.html (accessed on October 19, 2004).

Strepsiptera. Stylopids. http://www.ento.csiro.au/Ecowatch/Insects_Invertebrates/strepsiptera.htm (accessed on October 19, 2004).

"Strepsiptera: Twisted-Wing Parasites." Tree of Life Web Project. http://tolweb.org/tree?group=Strepsiptera&contgroup=Endopterygota (accessed on October 19, 2004).

Halictophagus naulti *parasitizes the corn leafhopper and may prove to be useful for controlling this pest. (Illustration by Bruce Worden. Reproduced by permission.)*

Class: Insecta

Order: Mecoptera

Number of families: 9 families

order
CHAPTER

PHYSICAL CHARACTERISTICS

Mecopterans measure 0.08 to 0.86 inches (2 to 22 millimeters) in length. They are small to medium sized insects that vary considerably in shape. The common name "scorpionfly" refers to male mecopterans with swollen, stinger-like reproductive organs on the tip of their abdomens. These organs are sometimes held over the back just like a scorpion. However, scorpionflies are unable to sting. Hangingflies have long slender bodies and resemble crane flies with four slender wings. Other species known as earwigflies are flat with finely veined wings. Their abdomens are tipped with long pincher-like projections. Snow scorpionflies are small insects measuring only 0.08 to 0.29 inches (2 to 7.4 millimeters) long. The males use their slender, hook-like wings to grasp the nearly wingless females while mating.

Most mecopterans have downward projecting beaks with chewing mouthparts at the tip. The antennae are long and threadlike. They have both compound eyes, or eyes with multiple lenses, and simple eyes, or eyes with only one lens. The four narrow wings, if present, are clear and often banded, spotted, or have darkened patterns along the veins. The forewings and hind wings are similar in size and appearance. In some species the wings are either very narrow, almost as wide as they are long, very short, or absent. All mecopterans have relatively long and slender legs. Unable to support themselves with their thin legs, hangingflies prefer to hang from twigs and leaves by their front legs. The abdomen has nine visible segments and is usually slender and narrow toward the rear. Male abdomens are sometimes tipped with special reproductive organs or claspers.

The larvae (LAR-vee), or young, do not resemble the adults at all. There are three distinctive body types. Many resemble caterpillars and have distinct heads with downward projecting mouthparts and eight pairs of fleshy false legs on their abdomens. Others are c-shaped and grub-like, lacking false legs. A few species have slender bodies without false legs. Some species do not have eyes, while others have seven simple eyes on each side of the head. Many other species have compound eyes with 30 or more lenses on each eye. This is unique among insects whose larvae do not resemble the adults, since most others have only simple eyes.

The legs, wings, antennae (an-TEH-nee) or sense organs, and mouthparts of all mecopteran pupae (PYU-pee), the life stage between larvae and adults, are distinct. These appendages are not attached to the pupa along their entire length. The pupae are not enclosed in a cocoon.

GEOGRAPHIC RANGE

Mecopterans are found on all continents except Antarctica. Some species even live in the northern polar regions of North America and Eurasia. Most species are found in Southeast Asia and Indonesia. There are about 550 species of mecopterans worldwide, with 81 species in the United States and Canada.

HABITAT

Mecopterans live mostly in cool, moist habitats, especially in shady forests near springs, streams, and rivers. Adults are usually found resting on leaves and other vegetation. The larvae usually live in the soil or leaf litter, although a few species are aquatic and live in streams. Adult snow scorpionflies are found on ice, snow, and stones near clumps of moss. Their larvae develop in moss.

DIET

Mecopterans eat both plant and animal tissues. The adults and larvae of scorpionflies scavenge mostly dead insects. The adults are known to steal insects trapped in spider webs. They also feed on pollen, nectar, and fruit juice. Adult hangingflies are predators (PREH-duh-ters) or hunters and seize aphids, caterpillars, flies, moths, and sometimes spiders with their hind

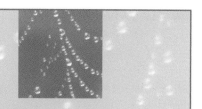

feet. Their larvae eat mostly dead insects and some decaying parts of plants. Adults and larvae of snow scorpionflies eat mosses. Short-faced scorpionfly adults graze the surfaces of leaves, but it is not known what their larvae eat. Aquatic scorpionfly larvae feed on the aquatic larvae of flies (Diptera) known as midges, but the diet of the adults is unknown.

BEHAVIOR AND REPRODUCTION

Mecopterans are secretive animals and are usually active during the day. Scorpionflies and hanging scorpionflies spend their time resting on or hanging from leaves. They are weak flyers and take to the air for only short distances. Earwigflies sometimes hide under logs and rocks and are often attracted to lights at night.

Courtship and mating usually occurs early in the evening or after dark. The males of many species offer a dead insect as food to females during courtship. They will sometimes steal insects caught in spider webs. If a suitable dead insect is not available, the male may try to steal one from another courting male, or he may spit up a blob of saliva and offer it to the female instead. Once he has a gift he flaps his wings and releases a pheromone (FEH-re-moan), which is a scent to attract females. The pheromones also attract other males who may try to steal his gift. Females select mates on the basis of the size and quality of their gift. In some species, males pretend to be females and then steal the gift of males attempting to court them. The thief then mates with a female while she eats his gift of stolen food. In some species of scorpionflies (*Panorpa*) the males use a special clamp on their abdomens to grab the edges of the female's wings to prevent her from flying away. Mating sometimes lasts for several hours. The gift of food provides the female with nourishment and helps to stimulate egg production. At times a male will simply seize the female's wings with his abdominal clamp and mate with her without offering her anything to eat.

The life cycle of mecopterans includes four very distinct stages: egg, larva, pupa, and adult. Eggs are laid in the ground, rotten wood, or leaf litter. The eggs hatch in a week or two. In some species, the eggs are laid in the fall and do not hatch until the following spring. The larvae molt, or shed their exoskeletons or hard outer coverings four times, reaching the pupal stage in anywhere from a month to two years. Mature larvae dig a small chamber in the soil in which they undergo the change. Adults live for about a month in the wild and two months or longer in captivity.

MECOPTERANS AND PEOPLE

Scorpionflies, hangingflies, and their relatives are seldom noticed by most people. They do not sting or bite.

CONSERVATION STATUS

No species of Mecoptera is considered endangered or threatened. However, studies have shown that populations in North America, Mexico, and Java are getting smaller as a result of habitat destruction caused by human activity.

Panorpa nuptialis

NO COMMON NAME
Panorpa nuptialis

Physical characteristics: The bodies of the adults are reddish brown. The yellow wings are marked with broad black or brown bands. The larvae are ringed with dark spots and short bristles and resemble caterpillars.

Geographic range: *Panorpa nuptialis* is found in the south-central United States and northern Mexico.

Habitat: The adults rest on dense vegetation in open fields and pastureland. The larvae live in the soil of these habitats.

Adult Panorpa nuptialis *rest on dense vegetation in open fields and pastureland. The larvae live in the soil of these habitats. (Illustration by Wendy Baker. Reproduced by permission)*

Diet: Both adults and larvae scavenge dead or dying soft-bodied insects.

Behavior and reproduction: Courting males occasionally offer saliva secretions to the female. Females lay their eggs in cracks in the soil. The larvae reach the pupal stage in about a month. They over-winter as pupae. Adults emerge in late fall and live nearly a month.

***Panorpa nuptialis* and people:** This species does not impact people or their activities.

Conservation status: This species is not considered endangered or threatened. ■

FOR MORE INFORMATION

Books:

Tavolacci, J., ed. *Insects and Spiders of the World.* Volume 8: *Scorpion Fly-Stink Bug.* New York: Marshall Cavendish, 2003.

Periodicals:

Byers, G. W., and R. Thornhill. "Biology of the Mecoptera." *Annual Review of Entomology* 28 (1983): 203–228.

Web sites:

"Mecoptera. Scorpionflies." Ecowatch. http://www.ento.csiro.au/Ecowatch/ Insects_Invertebrates/mecoptera.htm (accessed on October 21, 2004).

Mecoptera. Scorpionflies/Hangingflies. http://www.cals.ncsu.edu/course/ent425/compendium/mecopt 1.html (accessed on October 21, 2004).

Mecoptera Page. http://members.tripod.com/buggyrose/ipm/81mecoptera.html (accessed on October 21, 2004).

order

CHAPTER

PHYSICAL CHARACTERISTICS

Adult fleas are small insects usually measuring 0.04 to 0.3 inches (1.0 to 8 millimeters). The females have shorter antennae (an-TEH-nee) or sense organs and are usually larger than the males. The bodies of fleas are flat from side to side, allowing them to move easily between the fur and feathers of their mammal or bird hosts. Their tubelike mouthparts are used to pierce skin and suck blood. The eyes, if present, are simple and made up of a single lens each. The head and thorax, or midsection, sometimes have special comblike structures, while the legs are spiny. These features help to protect their bodies from damage, allow the fleas to cling to hair and feathers, and prevent them from being removed by the grooming activities of their hosts. The spiny and hairlike structures of bird fleas are longer, more slender, and more numerous than those of mammal fleas. The legs of fleas are used for moving through hair and feathers. Fleas are excellent jumpers and use this method to find new hosts. The abdomen is ten-segmented. In some species the abdomen of the females expands up to one hundred times its original size to accommodate either a blood meal or hundreds of developing eggs. They actually grow new tissue to allow their abdomens to expand without molting, or shedding their exoskeletons or hard outer coverings.

The legless, wormlike larvae (LAR-vee) or young do not resemble the adults at all. They range from 0.02 to 0.4 inches (0.5 to 10 millimeters) in length. Their bodies have a distinct head, a three-segmented thorax, and a ten-segmented abdomen.

phylum

class

subclass

● **order**

monotypic order

suborder

family

The legs, wings, antennae, and mouthparts of all flea pupae (PYU-pee) are distinct. These appendages are not attached to the pupae along their entire length. The pupae are surrounded by a silk cocoon and measure 0.008 to 0.4 inches (0.2 to 10 millimeters) long. The pupa is the life stage of the flea between larva and adult.

GEOGRAPHIC RANGE

Fleas are found on all continents, including Antarctica. There are 2,575 species of fleas worldwide, 258 of which occur in North America.

HABITAT

About 5 percent of all flea species occur on birds, while the remaining 95 percent parasitize, or live off of, mammals. They usually do not parasitize amphibians and reptiles. Fleas parasitize hosts in nearly all habitats where their hosts live and are found not only on their bodies but also in their burrows and nests. Bird fleas only parasitize species that reuse their nests year after year, including swallows, seabirds, some ground-dwelling species, and those living in tree holes and cavities. A few flea species that live in coastal, warm and moist, and tropical regions are free-living. Cat, dog, and human fleas all regularly spend time away from their hosts and are commonly found on the floors of homes, foot paths, animal pens, and pet beds. Most larvae are free-living and do not make their home on the body of a bird or mammal. They are usually found in pet beds and nests.

DIET

Free-living larvae scavenge scabs, flakes of skin, dried blood produced as waste by adult fleas, and other bits of tissue found in the host's nest. Some larvae live on the body of an animal, where they eat bits of skin and other tissues and fluids. *Uropsylla tasmanica* is the only larva known to burrow into the skin of its host, the Tasmanian devil. A few species prey on other insects that live in the host nest.

Adult fleas feed on host blood. Some species suck blood directly from a capillary (KAH-peh-LEH-ree), a small blood vessel just under the skin that connects arteries and veins. Others simply cut into the capillary and suck up the blood that pools on the surface of the skin. Males and females require a blood meal to produce sperm and eggs. Females usually drink more blood than males.

BEHAVIOR AND REPRODUCTION

The survival of every flea species depends on its ability to find a suitable host. Some species remain in the pupal stage for long periods of time to survive cold weather or to wait until a host comes by. The vibrations of an approaching host often trigger adults to emerge from their pupae (PYU-pee). Although fleas cannot see very well, they do respond to moving shadows by jumping. They are also attracted to the body heat and carbon dioxide, a respiratory gas exhaled by potential hosts. Cave-dwelling species instinctively crawl upward on the walls of their homes to find bats roosting on the ceiling.

Males deposit sperm directly into the reproductive organs of the females. The mating behavior of fleas differs from species to species. In many fleas the male grabs the sides of the female's abdomen with suckerlike structures on the inner surface of his antennae. He may also grasp her hind legs with his. With special claspers at the tip of his abdomen he locks his body to the tip of the female's abdomen.

The reproductive cycles of fleas are usually timed to match the reproductive cycles of their mammal hosts or the nesting and migratory habits of bird hosts. This way, hatching flea larvae will have plenty of young animals available to provide them with food.

The life cycle of fleas includes four very distinct stages: egg, larva, pupa, and adult. Some species lay eggs on the host or in the host's burrow or nest. Others deposit their eggs outdoors in soil rich with decaying plants, in carpets, or in animal beds. The larvae usually molt three times before reaching the pupal stage. Depending on species, temperature, and humidity, flea larvae may take a few weeks to several months to reach adulthood. Adults may live a few weeks to three years.

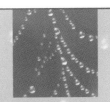

BETTER VERTICAL LEAP

A flea can jump one hundred times its body height. That is like a human being jumping 600 feet (182.8 meters) straight up. Instead of muscles, fleas rely mostly on tiny, springlike pads at the bases of their back legs. Made of a rubberlike protein called resilin (REH-zih-lihn), the pads are squeezed as the back legs are pulled up close to the body. When the legs are suddenly extended, energy stored from the squeezing is released, propelling the flea into the air.

FLEAS AND PEOPLE

The bites of the dog, cat, and human fleas are very annoying and may cause itching and allergic reactions in sensitive people. Scratching flea bites often causes further discomfort and leads to infections. Some fleas carry diseases that infect both humans and pets. Plague and other diseases are spread either through the bites of infected fleas or by rubbing the waste of infected fleas into the bite wounds. Eating fleas infected with parasitic worms and blood protozoan parasites can spread these harmful organisms to humans, dogs, rabbits, rats, and other animals.

CONSERVATION STATUS

There are no fleas that are considered endangered or threatened. However, flea species that feed only on one host species are vulnerable to extinction if their hosts were to become threatened by extinction. In these cases the fleas would share the fate of their hosts. No one has yet attempted to identify or list fleas that feed only on species listed by the World Conservation Union (IUCN).

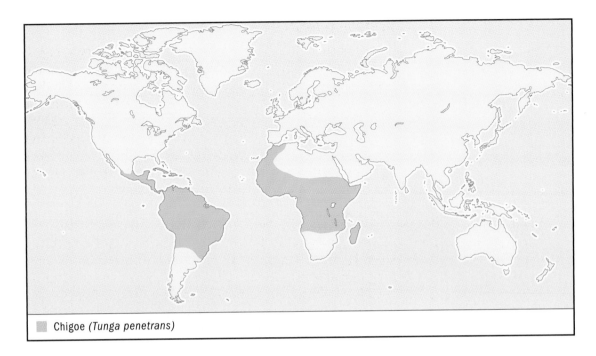

Chigoe (*Tunga penetrans*)

CHIGOE
Tunga penetrans

Physical characteristics: The chigoe's body is straw-colored or yellowish. Adults measure up to 0.04 inches (1.0 millimeters) long, but females filled with eggs may reach 0.16 inches (4.0 millimeters). The front of the head is sharply pointed. They lack comblike structures or spines on their legs. The top of each abdominal segment has a single row of hairlike structures. The last four pairs of spiracles, or breathing holes, are large. The base of each back leg has a distinct toothlike projection.

Geographic range: This species lives in the southern United States, Central and South America, the West Indies, and tropical Africa.

Habitat: Chigoes are usually found in places where there is human filth.

Diet: Both males and females bite humans occasionally. They prefer the feet, usually infesting tender areas between toes, under the nails, or along the soles. They will also attack other parts of the body.

Both male and female chigoes bite humans occasionally. They prefer the feet, usually infesting tender areas between toes, under the nails, or along the soles. (©Eye of Science/Photo Researchers, Inc. Reproduced by permission.)

Only females filled with eggs attach themselves permanently to their hosts.

Behavior and reproduction: Adults will pass through clothing to feed.

After mating the female finds a host and becomes permanently attached. The wound becomes irritated and surrounds the female with swelling tissues. Her body is now filled with eggs. She releases the eggs into the environment where they hatch. The larvae reach the pupal stage in about ten to fourteen days. Under good conditions the adults emerge after about ten to fourteen days.

Chigoes and people: Bites cause extreme irritation. Attached females may form bumps filled with pus on the host's skin. This may lead to infection and the loss of skin and tissue on toes. Extreme cases may result in the removal of toes by a doctor. Embedded females must be removed to help the wound to heal.

Conservation status: This species is not considered endangered or threatened. ■

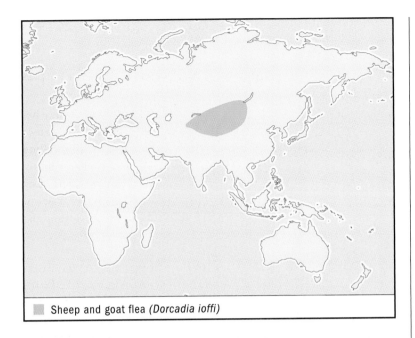

Sheep and goat flea (*Dorcadia ioffi*)

SHEEP AND GOAT FLEA
Dorcadia ioffi

Physical characteristics: The body of a sheep and goat flea has light and dark brown markings.

Adult males grow to 0.13 inches (3.3 millimeters) in length, while females are 0.18 inches (4.5 millimeters). Females swollen with eggs may reach 0.6 inches (16 millimeters). The head and thorax lack combs. The mouthparts are very long.

Geographic range: They are found in parts of China, Mongolia, and Russia.

Habitat: They prefer pastures and agricultural fields where domestic sheep, cattle, goats, and similar wild animals live.

Diet: Adults suck blood from their hosts.

Behavior and reproduction: Males attach themselves to skin on the sides of the neck. The legs of females filled with blood are almost

Female sheep and goat fleas that are filled with eggs often attach themselves to their hosts just inside the nostrils. (Illustration by Bruce Worden. Reproduced by permission.)

useless, so they wriggle through their host's fur like a worm to get around. Females filled with eggs often attach themselves to their hosts just inside the nostrils.

During the winter a single host animal may have as many as one hundred to two hundred fleas, mostly females. The dark oval eggs are dropped into the environment in spring and begin to hatch as temperatures become warmer. The larvae become pupae in late summer, and the adults emerge in early winter. The entire life cycle takes about nine months.

Sheep and goat fleas and people: This species does not bite humans but will attack their animals.

Conservation status: This species is not considered endangered or threatened. ■

FOR MORE INFORMATION

Books:

Berenbaum. M. R. *Bugs in the System: Insects and Their Impact on Human Affairs.* Reading, MA: Addison-Wesley Publishing Company, 1995.

Tavolacci, J., ed. *Insects and Spiders of the World.* Volume 4: *Endangered Species-Gypsy Moth.* New York: Marshall Cavendish, 2003.

Periodicals:

Conniff, R. "Body Beasts." *National Geographic* 194, no. 6 (December 1998): 102–115.

Rothschild, M. "Fleas." *Scientific American* 213 (1965): 44–53.

Web sites:

Flea News. http://www.ent.iastate.edu/FleaNews/AboutFleaNews.html (accessed on October 22, 2004).

Fleas of the World. http://www.fleasoftheworld.byu.edu (accessed on October 22, 2004).

Fleas (Siphonaptera): Introduction. http://www.zin.ru/Animalia/Siphonaptera/intro.htm (accessed on October 22, 2004).

"Siphonaptera. Fleas." Ecowatch. http://www.ento.csiro.au/Ecowatch/Insects_Invertebrates/siphonaptera.htm (accessed on October 2, 2004).

order
CHAPTER

PHYSICAL CHARACTERISTICS

Adult dipterans have large compound eyes, or eyes with multiple lenses, that often meet over the top of the head in males but are usually separated in females. There are two basic kinds of antennae (an-TEH-nee), or sense organs. Dipterans that have long antennae with six or more segments include mosquitoes, crane flies, midges, punkies, and no-see-ums. Those with short antennae include bee flies, flesh flies, horse and deer flies, house and stable flies, hover flies, and robber flies. The mouthparts are long and are used for sucking liquids. In predatory and blood-sucking species, such as robber flies and mosquitoes, the jaws form stiff, needle-like structures that pierce the exoskeleton or hard outer covering of other animals. They then form a straw to draw bodily fluids from the prey. In houseflies and others, the mouthparts are soft and fleshy with sponge-like structures at the tip and are used for sopping up liquids. Some flies with short antennae have a special air-filled sac. This sac is inflated only once and is used to help the young adult burst out of the pupa (PYU-pah).

An important feature that distinguishes adult flies from all other insects is the presence of only two wings. They are attached to the middle section of the thorax or midsection, which is enlarged to hold the flight muscles inside. The second pair of wings is reduced in size and resembles small clubs. They are used as balancing organs during flight. Flies that live on the bodies of animals, such as bat flies, as well as some other species, are wingless. In winged species, the bases of the wings may or may not have flaplike lobes at their bases.

The legs are variable, depending on the habits of the fly. Some are spiny and are used to capture insect prey while flying. The legs of some males are used to grasp females while mating or in elaborate courtship behaviors. Parasitic species have legs that help them cling to feathers or hair. Many species of dipterans have legs equipped with combs and brushes for grooming. The feet of all species are five-segmented and are incredibly sensitive. Some flies actually taste their food with their feet. House flies have oily and bristly pads on their feet allowing them to walk upside down on ceilings or climb smooth surfaces such as glass.

The fly abdomen has eleven segments and may be long and slender or shorter and thicker. The last two or three segments vary considerably in different species and are used for mating and egg laying.

The legless larvae (LAR-vee), or young, never resemble the adults. They are long and are either nearly cylinder-shaped or tapered at both ends. In mosquitoes the thorax is much larger than the head or abdomen. Across their bodies are swollen regions usually covered with short spines. These bumps and ridges are rough to help the larvae to get a grip and move through soil, mud, wood, water, or flesh. In species with adults that have long antennae, the larval head is distinct and nearly round and has jaws that chew from side to side. In all other flies the small pointed head is less distinct or not distinct at all and has jaws that move up and down. In these species most of the head can be withdrawn inside the thorax. Simple eyes, or eyes with only one lens, and antennae of fly larvae are greatly reduced in size or absent.

The thorax and abdomen are soft. They may or may not have spiracles along their sides, breathing holes that connect to the respiratory system. Aquatic species have only a single pair of spiracles located at the tip of the abdomen. These are sometimes mounted on a long, snorkel-like extension, allowing them to remain underwater as they breathe air directly from the surface. For example, rat-tailed maggots, larvae of drone flies, live in the bottom of ponds and breathe through a long tube resembling a rat's tail. Other aquatic species have snorkel-like extensions fitted with tiny saws used to tap into air pockets in the tissues of underwater plants.

The pupae of flies with long antennae show hints of adult features. Their legs and wing pads are clearly visible and are not completely attached to the body. In other groups of flies the pupae are smooth and resemble seeds because they are wrapped inside the old exoskeletons of the mature larvae.

GEOGRAPHIC RANGE

Flies, midges, and mosquitoes are found on all continents including Antarctica. There are about 124,000 species of flies worldwide, with about 5,127 species in the United States and Canada.

HABITAT

Adults and larval dipterans live in nearly all habitats on land and in freshwater. Almost all adults are found on land and move about freely. However, louse flies spend most of their lives on their host animals. Dipteran larvae are found in fresh and brackish, or salty, water, wet soil and leaves, and other wet places. Some species live as external parasites on animals or bore through the tissues inside leaves. Larval shore flies live along the edges of hot springs and geysers where temperatures are more than 112°F (44.4°C). Others develop in pools of crude oil or inside the nests of ants, bees, and wasps. The pupae are usually found in the same habitats as the larvae. Aquatic species usually become pupae in the water, but species found along the water's edge sometimes prefer pupal sites away from water.

DIET

The larvae of many species eat plant materials such as leaves, fruits, or roots of plants. Aquatic species filter bits of plant matter from the water or scrape algae (AL-jee) off leaves, rocks, and wood. Predators, parasites, and scavengers eat rotting plant materials and animals or animal waste. Those species that live as external parasites attack insects, spiders, and centipedes.

Adults suck or lap up all kinds of plant and animal fluids from living or dead organisms. Only female mosquitoes, no-see-ums, black flies, and horse flies bite humans and other animals because they need a blood meal to start the development of their eggs.

BEHAVIOR AND REPRODUCTION

Many species gather in mating swarms, usually around a large, stationary object such as a shrub, tree, boulder, or house. Others use open, well-lit areas such as a sunny patch in the forest or along a road. March flies, also known as lovebugs, form large mating swarms along roads in Central and South America, as well as in parts of the southeastern United States.

Many species of hover flies, bee flies, fruit flies, and robber flies mimic the distinctive colors and shapes of ants, bees, and wasps. These flies not only look like stinging insects, but they act like them too. Resembling harmful insects allows mimics to fool potential predators and live longer so they can mate and reproduce.

Before mating, many flies engage in courtship behaviors that include leg and body movements or wing flapping. In some dance flies, males offer females a dead insect as food. Mating usually starts with the couple facing the same direction but ends with the male and female facing opposite directions. A few species reproduce by parthenogenesis (PAR-thuh-no-JEH-nuh-sihs), a process where the larvae develop from eggs that have not been fertilized.

The life cycles of flies include four very distinct stages: egg, larva, pupa, and adult. Females lay their eggs on or near the right kind of food for the larvae. Fruit fly females use their long needle-like ovipositor, or egg-laying tube, to pierce the skin of fruit and lay their eggs inside. Parasitic species lay their eggs in, on, or near their hosts. Flies with aquatic larvae lay their eggs in the water or on nearby rocks and vegetation. Mosquitoes lay their eggs singly or in groups that form floating rafts on the surface of the water. The eggs usually hatch in a few days or weeks. The larvae molt, or shed their exoskeletons, four to nine times before reaching the pupal stage. The larvae may take just a few weeks to up to two years to reach maturity. The adults may live for several weeks or more.

DIPTERANS AND PEOPLE

Flies are extremely important animals in the environment. Many species of animals depend on both the adults and larvae as sources of food. Many flower-visiting species are significant as pollinators of plants. Some are considered directly beneficial to humans. For example, the larvae of some flies prey on aphids in gardens and crops, while others eat the tissues of plants that are considered weeds. The presence of certain kinds of flies can be used as indicators of water quality. The presence of midge larvae known as blood worms indicates a polluted environment. The fruit fly, *Drosophila melanogaster*, is the most intensely

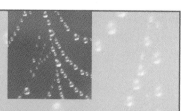

studied animal on Earth and is essential to genetic research. Several groups of flies that breed in decaying flesh have proven useful in helping police detectives to investigate human deaths. These flies have very specific food, temperature, and habitat requirements that can be used to establish not only the time of death but also if the body has been moved after death.

Flies are better known as pests because they are the most important carriers of disease that plague humans and other animals. These diseases have affected the movements of humans and changed the course of history. For example, tsetse flies prevented Europeans from colonizing parts of Africa because they spread deadly sleeping sickness in humans and nagana in cattle. Mosquitoes carry four different kinds of *Plasmodium*—protozoan single-celled animals that cause yellow fever, dengue fever, and malaria—and infect people with their bites. Even today more people die from malaria every year than all other diseases, car accidents, and wars combined. Until the use of insecticides, medicine, and the occasional window screen, humans were unable to live in some lowland areas without getting sick. Horse and deer flies infect wild and domesticated hoofed animals with several deadly diseases. In the tropics, blood-sucking black flies infect humans with parasitic worms that can cause blindness, while sand flies spread protozoans that, if left untreated, destroy all kinds of tissue and lead to death.

The mere presence of the larvae of bat flies, flesh flies, and bottle flies can cause health problems, especially in animals other than humans. Myiasis (my-EYE-ah-sis) is the infestation of an animal by fly larvae. The larvae of some species live in a wound and feed on the host's living or dead tissue and body fluids. Other species live inside the body where they feed on food inside the host's digestive system.

Still other species are attracted to eyes or food. Eye gnats (*Hippelates*) and face flies (*Musca autumnalis*) are attracted to the moisture produced around eyes. House flies (*Musca domestica*), little-house flies (*Fannia*), and latrine flies

(*Chrysomyia*) breed in filth, such as animal waste and garbage. They are considered not only a nuisance but also a potential health hazard when the adults are attracted to food at outdoor parties and picnics.

The larvae of fruit flies chew their way through citrus and other fruit and vegetable crops and are among the most destructive of all agricultural pests. Millions of dollars are lost every year because of the damage they cause, and millions more are spent on efforts to control them. The larvae of other crop pests, such as gall gnats, leaf miner flies, and root miner flies, weaken plants by boring through stems, leaves, and roots.

CONSERVATION STATUS

The World Conservation Union (IUCN) lists seven species of dipterans. Three species are listed as Extinct, or no longer in existence. The sugarfoot moth fly from the United States and the giant torrent midge from Australia are both listed as Endangered, or facing a very high risk of extinction in the wild. The Tasmanian torrent midge from Australia is listed as Critically Endangered, or facing an extremely high risk of extinction in the wild, because of the construction of a hydroelectric dam in its habitat. Belkin's dune tabanid fly, a horse fly from Mexico and the United States, is considered Vulnerable, or facing a high risk of extinction in the wild, because its habitat is being destroyed by development. The Endangered Delhi Sands flower-loving fly is the only fly listed by the United States Fish and Wildlife Service. Its habitat is disappearing due to development and is also being destroyed by trash dumping and pesticide use.

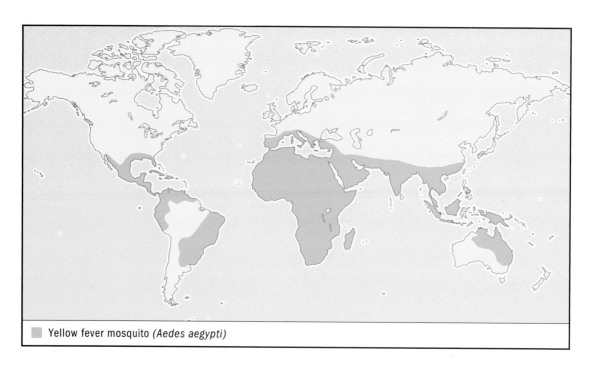

■ Yellow fever mosquito (*Aedes aegypti*)

YELLOW FEVER MOSQUITO
Aedes aegypti

Physical characteristics: This small mosquito measures 0.1 to 0.15 inches (3 to 4 millimeters) long. It is black with a u-shaped patch of white scales on the back of the thorax and white rings on the legs. The wings are clear with scales along the edges. The white eggs soon turn black after they are laid.

Geographic range: This species is originally from Africa but is now established in all tropical and subtropical regions of the world.

Habitat: Yellow fever mosquitoes live in hot, humid habitats and often breed near human dwellings, especially in towns and cities. Females search for blood meals early in the morning or late afternoon. They prefer human hosts and generally bite around the ankles. They rest in poorly lit cabinets, closets, and cupboards. The eggs are laid singly along the water's edge. The larvae develop in standing water.

Diet: Both males and females depend on plant juices for their own nutrition. Only the females need a blood meal so that their eggs will develop. The larvae strain tiny bits of floating plant material from the water.

Behavior and reproduction: When resting, the back legs are curled up. They often clean these legs by rubbing them against one another. They also raise and lower their back legs, as well as cross and uncross them.

Yellow fever mosquitoes and people: This species is the most important transmitter of viruses that cause human dengue fever and urban yellow fever. It also spreads chikungunya virus in Asia.

Conservation status: This species is not considered endangered or threatened. ■

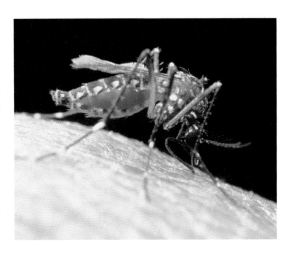

A female yellow fever mosquito is shown feeding on a human arm. The mosquito normally conceals her slender stylets, which can be seen here inserted in the skin as she removes blood from her victim. (©Martin Dohrn/Photo Researchers, Inc. Reproduced by permission.)

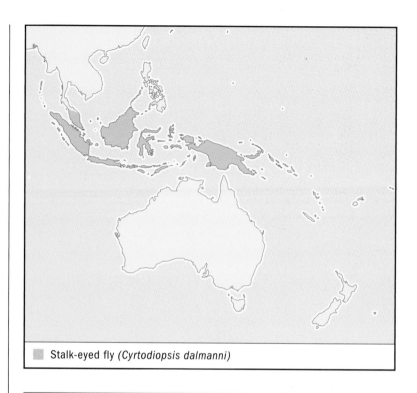

Stalk-eyed fly *(Cyrtodiopsis dalmanni)*

STALK-EYED FLY
Cyrtodiopsis dalmanni

Physical characteristics: This species is about the size of a house fly. The compound eyes, or eyes with multiple lenses, are located on the tips of horn-like structures, or stalks, that project from the sides of the head. The distance between each eye on a male is nearly equal to the length of its body. The eye-stalks of the females are much shorter.

Geographic range: This particular stalk-eyed fly is widespread in Southeast Asia.

Habitat: They live on damp, shady forest floors near streams.

Diet: The larvae eat plants, while the adults feed on nectar and other plant juices.

Behavior and reproduction: Males stake out rootlets on the ground and compete with one another for females. Males face one another and

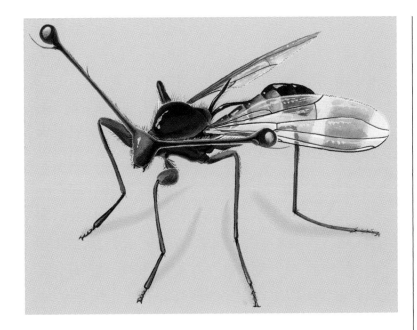

wrestle each other with their front legs. Eventually the male with the shortest eye-stalks backs down. Females prefer large-bodied males with long eye-stalks as mates. They are usually found in small groups. A single male will mate with up to twenty females in just thirty minutes.

Upon emerging from the pupa, stalk-eyed flies pump body fluids into both their wings and eye-stalks for up to fifteen minutes until they expand to their full lengths.

Stalk-eyed flies and people: These fascinating animals are observed by scientists who study courtship behavior.

Conservation status: This species is not considered endangered or threatened. ■

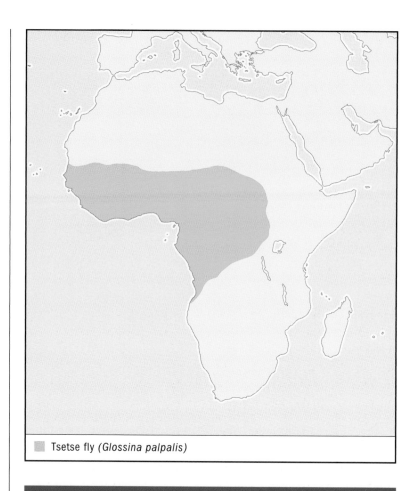

Tsetse fly (*Glossina palpalis*)

TSETSE FLY
Glossina palpalis

Physical characteristics: Adult tsetse flies are yellowish to brown, with forward-projecting, piercing mouthparts. They measure up to 0.47 inches (12 millimeters) in length. There is a hatchet-shaped cell in the center of each wing.

Geographic range: They live in western Africa.

Habitat: Tsetse flies are found in patches of dense vegetation along banks of rivers and lakes in hot, dry habitats. They also live in dense, wet, heavily forested equatorial rainforest.

Diet: Adults feed on the blood of birds, mammals, and reptiles.

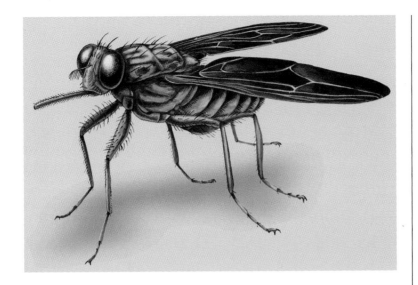

The tsetse fly is a major carrier of sleeping sickness in humans and nagana in animals. (Illustration by Jonathan Higgins. Reproduced by permission.)

Behavior and reproduction: Host animals are located primarily by sight, rather than smell. The female keeps a single egg for nine to twelve days inside her body, where it molts three times. The larva is then deposited in the soil and pupates. The pupal stage lasts four to five weeks. The adult emerges from the pupa with the aid of a special, inflatable sac on the head. Females are ready to mate two or three days after emerging, but males may take up to several days more. Adults are long-lived, with males living six weeks and females up to fourteen.

Tsetse flies and people: This species transmits a protozoan, or one-celled animal, that causes nagana in horses and cattle, and sleeping sickness in humans.

Conservation status: This species is not considered endangered or threatened. ■

■ Spider bat fly (Basilia falcozi)

SPIDER BAT FLY
Basilia falcozi

Physical characteristics: Adult spider bat flies have flat bodies, no wings, and resemble six-legged spiders. They have long legs with strong claws. The shiny pupae are black and flattened.

Geographic range: This species is found in Australia.

Habitat: They live on the bodies of cave-dwelling broad-nosed, bent-winged, and big-eared bats.

Diet: Spider bat flies feed on the blood of bats.

Behavior and reproduction: Adults spend most of their lives on the body of their bat host. Females leave the host to deposit a single, fully developed pupa on cave walls and trees near bat roosts. Females will deposit several pupae during their lifetime. Adults emerge from the pupae when they sense the body heat of a nearby bat.

Spider bat flies and people: This species does not impact people or their activities.

Conservation status: This species is not considered endangered or threatened. ■

Spider bat flies live on the bodies of cave-dwelling broad-nosed, bent-winged, and big-eared bats. (Illustration by Jonathan Higgins. Reproduced by permission.)

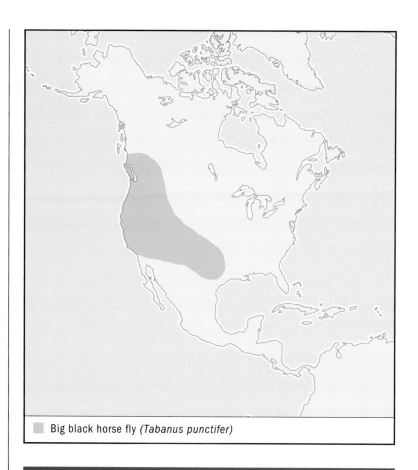

Big black horse fly (Tabanus punctifer)

BIG BLACK HORSE FLY
Tabanus punctifer

Physical characteristics: Adult big black horse flies are large, heavy-bodied flies and measure 0.35 to 1.1 inches (9 to 28 millimeters) in length. Their wide heads have bulging, brightly colored eyes. The thorax or midsection is gray, while the abdomen is black. The wings are blackish. The larvae are cylinder-shaped and have fine wrinkles along the length of the body.

Geographic range: This species is found in western Canada and the United States, from British Columbia south to California, east to Kansas and Texas.

Habitat: Adults live near ponds, streams, and marshes, while the larvae develop in mud or moist soil along the edges of these habitats.

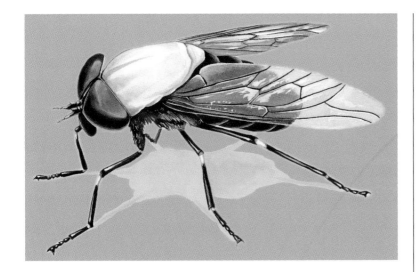

Adult big black horse flies eat mostly nectar and pollen. Females require a blood meal before they can lay eggs. They suck blood from livestock and humans. (Illustration by Jonathan Higgins. Reproduced by permission.)

Diet: Adults eat mostly nectar and pollen. Females require a blood meal before they can lay eggs. They suck blood from livestock and humans. The larvae prey on other insect larvae, snails, and earthworms.

Behavior and reproduction: Females land on exposed skin to feed. They lay up to one thousand eggs in masses three or four layers deep. The masses are laid on leaves, rocks, or other objects near water or moist areas and are covered with a jellylike material. Hatching larvae fall into the water or on moist soil. They pupate at the margins of pools or other drier areas in the habitat.

Big black horse flies and people: Horse flies are a nuisance to horses and mules because of the painful bites of the female. They will also bite people.

Conservation status: This species is not considered endangered or threatened. ■

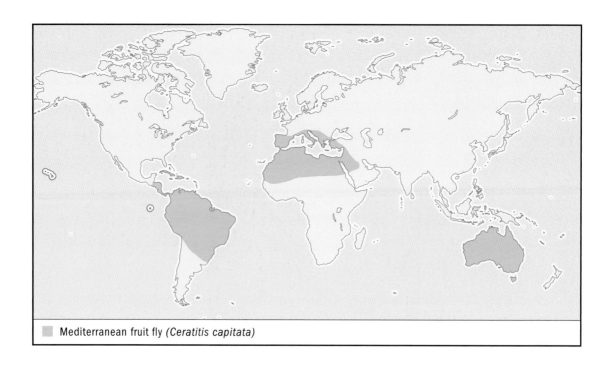

Mediterranean fruit fly (Ceratitis capitata)

MEDITERRANEAN FRUIT FLY
Ceratitis capitata

Physical characteristics: Adult Mediterranean fruit flies measure 0.14 to 0.2 inches (3.5 to 5 millimeters) in length. The eyes are iridescent (IH-rih-DEH-sent), or shiny and multicolored. The wings are broad with yellow patterns. The females have a distinctive egg-laying tube, or ovipositor, on the tip of the abdomen. The larvae are white and narrow toward the head, becoming wider toward the rear. The tip of their abdomen is broad and flat. The dark reddish brown pupae are cylinder-shaped and about 0.12 inches (3 millimeters) in length.

Geographic range: This species is native to Africa. During the past one hundred years it has become established in countries in the Mediterranean region, including Spain, Italy, Greece, Jordan, Turkey, parts of Saudi Arabia, and most countries along the North African coast. It is also found in Portugal and the Hawaiian Islands. It is occasionally found in California and Florida in the continental United States, as well as in Mexico, Guatemala, and Chile.

The Mediterranean fruit fly is a major agricultural pest in temperate and subtropical regions worldwide. It attacks more than two hundred different kinds of fruit crops. (Illustration by Jonathan Higgins. Reproduced by permission.)

Habitat: The adult Mediterranean fruit flies are found wherever fruit trees grow. The larvae bore inside of fruit.

Diet: Larvae feed within the flesh of citrus, peach, and guava, among many other fruits. The adults sop up fruit juices, honeydew, and plant sap.

Behavior and reproduction: Adults fly only short distances, but winds may carry them up to several miles (kilometers) away.

Females lay one to ten eggs beneath the skin of ripening fruit. They may lay up to three hundred eggs in their lifetime. Eggs hatch after two or three days and molt twice within six to ten days. Mature larvae leave the fruit and burrow 1 to 2 inches (2.5 to 5 centimeters) into the soil to pupate. Adults emerge in about ten days. Males defend leaves on fruit trees as territories and release pheromones (FEH-re-moans), chemical scents attractive to females. Courtship includes brief wing flapping and head movements.

Mediterranean fruit flies and people: The Mediterranean fruit fly is a major agricultural pest in temperate and subtropical regions worldwide. It attacks over two hundred different kinds of fruit crops. Fly infestations in North, Central, and South America are eradicated by flooding the area with thousands of sterile males. Sterile males are exposed to low doses of radiation and cannot produce sperm. Although sterile, these males will still mate with females, but their eggs will not be fertilized.

Conservation status: This species is not considered endangered or threatened. ■

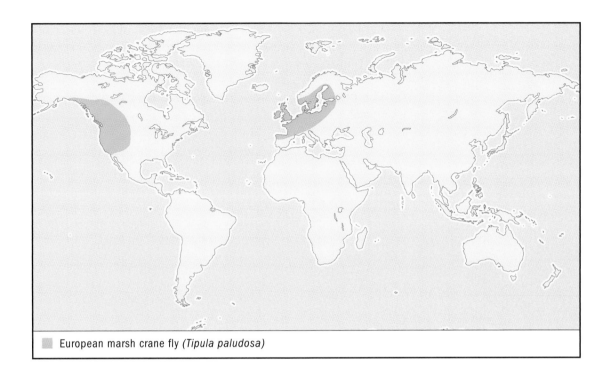

European marsh crane fly (*Tipula paludosa*)

EUROPEAN MARSH CRANE FLY
Tipula paludosa

Physical characteristics: Adult European marsh crane files resemble giant, grayish brown mosquitoes with brown legs. They measure about 1 inch (25 millimeters) in length. Their narrow wings span 0.7 to 0.9 inches (17 to 25 millimeters). The gray larvae are known as leather jackets because their exoskeleton is tough and leathery. Mature larvae measure 1.1 inches (30 millimeters). The brown, spiny pupae are about 1.3 inches (33 millimeters) in length.

Geographic range: Native to northern Europe, they are now found in western Canada and the United States.

Habitat: This species lives in areas with mild winters, cool summers, and rainfall averaging about 23.5 inches (600 millimeters) a year. They prefer wet lawns, pastures, hay fields, and grassy banks along drainage ditches.

Diet: The larvae eat rotting vegetable matter, grass seedlings and roots, and the bases of other young plants.

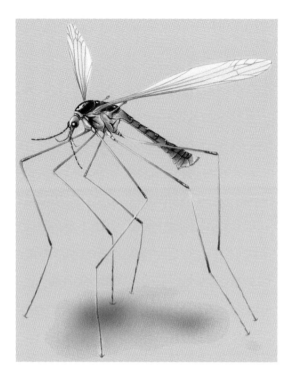

Behavior and reproduction: Adults are weak fliers and are attracted to lights at night. They may accidentally enter houses and buildings.

Adults are most common in late summer. Females lay up to 280 black, shiny eggs in the soil, usually at night. They hatch within two weeks and grow rapidly to a maximum length of 1.1 inches (30 millimeters). They pupate in the soil in mid-July. The pupal stage lasts about two weeks. The adults emerge at sunset, leaving the pupal case partially sticking out of the soil, and mate immediately. Males live about seven days; females, four to five. There is one generation per year.

European marsh crane flies and people: The larvae strip the root hairs and kill parts of small trees in nurseries by chewing all the way around some stems.

Conservation status: This species is not considered endangered or threatened. ■

The European marsh crane fly lives in areas with mild winters, cool summers, and rainfall averaging about 23.5 inches (600 millimeters) a year. They prefer wet lawns, pastures, hay fields, and grassy banks along drainage ditches. (Illustration by Jonathan Higgins. Reproduced by permission.)

FOR MORE INFORMATION

Books:

Conniff, R. *Spineless Wonders, Strange Tales from the Invertebrate World.* New York: Henry Holt and Company, 1996.

Hubbell, S. *Broadsides from the Other Orders. A Book of Bugs.* New York: Random House, 1993.

Oldroyd, H. *The Natural History of Flies.* New York: W.W. Norton and Company, 1965.

Tavolacci, J., ed. *Insects and Spiders of the World.* Volume 4: *Endangered Species-Gypsy Moth.* New York: Marshall Cavendish, 2003.

Periodicals:

Gerster, G. "Fly of the Deadly Sleep. Tsetse." *National Geographic* 170, no. 6 (December 1986): 814–832.

Moffett, M. W. "Flies That Fight." *National Geographic* 192, no. 5 (November 1997): 68–77.

Web sites:

"Beetles. True flies, including mosquitoes." BioKids. Critter Catalog. http://www.biokids.umich.edu/critters/information/Diptera.html (accessed on October 25, 2004).

"Diptera. Flies, mosquitoes." Ecowatch. http://www.ento.csiro.au/Ecowatch/Diptera/diptera.htm (accessed on October 25, 2004).

The Young Diptera Site. http://www.sel.barc.usda.gov/Diptera/youngent.htm (accessed on October 25, 2004).

Videos:

Bug City. Flies and mosquitoes. Wynnewood, PA: Schlessinger Media, 1998.

order

PHYSICAL CHARACTERISTICS

Adult caddisflies are slender, mothlike insects that are usually drab in color, although some species are very brightly marked. They measure 0.048 to 1.76 inches (1.2 to 40 millimeters) in length. Both compound and simple eyes are present. Compound eyes have multiple lenses; simple eyes have only one. The chewing mouthparts are made up of long, fingerlike appendages on either side of very small jaws. The antennae (an-TEH-nee), or sense organs, are long, threadlike, and held together out in front of the body. Both the head and the thorax, or midsection, have wartlike bumps. All four wings are similar to one another in size and appearance. They are folded like a roof over the body when at rest. Most of the wing veins are straight and have very few branches, or cross-veins. The females of some species have very small wings and cannot fly. The legs are long, slender, and have scattered spines. The ten-segmented abdomen is tipped, with reproductive organs that vary in shape.

The larvae (LAR-vee), or young, resemble caterpillars. Their heads are distinct and hard with strong jaws. Each of the three segments of the thorax has a pair of well-developed legs. A thick plate covers one or more of the thoracic segments. The long, soft ten-segmented abdomen is slender or plump and sometimes has gills along the sides. The last abdominal segment has a pair of leglike structures.

GEOGRAPHIC RANGE

Caddisflies are found on all continents except Antarctica. Most species have relatively small ranges, and many are found only in one or a few countries. There are more than 11,000 species worldwide, with about 1,400 species known in the United States and Canada.

HABITAT

Most caddisfly larvae and pupae (PYU-pee), the life stage between larva and adult, are found in freshwater, but there are a few species that live on land or in the sea. The larvae of freshwater species usually live in cold clean flowing waters, but some species prefer warmer slower waters. They are very particular about water temperature and speed, dissolved minerals and pollutants, as well as the amount of sunlight. Several species can live together in a stream or river because each occupies habitats within the water that do not overlap. Predatory species wander about freely in the environment hunting for food animals, but many plant-feeding species live in protective cases built from pebbles, sand, or bits of vegetation from the bottom and held together with silk. A marine species from Australia and New Zealand spends part of its larval life eating tissues inside the body cavity of a living sea star (starfish). Later it leaves its host to build a case from seaweed.

The adults are usually active at night. They spend their days hiding in moist, cool habitats and are often found on vegetation growing along river banks.

DIET

Adult caddisflies eat only plant fluids such as nectar or sap. Depending on the species, the larvae eat bits of plant materials on the bottom or in the water, living plants, living and dead animals, or most or all of the above. Species that do not build cases usually feed on tiny bits of plants or prey on other insects. Case builders shred leaves, graze on living plants, or scrape algae (AL-jee) from rocks, wood, and other surfaces. Some species use their jaws to pierce threadlike algae and suck its fluids, one cell at a time.

BEHAVIOR AND REPRODUCTION

All caddisfly larvae spin silk to make nets to capture food floating in the water or build protective shelters. Shelters may be silken bags or made with small pebbles, sand, or plant materials attached together with silk to form a case. The materials used and the shape of the case vary with each species. The larvae can be categorized into five groups based on their case-building behavior. Free-living forms construct shelters only for pupation. Saddle-case makers build cases resembling tortoise shells. Purse-case makers are free-living until they are ready to pupate. Then they build silken purselike or barrellike cases. Net-spinners build a fixed silken retreat on the rocky bottoms of swift streams with a weblike net to capture bits of plants and animals floating in the water. Tube-case builders are probably the most familiar. They use bits of leaves, twigs, or small gravel to construct portable cases. With only their head, thorax, and legs sticking out of the case, the larvae drag themselves across the stream bottom to search for food. The ability of caddisfly larvae to build their own shelters allows them to live in a variety of aquatic habitats.

Caddisflies are ready to mate as soon as they emerge from their cocoons. Some females attract males with chemical scents or pheromones (FEH-re-moans). In other species, males gather in swarms and engage in dances to attract females. Some species also make sounds, but these have different meanings among different species. For example, drumming sounds may drive some species to mate, but in others the same sounds are part of a defensive behavior that signals an attack. Many species also flap or spread their wings as a part of courtship, but males of other species may use these movements as a sign of attack toward other males.

Males transfer sperm or a sperm packet directly to the reproductive organs of the females. Mating usually takes place near the larval habitat, either on streamside vegetation or on the ground. They may stay together for just a few minutes or several hours. Both males and females may mate several times with other partners.

The life cycles of caddisflies includes four very distinct stages: egg, larva, pupa, and adult. The adult female can stay under the water up to thirty minutes as she glues her eggs to rocks and plants. In some species the female carries her eggs on the tip of the abdomen. She then flies upstream, dipping her abdomen into the water to deposit the eggs. Other species simply lay their eggs on plants hanging over the water. Case-builders usually pupate inside their shelters. Even species that do not build shelters use silk to make a cocoon before pupating inside. Some species cover their cocoons with small loosely stacked pebbles.

After emerging from its pupa the adult cuts its way out of the cocoon and swims to the surface. The adults are mostly active in spring and summer, but a few species emerge in the winter. They live for only a short time and spend most of their time looking for a mate. Many species are attracted to lights at night. Since larvae are usually washed downstream by the water current, many species will fly short distances upstream to lay their eggs.

CADDISFLIES AND PEOPLE

Some South American native peoples use larval cases as earrings and as beads for necklaces. Beginning in the 1980s, the visual artist Hubert Duprat utilized caddisflies to create unique sculptural forms. He first removed larvae from their natural habitat, and then he provided the larvae with different colored pebbles, sand, or ground up seashells or glass materials. The caddisflies used these materials to build "jeweled" cases. Since then other companies have used this method to make earrings, necklaces and other types of jewelry.

Salmon and other fishes eat caddisfly larvae, pupae, and adults. Fly fishermen make all sorts of lures that mimic the various stages of caddisfly development and use them instead of bait to catch fish.

A few species of caddisflies are considered pests. Some chew on wood structures in the water, while others nibble on rice plants and aquatic ornamental plants sold in nurseries. The adults are often attracted by the thousands to lights, clogging air conditioners with their bodies. Others lay their eggs on the shiny road surface, mistaking it for water. Thousands of crushed eggs make the roads slippery and a hazard to drivers.

CONSERVATION STATUS

Four species of caddisflies are listed as Extinct by the World Conservation Union (IUCN). These four species no longer exist. All caddisflies are vulnerable to changes in water quality. Since

WHEN IS A FLY NOT A FLY?

The common names for true flies (Diptera), such as bee fly, crane fly, fruit fly, hover fly, house fly, and robber fly, always have two words. But insects that are not dipterans have common names that are written as one word, like butterfly (Lepidoptera), caddisfly (Trichoptera), dobsonfly (Megaloptera), dragonfly and damselfly (Odonata), mayfly (Ephemeroptera), sawfly (Hymenoptera), scorpionfly (Mecoptera), snakefly (Raphidioptera), and stonefly (Plecoptera).

many species are found only in a small region, the slightest disturbance in their environment may have a devastating effect on the entire population. Because of their sensitivity to water pollution, the presence or absence of caddisfly larvae is used as an indicator of water quality.

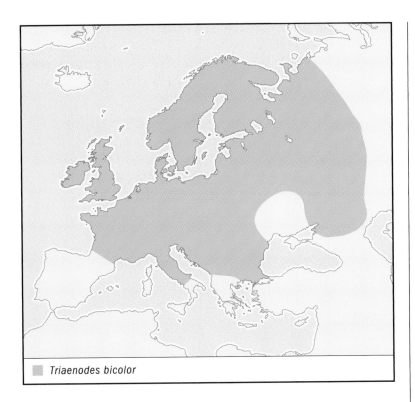

Triaenodes bicolor

NO COMMON NAME
Triaenodes bicolor

Physical characteristics: The larvae of this species measure 0.34 to 0.52 inches (8.5 to 13.0 millimeters) in length. They are brownish yellow in color. The adults have slender brown bodies. The antennae are very long.

Geographic range: This species lives in Europe and western Russia.

Habitat: The larvae are found on plants growing in shallows close to the river bank, usually at depths of 7.87 to 59.05 inches (0.2 to 1.5 meters).

Diet: The larvae eat green plants.

Behavior and reproduction: The larvae build cases with long bits of plant material arranged in a spiral. The cases become narrow at the

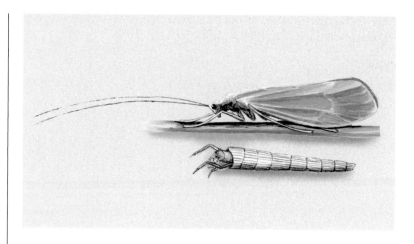

Shown here are the adult (top) and larvae (bottom) Triaenodes bicolor species. The larvae build cases with long bits of plant material arranged in a spiral. The cases become narrow at the end and measure 0.6 inches (15 millimeters) in length. (Illustration by Wendy Baker. Reproduced by permission.)

end and measure 0.6 inches (15 millimeters) in length. Mature larvae remodel their cases just before pupation.

Females lay their eggs in a spiral pattern on aquatic plants.

Triaenodes bicolor and people: This species is a pest in cultivated rice fields.

Conservation status: This species is not considered endangered or threatened.   ∎

FOR MORE INFORMATION

Books:

LaFontaine, G. *Caddisflies.* New York: The Lyons Press, 1994.

Tavolacci, J., ed. *Insects and Spiders of the World.* Volume 2: *Beetle-Carpet Beetle.* New York: Marshall Cavendish, 2003.

Wiggins, G. *Larvae of the North American Caddisfly Genera (Trichoptera).* 2nd ed. Toronto and Buffalo, New York: University of Toronto Press, 1996.

Periodicals:

"Surprising Snapshot of a Long-lost World. Geographica." *National Geographic* 190, no. 4 (October 1996).

Web sites:

"Trichoptera. Caddisflies." Ecowatch. http://www.ento.csiro.au/ Ecowatch/Trichoptera/Trichoptera.htm (accessed on October 27, 2004).

"Trichoptera. Caddisflies." Tree of Life Web Project. http://tolweb.org/ tree?group=Trichoptera&contgroup=Endopterygota#top (accessed on October 27, 2004).

"The Trichoptera (Caddis Flies)." Earthlife. http://www.earthlife.net/insects/trichopt.html (accessed on October 27, 2004).

Videos:

Bug City. Aquatic Insects. Wynnewood, PA: Schlessinger Media, 1998.

BUTTERFLIES, SKIPPERS, AND MOTHS
Lepidoptera

Class: Insecta

Order: Lepidoptera

Number of families: 122 families

phylum

class

subclass

 order

monotypic order

suborder

family

PHYSICAL CHARACTERISTICS

Adults come in a wide variety of shapes, sizes, and colors. Their bodies are long and slender or plump and are either brightly or drably colored. The smallest species are leaf-miner moths with wingspans measuring 0.17 inches (4.5 millimeters). The largest moth is from the American tropics with a wingspan of up to 11.02 inches (280 millimeters). The smallest known butterfly species are *Micropsyche ariana* from Afghanistan and the Western pygmy blue of the United States. Both have wingspans of 0.39 to 0.75 inches (10 to 19 millimeters). The largest butterfly is the Queen Alexandra's birdwing of New Guinea. Females are larger than males and have wingspans measuring up to just over 7 inches (129 millimeters).

Most adults have a long coiled tubelike tongue called the proboscis (pruh-BAH-suhs). The proboscis is used for sucking up fluids. It is sometimes longer than the body and is coiled up and stored under the head when not in use. In some moths the proboscis is strong enough to pierce the skin of fruit. Some moths do not have a proboscis, and a few species have jaws. The mouthparts usually include a pair of fingerlike structures covered with scales called palps. The antennae (an-TEH-nee), or sense organs, of moths are long and threadlike or feathery. Those of butterflies are long, slender, and swollen at the tips. Skippers also have long slender antennae, but the tips are hooked. All adults have a pair of large compound eyes, or eyes with multiple lenses, and some also have a pair of simple eyes, or eyes with one lens.

Nearly all lepidopterans (leh-pe-DOP-teh-runs) have four wings, but a few species, especially the females, are wingless. The wings are usually large when compared to the size of the body and are densely covered with tiny flat hair-like structures called scales. Thousands of scales are arranged on the wings like overlapping shingles on a roof and give lepidopterans their colors and patterns. The wings are similar in size and texture, but the forewing colors of many moths are usually bolder than the hind wings. The wing veins, which can only be seen when the scales are removed, vary in pattern. Smaller moths have only a few veins in each wing. The leading edge of the forewing is reinforced with several veins to give it strength.

The forewings and hind wings work together while the insect is in flight. In ghost moths there is a flap near the base of the forewing that overlaps and connects with the base of the hind wing. In most other moths, the portion of the hind wings closest to the body, called the base, has a cluster of hairs that fits into a special structure on the base of the forewing. Butterflies, nearly all skippers, and a few moths have hind wings with a stiff flap near the base that overlaps the base of the forewing.

The soft, ten-segmented abdomen is covered with scales and lacks any long projections on the tip.

The larvae (LAR-vee) or young, usually known as caterpillars, do not resemble the adults at all. Their bodies are long, soft, and fleshy. The nearly round head is distinct, hard, and has powerful jaws. The antennae are small and not easily seen. Two silk glands are located inside the lower lip. The silk comes out through a single opening on the lip. The six true legs are located on the thorax, or midsection. Each leg is five-segmented and usually tipped with a single claw. The underside of the abdomen has a series of paired false legs called prolegs, which are fleshy structures usually tipped with a series of hooks. These hooks allow caterpillars to grip leaves, twigs, and other objects. The surfaces of their wrinkled bodies are smooth or covered with scales, fleshy bumps, spines, or tufts of hair. These coverings sometimes help to protect the caterpillars from potential predators (PREH-duh-ters), or animals that hunt them for food. The needlelike spines are sometimes hollow, attached to poison glands, and capable of delivering burning stings. The hairs of some species are especially irritating to people if they get into the eyes, nose, or mouth.

The features of the adult are clearly visible in the pupae (PYU-pee), or the life stage between larva and adult. The legs and wings are tightly fastened to the body along their entire lengths. The pupae of moths are usually brownish and smooth. The pupa of a butterfly is called a chrysalis (KRIH-suh-lihs). Chrysalises come in a variety of colors and are sometimes distinctly sculptured. The pupae are sometimes wrapped in a silk cocoon, especially in some moths. The chrysalises of many butterflies are attached to branches and the undersides of leaves. They have a small cluster of hooks located on the very tip of the abdomen that they use to grab a buttonlike pad of silk spun by the caterpillar. Swallowtail butterflies also secure their chrysalises with an additional strand of silk like a belt wrapped around the body. Many moths do not use any silk at all and pupate, or change into pupae, in the ground or under tree bark.

GEOGRAPHIC RANGE

Lepidopterans are found on all continents except Antarctica. Most species are found in the tropics. There are about 160,000 species of butterflies and moths worldwide, the vast majority of which are moths. Of the 12,000 species of Lepidoptera known in the United States and Canada, only 760 are butterflies.

HABITAT

All the life stages of lepidopterans are found in a wide variety of habitats on land, usually on or near caterpillar food plants or adult nectar sources. Some moth caterpillars live on aquatic plants in ponds and streams. Some caterpillars of butterflies known as blues live inside ant nests.

Adults are also widespread. They are found resting on foliage, tree trunks, or visiting flowers or patches of moisture. Some species gather in large groups on shrubs, trees, or near cave entrances.

DIET

Nearly all lepidopterans feed on flowering plants, but a few species prefer algae (AL-jee), or tiny plantlike organisms, growing underwater, funguses, mosses, or pine trees and their relatives. Most larvae will eat the tissues of just one or a few closely related plant species, but a few will feed on many kinds of plants. Most species feed on the outside of plants. Depending on the species they devour leaves, flowers, seeds, or buds. A few species of moth larvae roll up leaves to create a shelter to feed inside in safety. Some moth species bore into plants, eating wood inside tree trunks or softer tissues inside vine stems. A few moth and butterfly species are predators and attack flies, aphids, and scale insects. Butterfly larvae living inside ant nests eat the eggs, larvae, and pupae of their hosts. Other moth species steal insects from insect-eating pitcher plants or from spider webs. The caterpillars of clothes moths eat cloth, wool, fur, and feathers, while those of Indian mealmoths prefer dried fruit and stored grains. Still others scavenge the waste of birds and mammals.

Most adults drink nectar, fruit juices, and plant sap and will sometimes supplement their diets with pollen. Some will also take up mineral-rich fluids from mud, dead animals, and both liquid and solid animal waste. A few prefer fluids such as tears around the eyes of animals. An Asian moth, *Calpe eustrigiata*, prefers to feed on blood and uses its proboscis to pierce the skin of animals. The few species with chewing mouthparts eat pollen. Those adults without mouthparts must rely on the food they ate as caterpillars for energy.

BEHAVIOR AND REPRODUCTION

Butterflies and moths have to be warm (77 to 79°F or 25 to 26°C) in order to fly. They depend on the temperature of their environment to maintain their body temperature. Butterflies living in cooler climates use their wings to warm their bodies. They bask in the sun so their wings get maximum exposure to the warm light. In hotter climates butterflies can overheat, so they are usually active only during the cooler parts of the day, early morning, late afternoon, or early evening. During the heat of the day they rest in the shade.

Some larger thick-bodied moths, such as hawk moths, can generate their own heat to a limited degree by vibrating their wings. The heat generated by the flight muscles warms the thorax, but the abdomen does not need to be kept so warm. To avoid overheating some moths rely on hairy scales, internal air sacs, and other structures to separate the thorax and abdomen and keep the abdomen cooler.

Butterflies, skippers, and moths usually get together only to mate. However, some species do gather in large groups to find a more comfortable climate. Only about 200 species of butterflies and moths regularly migrate long distances, returning to the areas where they breed. The Jersey tiger moth escapes the summer heat by gathering in large numbers in cooler, wetter habitats. Monarchs in North America migrate by the thousands or millions each year to the coast of California or the volcanic mountains of southern Mexico to escape cold winters. In spring they fly east from coastal California, or north from Mexico, laying their eggs on milkweeds as they go. Individuals seldom make the entire return trip. Instead, this is accomplished by their offspring. It takes three to five generations of monarchs each year to repopulate the continent. The last generation in late summer or early fall is the one that migrates to warmer climates.

Caterpillars display a wide range of defensive behaviors to avoid being eaten by birds and other animals. For example, bagworms build a protective case of silk and cover it with twigs, leaf fragments, and sand. Others have colors and textures that help them blend in with surrounding twigs, leaves, and flowers. When startled, some species whip back and forth, rear up to expose large fake eye spots, vomit bright-colored fluids, or pretend to be dead and drop to the ground.

Both adults and larvae of some species have bright colors or distinctive patterns that warn predators of their bad taste. Other caterpillars are covered with irritating hairs or stinging spines. Giant leopard moths from the eastern United States are boldly marked insects with large black spots on a white background. When threatened they release a foul-smelling yellow fluid from special glands in their thorax. Mimics also have bright colors to fool experienced predators into thinking that they taste bad or are otherwise harmful. For example, some larvae mimic snakes in both appearance and behavior. Many day-active moths have slender black and yellow bodies with clear wings and resemble stinging bees and wasps. Bright warning colors are of little use to some night-flying moths, so they produce high-pitched sounds as part of their defense system that warns bats of their bad taste.

Male butterflies locate mates either by establishing and defending territories or by actively flying about the environment in search of females. They rely mostly on eyesight to find a mate but will also release pheromones (FEH-re-moans), or chemical scents that attract females. After locating a female the male will chase her until she drops to the ground. Depending on the species, before they mate he will move his antennae, flap his wings, and release pheromones from brushy tufts of hairs located on the thorax, wings, legs, or abdomen.

Most lepidopterans must mate to produce offspring, but some European bagworm moths reproduce by parthenogenesis (PAR-thuh-no-JEH-nuh-sihs), where caterpillars hatch and develop from unfertilized eggs. In moths, females release pheromones from their abdominal glands to attract males. The feathery antennae of some male moths are so sensitive that they can locate a female over a distance of several miles (kilometers). Courtship is usually very brief.

The life cycle of lepidopterans includes four very distinct stages: egg, larva (caterpillar), pupa, and adult. Females may lay their eggs singly or in batches inside plant tissues, glue them to all kinds of objects, or simply drop them from the air. In cooler regions the eggs may overwinter, or last through the winter, and will not hatch until the following spring or summer. The larvae molt, or shed their exoskeletons, or hard outer coatings, five or six times before reaching the pupal stage. Depending on the species, temperature, and the availability and quality of food, the time between egg and adult may take anywhere from fifteen days to two years. Mature larvae search for a suitable site to pupate.

Adults often emerge from their pupae right after rains. This way they can mate and lay their eggs at the same time plants are developing new leaves, providing the caterpillars with plenty to eat. Moths secrete a fluid to dissolve a hole in the cocoon or use sharp structures on their head to cut their way through the silk. Most adults live for a few days or weeks, but some species, such as migrating monarchs, live several months. Some species, such as mourning cloaks and several species of North American anglewings, overwinter as adults and fly in early February and March.

LEPIDOPTERANS AND PEOPLE

Butterflies have appeared in ancient Egyptian and Chinese carvings, on Aztec pottery, and in countless paintings, sculptures, jewelry, textiles, glass, drawings, and poetry. They have been used to symbolize joy, sorrow, eternal life, or the frailty of life. In some parts of the world butterflies and moths are thought to represent the soul. In fact, *psyche*, the word for butterflies and moths in Greek, means "soul."

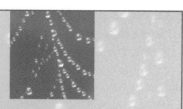

Many lepidopterans are directly beneficial to humans. The best known example is the silkworm. They are raised commercially on farms so that silk from their cocoons can be harvested to manufacture textiles. Other lepidopterans are useful, too. Flower-visiting adults are important pollinators of flowers, while some caterpillars eat pest insects, such as aphids and scale insects, and others parasitize plant hoppers. The eggs of some moths are used to raise large numbers of a parasitoid wasp *Trichogramma*, which is then released to control the caterpillars of another moth species that is a pest of crops. The larvae of a South American moth are used in South Africa and Australia to control cactus, which is considered a weed outside of its normal range in the New World. In many parts of the world, caterpillars, rich in protein, are considered a part of a balanced human diet.

Yet the feeding habits of many caterpillars have led humans to consider them major pests. Leaf-rollers, webworms, leaf miners, cutworms, armyworms, underground grass grubs, vine borers, carpenterworms, gypsy moth caterpillars, tent caterpillars and their relatives attack crops, garden plants, and forests managed for timber. Still others destroy clothing and stored foods.

CONSERVATION STATUS

The World Conservation Union (IUCN) lists 303 species of lepidopterans, 176 of which are listed as Critically Endangered, Endangered, or Vulnerable. Critically Endangered means facing an extremely high risk of extinction in the wild; Endangered means facing a very high risk of extinction in the wild, and Vulnerable means facing a high risk of extinction in the wild. The United States Fish and Wildlife Service also lists twenty-five of these species, mostly butterflies, as Endangered, or in danger of extinction throughout all or a significant portion of their range. Giant birdwing butterflies and other species are listed by the Convention on International Trade in Endangered Species (CITES).

Butterflies are familiar animals that attract considerable attention. Unlike most insects, they are admired and appreciated by the general public. Because of this, many species have been given protection by local, state, national, and international agencies. Butterfly collecting is often thought to be the most serious threat to their populations, but this is simply not true. As with all species, it is the destruction of their habitats that makes them vulnerable to extinction.

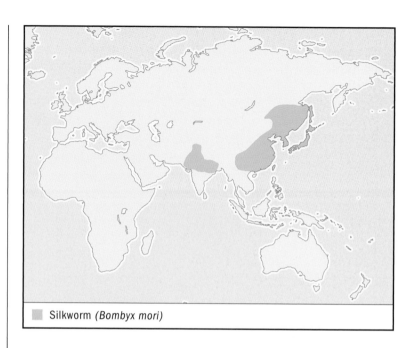

Silkworm (*Bombyx mori*)

SILKWORM
Bombyx mori

Physical characteristics: Mature caterpillars measure 1.5 inches (40 millimeters) and are grayish with brown marks on the thorax. They have a short horn near the tip of the abdomen. They spin a white or yellow cocoon for pupation. The color of the cocoon is determined by heredity and diet. The cocoon is made from one continuous silk thread that measures 1,000 to 3,000 feet (300 to 900 meters) long. The whitish adults are heavy bodied, rounded, and furry. Adult wingspan is 1.5 to 2.5 inches (40 to 60 millimeters). The forewings are hooked at their tips.

Geographic range: This species is originally from the north of China, the north of India, Japan, Taiwan, and Korea. They are now raised commercially in Europe and North and South America.

Habitat: The silkworm is the world's only completely domesticated insect. No populations are found in the wild. They are raised on farms near fields of mulberry trees.

Diet: Caterpillars feed only on mulberry leaves. The adults have no mouthparts and do not feed.

Silkworms are now raised commercially in Europe and North and South America. (©Pascal Goetgheluck/Photo Researchers, Inc. Reproduced by permission.)

Behavior and reproduction: The adults cannot fly. The domesticated larvae can survive only with human assistance.

Females lay 200 to 500 lemon-yellow eggs that eventually turn black. The eggs hatch in spring. The larvae molt four times in four to six weeks before spinning a cocoon. The mature caterpillar spends up to three or more days to spin an entire cocoon. Adults emerge in about three weeks, mate, and die in about five days. There is usually only one generation per year.

Silkworms and people: Silkworms were first domesticated in China. They are now raised for educational purposes in classrooms as well as to harvest their silk. The silk is obtained by boiling the cocoons in water to kill the pupa and unraveling the thread. Dead pupae are sometimes used as cockroach bait, fish food, or as fertilizer for mulberry trees.

Conservation status: This species is not considered endangered or threatened. ■

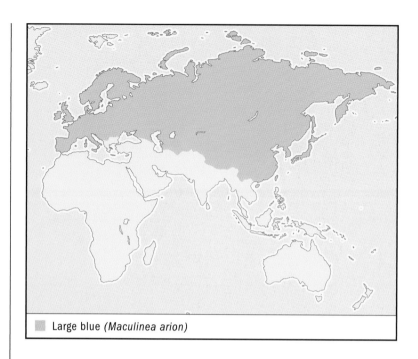

Large blue (*Maculinea arion*)

LARGE BLUE
Maculinea arion

Physical characteristics: Adult wingspan is 0.64 to 0.8 inches (16 to 20 millimeters) across. The upper side of the forewing is bright blue with large black spots. The underside of the forewing is grayish with large black spots and a bluish or greenish area near the base. The head of the larva is small and hidden. The legs are also hidden, and the body is covered with short hairs.

Geographic range: This species is found from western Europe to southern Siberia, Mongolia, and China.

Habitat: Large blues are found in dry, rugged, open grasslands where their host ants, *Myrmica sabuleti*, live. In the north, the ants prefer warm, south-facing slopes covered in short grass.

Diet: Younger larvae eat pollen and seeds of wild thyme and oregano, while the older caterpillars prefer ant eggs and larvae.

Behavior and reproduction: Females lay their eggs singly on flowers of thyme or oregano. Caterpillars feed on plants for about three

Large blues are found in dry, rugged, open grasslands where their host ants, Myrmica sabuleti, live. (Illustration by Michelle Meneghini. Reproduced by permission.)

weeks and then drop to the ground. From special glands they produce fluids that are attractive to ants. The ants pick up the caterpillars and carry them back to their nests. There the caterpillars prey on ant eggs and larvae. Pupation takes place in the nest. Adults emerge the following summer and live for about three or four weeks. They are active from June through August.

Large blues and people: Scientists study their relationships with ants to understand how different kinds of animals come to depend on each other. These studies provide useful information for the conservation of other species of blues whose caterpillars also depend on ants for their development.

Conservation status: This species is listed by the World Conservation Union (IUCN) as Near Threatened, or likely to qualify for a threatened category in the near future. Their populations have declined or disappeared in northern Europe. They have been reestablished in England and are still common in Siberia and the Far East. Their populations are threatened by the expansion of agricultural areas. ■

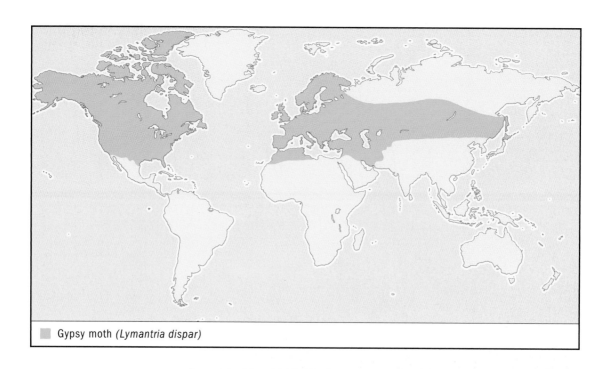

Gypsy moth (*Lymantria dispar*)

GYPSY MOTH
Lymantria dispar

Physical characteristics: Adult males are light to dark brown with irregular black markings. Their wingspan measures 1 to 1.5 inches (25.4 to 38.0 millimeters). They have wider feathery antennae. Females are all white with irregular black lines on the wings. Their wingspan is 2.24 to 2.68 inches (56 to 67 millimeters), and they have narrower feathery antennae. Mature larvae are 1.48 to 2.40 inches (37 to 60 millimeters) long. Their bodies are gray with a row of hair tufts down their backs. They have five pairs of blue spots followed by six pairs of red spots. The brown pupae are 0.76 to 1.0 inches (19 to 25 millimeters) long and have small circlets of hairs.

Geographic range: Gypsy moths are found throughout most of Eurasia. They have become established in northeastern North America.

Habitat: Gypsy moths live in forests and fields, as well as in towns and cities. The caterpillars are found on their food plants.

Gypsy moths lay batches of one hundred to one thousand eggs on virtually any surface, including automobiles and lawn and picnic furniture. (©Rod Planck/Photo Researchers, Inc. Reproduced by permission.)

Diet: The larvae eat more than five hundred different kinds of trees and shrubs, including pines, oaks, poplars, willows, and birches. The moths do not feed.

Behavior and reproduction: Males fly in late afternoon or at night in search of females. The females have wings but do not fly. However, females of Japanese populations are capable of flying.

Females attract males with pheromones during the summer. After mating they lay batches of one hundred to one thousand eggs on virtually any surface, including automobiles and lawn and picnic furniture. Eggs laid on moveable objects are often accidentally transported long distances. The eggs overwinter and hatch in spring. The caterpillars require 20 to 60 days before they can pupate. During this period male caterpillars molt five times, while females molt six. The life cycle, from egg to adult, takes about 20 to 60 days. The pupal stage lasts about 14 to 17 days.

Gypsy moths and people: The gypsy moth is an important forest pest in Europe, Asia, and the northeastern United States. There are laws in the United States and other countries designed to isolate known populations and prevent their spread into new areas.

Conservation status: This species is not considered endangered or threatened. ■

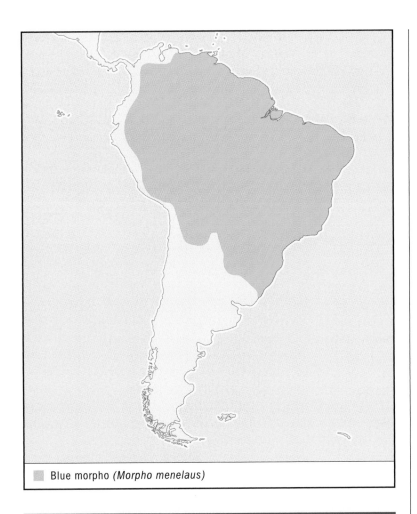

Blue morpho *(Morpho menelaus)*

BLUE MORPHO
Morpho menelaus

Physical characteristics: Both males and females have shiny blue wings that change color slightly depending on the angle of light. The upper sides of the male's wings are mostly bright blue. Female's wings are duller, with brown edges and white spots surrounding blue. The undersides of the wings of both males and females are brown with bronze eyespots. Their wingspans measure up to 6 inches (150 millimeters) across. The larvae are reddish brown with bright patches of lime green and reddish brown with white tufts of hair on the back.

Geographic range: This species is found in South America, from the Guianas to Brazil and Bolivia.

Habitat: This species lives in wet humid forests.

Diet: Adults suck juices from rotting fruit, while the larvae feed on the leaves of *Erythroxylum pilchrum.*

Behavior and reproduction: Adults fly through the forest in a series of blue flashes as their wings open and close. They are perfectly camouflaged when at rest with their wings closed. The males are very territorial and use their bright blue wings to scare off other males. The larvae feed at night. When threatened they release a strong smell from a gland that opens between their front legs.

Nothing is known of their reproductive behavior.

Blue morphos and people: The surface sculpturing of each scale on the morpho wings create the shimmering blue color that brightens or fades depending on the direction of the light. This quality has suggested security measures for use in paper money and credit cards to prevent them from being copied illegally.

Conservation status: This species is not considered endangered or threatened.   ■

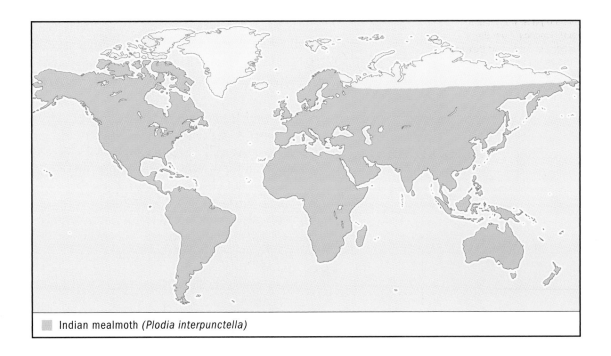

Indian mealmoth (*Plodia interpunctella*)

INDIAN MEALMOTH
Plodia interpunctella

Physical characteristics: Adults are small and slender, with a wingspan of 0.62 to 0.79 inches (16 to 20 millimeters). Each forewing is yellowish brown toward the base and reddish brown toward the tip. The hind wings are dull white and almost clear. The mature larvae measure 0.36 to 0.60 inches (9 to 15 millimeters). They have a yellow-brown head and shield over the front of the thorax. The rest of the body is dull white to pinkish.

Geographic range: Indian mealmoths are found on all continents except Antarctica.

Habitat: Indian mealmoths live outside and are attracted to lights at night but are usually seen in cupboards and pantries in homes. They also infest supermarkets and feed stores. The larvae are found in stored foods or pupating between shelves and walls or where walls and ceilings meet.

Diet: The larvae eat all kinds of stored foods, including pastas, cereals, dry pet food, and dried fruit.

Indian mealmoths are attracted to lights at night but are usually seen in cupboards and pantries in homes. They also infest supermarkets and feed stores. (Illustration by Patricia Ferrer. Reproduced by permission.)

Behavior and reproduction: Adults fly at night and are attracted to televisions and other sources of light in the home. The larvae tunnel into food and ruin it with their waste and trails of silk webbing.

The female lays eggs just three to four days after emerging from the pupa. The speed of larval development depends on temperature, humidity, and food quality and ranges from thirteen to 288 days. Multiple overlapping generations are found in homes and warehouses.

Indian mealmoths and people: The caterpillars infest stored foods in homes, supermarkets, and warehouses and are considered pests.

Conservation status: This species is not considered endangered or threatened. ■

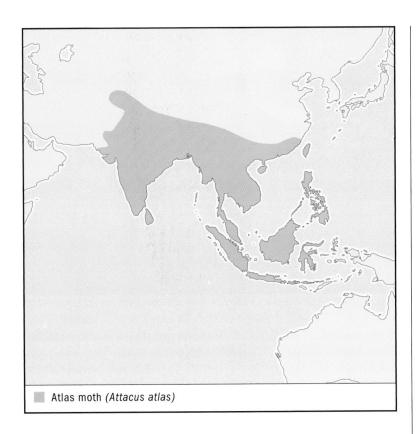

Atlas moth (*Attacus atlas*)

ATLAS MOTH
Attacus atlas

Physical characteristics: The atlas moth is one of the largest moths with a wingspan of 8 inches (200 millimeters). Their plump bodies are very hairy. Each wing is reddish brown and has a single triangle-shaped spot that does not have any scales and is clear. The tips of the forewings are curved. The antennae of the males are larger and more feathery than the females. The caterpillars are bluish green with shades of pink. They pupate in cocoons made up of broken strands of silk.

Geographic range: This species is found in the tropical regions of Asia, India, and southeast Asia.

Habitat: Atlas moths live in habitats from the lowlands to upper mountain forests.

Diet: The larvae feed on many kinds of trees, including Jamaican cherry, soursop, cinnamon, rambutan, guava, and citrus. The moths lack developed mouthparts and do not feed.

Behavior and reproduction: Atlas moths are attracted to lights at night. Females attract males with pheromones. Males can detect the faintest traces of these pheromones from as far as three miles (4.8 kilometers) away.

Females lay a few to several hundred eggs on the undersides of leaves and die soon afterward. The eggs hatch in about two weeks, depending on temperature. The pupal stage lasts about one month.

Atlas moths and people: The caterpillars are raised commercially, and the adults are sold as specimens to collectors. Their silk cocoons are used to make coin purses in Taiwan.

Conservation status: This species is not considered endangered or threatened. ■

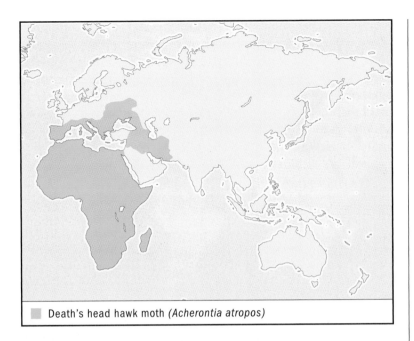

Death's head hawk moth *(Acherontia atropos)*

DEATH'S HEAD HAWK MOTH
Acherontia atropos

Physical characteristics: These moths have a skull-like pattern on the thorax. They are large and heavily built insects, with a wingspan of 4.4 to 4.8 inches (110 to 120 millimeters). Their long forewings are dark, while the hind wings are yellow with black lines near the edges. The hairy proboscis is short and thick. The abdomen has yellow and black bands. Mature larvae measure 4.8 to 5.2 inches (120 to 130 millimeters) long. Their bodies are yellow, green, or brown with a large horn toward the rear. The pupa is shiny, reddish brown, and measures 3.0 to 3.2 inches (75.7 to 80.0 millimeters).

Geographic range: They are found throughout Africa south of the Sahara Desert but occasionally migrate north to the Mediterranean Sea as well as central and northern Europe.

Habitat: The death's head hawk moth lives in dry and sunny locations, especially open shrubby habitats with plenty of plants in the nightshade family. This includes agricultural areas where potatoes are grown.

Death's head hawk moths use their short proboscis to feed on honey, rotting fruit, and tree sap. (Kim Taylor/Bruce Coleman Inc. Reproduced by permission.)

Diet: The larvae eat plants in the nightshade family and are particularly fond of potato. The adults use their short proboscis to feed on honey, rotting fruit, and tree sap.

Behavior and reproduction: The caterpillars are sluggish and usually move only when looking for a fresh leaf to eat. When threatened they click their jaws together and will sometimes bite. Adults are active just after sundown to midnight. Their days are spent resting on tree trunks, walls, or leaves on the ground. They are attracted to lights and sometimes to flowers. These moths often invade beehives to steal honey and defend themselves by smelling like a bee, raising their wings, and running and hopping about. When attacked, they force air out of their proboscis, making a squeaking noise. They also release a moldy smell from special hairs associated with glands on their abdomen.

Females lay eggs singly underneath old leaves of the caterpillar's food plant. They pupate inside a flimsy cocoon in a cavity dug deep in the soil.

Death's head hawk moths and people: This moth is considered to be an evil creature because of the skull pattern on the thorax and the loud squeaking sound that it makes when disturbed. It once was considered a symbol of war, pestilence, and death. It was featured on the cover of the book and appeared in the film *The Silence of the Lambs*.

Conservation status: This species is not considered endangered or threatened. However, it is less common today as a result of the use of pesticides. ■

FOR MORE INFORMATION

Books:

Brock, J. P., and K. Kaufman. *Butterflies of North America*. New York: Houghton Mifflin Co., 2003.

Coville Jr., C. *A Field Guide to the Moths of Eastern North America*. Boston: Houghton Mifflin, 1984.

Leverton, R. *Enjoying Moths*. London: T. and A. D. Poyser, 2001.

Pyle, R. M. *Handbook for Butterfly Watchers*. New York: Houghton Mifflin Company, 1992.

Sbordoni, V., and S. Forestiero. *Butterflies of the World.* Westport, CT: Firefly Books, 1998.

Scheer, J. *Night Visions. The Secret Design of Moths.* Munich: Prestel, 2003.

Periodicals:

Evans, A. V. "Butterfly Farming in Costa Rica." *Terra* 35, no. 5 (1998): 8–9.

Evans, A. V. "Spineless Wonders. The Beauty of Caterpillars." *Reptiles Magazine* 11, no. 6 (June 2003): 82–85.

Urquhart, F. A. "Found at Last: the Monarch's Winter Home." *National Geographic* 150, no. 2 (August 1976): 161–173.

Web sites:

"Butterflies and Moths. Lepidoptera." BioKids. *Critter Catalog.* http://www.biokids.umich.edu/critters/information/Lepidoptera.html (accessed on October 28, 2004).

"Lepidoptera. Butterflies, moths." Ecowatch. http://www.ento.csiro.au/Ecowatch/Lepidoptera/Lepidoptera.htm (accessed on October 28, 2004).

Videos:

Bug City. Butterflies and Moths. Wynnewood, PA: Schlessinger Media, 1998.

SAWFLIES, ANTS, BEES, AND WASPS
Hymenoptera

Class: Insecta

Order: Hymenoptera

Number of families: About 84 families

PHYSICAL CHARACTERISTICS

Adult hymenopterans (HAI-men-OP-teh-runs) range in size from 0.006 to 4.72 inches (0.15 to 120 millimeters) in length. The bodies of many wasps are slender, while those of bees are robust. They often have large compound eyes, each with many lenses. Some also have simple eyes, or eyes with one lens, located between the compound eyes. The distinct head has chewing mouthparts directed downward. The jaws are used for emerging from the pupa (PYU-pa), or cocoon, and for defense, killing prey, and nest construction. Bees have the combination of chewing and sucking mouthparts, allowing them to drink nectar from flowers.

All four wings are similar in texture, but the forewings, or those in front, are usually longer than the hind wings. The hind wings have a row of hooks along their leading edges that attach to the hind margins of the forewings while the insect is in flight. The legs are usually long and are used for running. In some species the legs are also used for digging. The midsection, or thorax, of sawflies and their relatives is broadly attached to the abdomen. However, ants, bees, and wasps have threadlike waists. In these groups the threadlike segments are made up of the first few segments of the abdomen. Winged species have four membranelike wings with relatively few veins.

The ovipositors, or egg-laying tubes, of hymenopterans have special sensory structures that help the female to find good places to lay her eggs. In some ants, bees, and wasps the ovipositor is not used for egg laying. Instead it is used as a defensive stinger. The stinger is hollow like a syringe and is capable of delivering a painful and venomous sting. The stingers of ants, wasps, and most bees are smooth so that they can be used repeatedly. However, the stings of honeybees can be used only once. Their barbed stingers remain in the flesh of the victim. As the honeybee pulls away, the stinger and internal organs are ripped from the abdomen and the insect soon dies.

The bodies of bees have several special features that allow them to collect pollen. Their bodies are covered with bristly and branched hairlike structures. The hind legs of many bees have special bristles that form either a brush or a basket allowing them to carry pollen. Leaf-cutter bees use brushes on the undersides of their abdomens for carrying pollen.

The larvae (LAR-vee), or young form, of sawflies and their relatives resemble caterpillars. They have distinct heads, three pairs of legs, and fleshy cone-shaped false legs on their abdominal segments. In all other Hymenoptera the larvae are wormlike and lack both legs and a distinct head. In parasitic species the mature larva is wormlike, but the previous stages may be very different in appearance. Parasites are completely dependent on other living organisms, or hosts, for food. Parasitic hymenopteran larvae spend their entire lives on the host. Their feeding activities usually do not kill the host.

The features of adult hymenoptera are clearly visible in the pupae (PYU-pee), or life stage between larvae and adults. The legs and developing wings are not firmly attached to the body along their entire length. Some species pupate within a silk cocoon.

GEOGRAPHIC RANGE

Hymenopterans are found on every continent except Antarctica. There are about 115,000 species of hymenopterans worldwide, with about eighteen thousand in the United States and Canada.

HABITAT

Hymenoptera occur in a wide variety of habitats where they are found in the soil and leaf litter or on grasses, shrubs, and trees. Most species are active on warm, sunny days, but some species are active at night, especially those that attack prey that are also active at night.

DIET

Most adults feed on pollen, nectar, and plant sap, as well as honeydew, the sugary waste produced by aphids, mealy bugs and hoppers (Hemiptera). Both adult and larval leaf-cutter ants depend on a special fungus as their primary source of food. The ants grow the fungus themselves in special underground chambers. Other hymenopterans eat living or dead animal tissues, especially insects. Many female parasitoids (PAE-re-SIH-toyds) feed on the body fluids of insects in order to produce eggs. Parasitoids are hymenopterans with lifestyles in between parasites and predators (PREH-duh-ters) that hunt for food. Parasitoids feed inside the body of a single living host, eventually killing it.

The larvae of most sawflies and their relatives feed on plant tissues. They feed on the outside of plants, but some bore into stems, fruits, and leaves. Horntail larvae bore through living tree trunks and rely on funguses to break down the wood so they can use it for food. Parasitic or parasitoid wasp larvae eat the tissues of their host insects. Other wasps live and feed in plant galls (gawls). Plant galls are swellings or abnormal growths that appear on roots, stems, leaves, and flowers. Infections, insects, mites, and other organisms produce galls. Many wasps feed their larvae chewed-up or paralyzed (PAE-ruh-laizd) insects and spiders. The paralyzing stings of these wasps do not kill the insects or spiders. Instead, the sting has chemicals that affects their nervous systems and prevents them from moving.

BEHAVIOR AND REPRODUCTION

Only some ants, bees, and wasps sting. In these species only the females can sting. They use their egg-laying tubes, or ovipositors, to deliver a painful venomous sting that burns and itches. The burning is caused by an acid that is released into the wound with the venom or poison.

The larvae of parasitoid wasps spend their lives with their hosts, while the adults are free to move about the environment. Using special chemicals produced inside their bodies, some parasitoid larvae paralyze their larval hosts and stop them from growing. In other species they allow the host larva to continue to feed and grow so that it reaches maximum size, but it will die before reaching maturity. Depending on species, parasitoids either feed on the inside or outside of the bodies of their hosts. Some species feed alone, while others attack their hosts in groups. There are even some hymenopteran parasitoids that attack other hymenopteran parasitoids.

The larvae of many wasps live as parasitoids inside the bodies of insect larvae. The adults freely move about the environment and are often seen on flowers. For example, female scoliid wasps attack beetle grubs in their burrows or underground pupal cases. After laying her eggs, the females leave. The larvae will hatch, feed, and develop without any assistance. These and other wasps may or may not use their stings to paralyze their larvae's future hosts.

Other wasp females must first locate, capture, and paralyze food for their larvae, usually caterpillars, crickets and katydids, and spiders. They then drag their victims to a cavity or crevice (KREH-vuhs) in the ground or stuff them into previously built nests. Metallic blue or green cuckoo bees, which are actually thick-bodied wasps, do not construct nests and rely on the food stores of other hymenopterans to feed their young. Potter wasps build a potlike mud nest and lay their eggs inside. Then they provide the nest with all the paralyzed spiders necessary to feed their young through pupation and seal it with more mud. Hornets, paper wasps, and yellow jackets continue to feed their larvae as they develop. Many bees also continue to feed their young as they develop, but they give them pollen and nectar instead of insects and spiders.

All ants, but only some bees and wasps, are truly social insects. Social insects live in colonies with multiple overlapping generations that share the duties of rearing the young, gathering food, defending the colony, and expanding and repairing the nest. The labor is divided among different castes, or forms. The worker caste takes care of most of the nest chores. Some species have a soldier caste. Soldiers are larger, more powerfully built individuals that defend the nest. Workers and soldiers are always sterile females and are unable to mate or reproduce. Only members of the reproductive caste, queens and males, can mate and reproduce. The males are short-lived and die soon after mating. Queens mate one or more times before they start a new colony and never have to mate again. They will store enough sperm in a special sac in their abdomen to fertilize thousands to millions of eggs. Social hymenopterans use mud, leaves, and chewed-up bits of wood that are formed into paper or a paperlike material to build their nests.

Males of parasitic species usually look for emerging females in places where their hosts live. They will sometimes fight with other males to defend these sites. Others form mating swarms to attract females. In most hymenopterans, the females release pheromones (FEH-re-moans), chemicals that are very attractive to males of the same species. Courtship is common among ants, bees, and wasps and involves touching each other with antennae (an-TEH-nee), or sense organs, and vibrating legs and wings.

The life cycles of hymenopterans include four very distinct stages: egg, larva, pupa, and adult. In some parasitic species, a single egg will develop into several individuals. In many species females determine the sex of their offspring by controlling which eggs are fertilized. Fertilized eggs become females, while unfertilized eggs develop into males. They can also speed up or slow down the growth of their populations by producing females or males.

Sawflies and their relatives lay their eggs on or in leaves, stems, wood, and leaf litter. The females of some sawflies will stand guard over their egg masses until they hatch. Mature larvae pupate inside plant tissues or in the soil. Most species produce only one generation each year and overwinter, or last through the winter, as larvae.

Parasitic and parasitoid females search for and select the right host by using highly sensitive organs on their antennae and ovipositors. Some females will use only one host or a few closely related host species. Others will lay their eggs on a variety of similar hosts, such as caterpillars, in a specific habitat. Most parasitoids lay their eggs on or in the body of the host. The females often have long ovipositors to lay eggs in cocoons, burrows, and other protected places.

The larvae of sawflies and their relatives molt, or shed their exoskeletons, or hard outer coverings, up to eight times before becoming a pupa. Females sometimes molt one more time than the males of their species. In all other Hymenoptera the larvae molt up to five times before reaching the pupal stage.

HYMENOPTERANS AND PEOPLE

Hymenopterans have long been a part of human culture. In ancient Egypt bees and wasps symbolized various gods. The ancient Greeks called the bee *Melitta* the Goddess Honey Mother. One of the largest ants in the world, *Dinoponera*, was used as a symbol of strength for several tribes in the Amazon. The Mixe people of Oaxaca, Mexico, believed that they would become more powerful if they ate ants and considered them symbols of courage, patience, and strength.

In modern times the Russian composer Nikolai Rimski-Korsakov (1804–1908) was inspired by the buzzing of flying bees and composed the famous "Flight of the Bumblebee." This music was written for strings and is performed as part of the opera, *The Tale of Tsar Saltan*, the story of a prince who is turned into a bee. Several Pokemon cartoons include characters inspired by hymenopterans.

Hymenopterans are also considered to be beneficial to humans. Many species of parasitoids and predators are used to control insect pests in gardens, agricultural fields, and managed forests. Bees are important pollinators. Honeybees also produce honey, which is used in the making of all kinds of foods. Beeswax is used for making candles, cosmetics, lip balm, polishes, and sealing wax.

In some parts of the world hymenopterans are considered an important part of the human diet. Boiling them breaks down their venom and softens their stings. Many species of ants and ant larvae are not only eaten but are considered to be a real treat. Aborigines, native people of Australia living in the desert, dig up honey pot ants as a source of sugar. Some of the workers of these ants spend their lives in underground chambers as living honey pots. When food is abundant, special workers are continually fed honeydew and nectar by other ants until their abdomens swell to the size of a small marble. They store the sweet stuff during times of plenty and feed it to their nest mates when food is scarce. Honey pot ants also live in the western United States and Mexico.

Hornets, paper wasps, and yellow jackets are often considered a nuisance when they build their paper nests on or near homes and office buildings. Nest-building Hymenoptera can be domestic nuisances. They inflict painful stings to protect their nests. Some people are highly allergic to stings and may die if stung. Southern imported fire ants have burning stings and are

THE MYTH OF THE WHITE ANT

Termites are sometimes called "white ants," but they are not ants at all, nor are they closely related to them. Most ants are dark and hard-bodied, while termites are soft and pale. Ants have a narrow waist, while termites are thick-waisted. Ants have antennae distinctly bent like an elbow, while those of termites are short and beadlike. Moreover, worker ants are always females, while worker termites are both males and females.

considered a nuisance if their colonies are established close to homes and parks. Their nest mounds sometimes make it difficult to use harvesting equipment in some agricultural fields. They also attack and kill nestlings and other small animals and can have a devastating effect on the local populations of all kinds of animals, including other insects.

Only a few species of Hymenoptera are considered pests that harm forests and crops. Sawfly larvae cause damage to forests, orchards, and ornamental trees. Wood-boring larvae, in association with funguses, can cause extensive damage to plantations of fir trees. A few ant species are also considered pests. For example, the leaf-cutter ants strip crops and garden plants of their leaves and flowers. Other species protect other crop pests, such as sap-sucking insects, from predators and parasitoids.

CONSERVATION STATUS

One hundred and fifty-one species of hymenopterans are listed by the World Conservation Union (IUCN). Three species are listed as Critically Endangered, or facing an extremely high risk of extinction in the wild; 139 are Vulnerable, or facing a high risk of extinction in the wild; 7 are Near Threatened, or likely to qualify for a threatened category in the near future; one is Data Deficient, which means there is inadequate information to make a direct or indirect assessment of risk of extinction; one is Least Concern, or does not qualify for a threatened category.

Like all organisms, hymenopterans are particularly sensitive to the misuse of pesticides and habitat destruction. All humans are especially dependent on the pollination services of bees and wasps. The reduction or loss of their populations will greatly hurt efforts to grow vegetables, fruits, and flowers, as well as fodder for domestic animals.

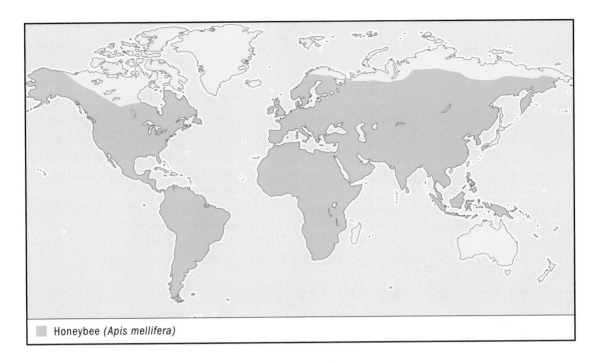

Honeybee (Apis mellifera)

HONEYBEE
Apis mellifera

Physical characteristics: Workers measure 0.37 to 0.62 inches (9.5 to 15.8 millimeters) in length, while male drones are 0.62 inches (15.8 millimeters), and queens are 0.75 inches (19.5 millimeters). Their bodies are golden brown and black, with bands of pale orange or yellow on the abdomen. The head, antennae, and legs are nearly black. Fine, hairlike structures cover the thorax and appear less so on the abdomen. The wings are clear. Honeybees have special bristles on the outside of the back legs that form pollen baskets.

Geographic range: Honeybees are found on all continents except Antarctica.

Habitat: Colonies of honeybees often live in manmade commercial hives, but wild colonies generally prefer tree hollows and other sheltered spaces.

Diet: Adults and larvae eat honey and a mixture of honey and pollen called beebread. The larvae of queen bees are also fed royal jelly, a

This honeybee has pollen attachted to its leg. (©James H. Robinson/Photo Researchers, Inc. Reproduced by permission.)

nutritious substance produced by special glands located in the heads of the workers.

Behavior and reproduction: Honeybees are social insects that live in colonies made up of a queen and up to eighty thousand workers. During the warmer months there may also be a few hundred males or drones. The queens live four or five years. They lay up to two thousand eggs per day or about two million in a lifetime. The drones mate with new queens. The workers care for the queen and young, forage for food, defend the colony, and expand the hive, by building new combs. The combs are made from wax produced as flakes from special glands in each worker's abdomen. The workers use their jaws to shape the wax into cells and combs. Each comb is made up of two layers of six-sided cells and hangs straight up and down in the nest. The cells are used to rear the larvae and to store honey and pollen. Queen cells are built at the lower edges of combs and are peanut-shaped. Honeybee colonies live for several years. The queen and workers spend the winter inside the hive.

Honeybees form new colonies by swarming. Just before the new queens emerge from their cells, the old queen leaves the hive with about half the workers to search for a new site to start a hive. The new queens fly into the air to mate one or more times with different drones. They will return to the hive of their birth, but only one queen will eventually take over the hive. The other queens are stung to death by the ruling queen or by the workers.

Unfertilized eggs develop into drones. Fertilized eggs develop into females, either workers or queens. Larvae develop into queens only if they are continually fed royal jelly by the workers.

Honeybees and people: Many crops around the world depend on honeybees for pollination. Honeybees are raised commercially to harvest their honey, wax, pollen, venom, and other products.

Conservation status: This species is not considered endangered or threatened. However, many populations have suffered serious losses due to mite infestations. ■

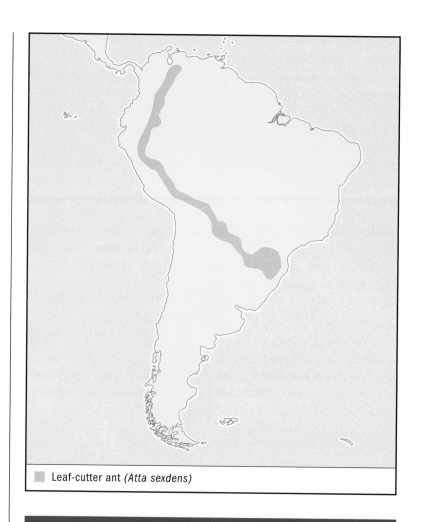

Leaf-cutter ant (*Atta sexdens*)

LEAF-CUTTER ANT
Atta sexdens

Physical characteristics: The bodies of larger workers and soldiers measure 0.43 to 0.47 inches (11 to 12 millimeters) in length. The surfaces of their reddish bodies are rough in texture. The back of the thorax has three pairs of spines. Males and queens have wings, but all workers and soldiers are wingless. There are three distinct classes of workers based on size.

Geographic range: This species is found in Central and South America, including Costa Rica, Panama, Colombia, Venezuela, Guiana, Ecuador, Peru, Bolivia, Brazil, Paraguay, and Argentina.

Habitat: Ant colonies are found on the floor of rainforests, tropical deciduous forests, and tropical scrub forests.

Diet: Both adults and larvae of leaf-cutter ants eat a special fungus that is grown by the workers.

Behavior and reproduction: Leaf-cutter ants are social insects that live in large underground colonies. Workers use their sharp jaws to cut sections of many kinds of green leaves and carry them back to the nest. The leaves are chewed up to form compost for growing a species of fungus for food. Depending on their size, workers perform various tasks, including caring for the larvae, expanding the nest, cutting leaves, and defending the nest. The fungus gardens are located in underground chambers just beneath the surface. There are also special chambers for waste and unused plant materials. Each nest has tunnels leading to the surface that help to keep the air below cool and fresh.

New queens leave their colonies to fly into the air and mate with as many as eight males. From these matings she will begin a new colony, laying up to 150 million eggs in ten or more years. Leaf-cutters do not replace their queens, and the colony will survive only as long as she lives.

Leaf-cutter ants and people: Leaf-cutter ants are sometimes considered serious pests because they attack crops. Because mature colonies contain millions of individuals, they dominate the habitats where they occur. These ants are eaten by people in parts of Mexico.

Conservation status: This species is not considered endangered or threatened. ■

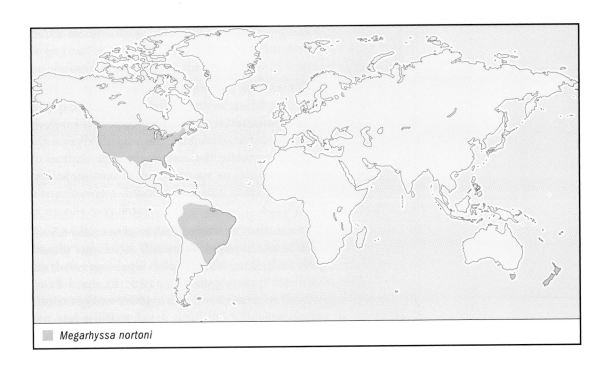

Megarhyssa nortoni

NO COMMON NAME
Megarhyssa nortoni

Physical characteristics: These large wasps measure 0.59 to 1.77 inches (15 to 45 millimeters) in length. The female ovipositor is often twice as long as the body. Some wasps measure more than 6.29 inches (130 millimeters), including the ovipositor. They are black, reddish brown, and yellow and have round yellow spots down the side of the abdomen.

Geographic range: This species is native to the United States and has been introduced into New Zealand, Tasmania, and Brazil.

Habitat: These wasps are found in pine forests and plantations.

Diet: Adult wasps drink nectar, but the larvae eat the wood-boring larvae of horntails.

Behavior and reproduction: The larvae are parasitoids on a wood-

boring wasp larvae. They feed inside the bodies of mature horntail larvae.

Horntails lay their eggs in pine trees and introduce a special wood-digesting fungus at the same time. The horntail larvae bore through and eat the wood that has been broken down by the fungus. The smell of the fungus attracts female *Megarhyssa* to trees infested with horntail larvae. Female *Megarhyssa* use their long ovipositors to bore through the wood to lay an egg on or near the horntail larvae. The parasitoid larva develops and pupates inside the body of its host.

Megarhyssa nortoni and people: *Megarhyssa nortoni* does not bite or sting. It has been imported into various parts of the world to help control horntail forest pests. They are sometimes used with another hymenopteran parasitoid, *Ibalia leucospoides*, which attacks the young horntail larvae.

Conservation status: This species is not considered endangered or threatened. ■

Velvet ant *(Mutilla europaea)*

VELVET ANT
Mutilla europaea

Physical characteristics: Velvet ants are brownish red with an iridescent blue-black abdomen marked with white bands. They measure 0.47 to 0.55 inches (12 to 14 millimeters) in length. Females are wingless and resemble ants, but the males have wings. Both appear as if their bodies are covered with hair.

Geographic range: This species is found in Europe.

Habitat: Adult females are usually on the ground in open, sandy habitats.

Diet: Adult velvet ants drink nectar, while the larvae eat pollen and nectar, as well as the larvae and pupae of bumblebees.

Behavior and reproduction: Velvet ants mate in the air, with the winged male carrying the wingless female. Females crawl into the un-

derground nests of bumblebees and lay their eggs. Mature velvet ant larvae spin their cocoons inside bumblebee pupal cells.

Velvet ants and people: Females inflict an incredibly painful sting and are sometimes considered minor pests because they attack bumblebees.

Conservation status: This species is not considered endangered or threatened. ■

Female velvet ants can inflict an incredibly painful sting. (Jane Burton/Bruce Coleman Inc. Reproduced by permission.)

Tarantula hawk (*Pepsis grossa*)

TARANTULA HAWK
Pepsis grossa

Physical characteristics: This slender wasp with long, spiny legs measures 0.94 to 2 inches (24 to 51 millimeters) in length. The species is black with mostly blue-green reflections, sometimes with a violet or coppery tinge. The black antennae are orange at the tip. The wings are usually black with blue-violet reflections, but they are sometimes yellowish or orange with dark borders.

Geographic range: Tarantula hawks are found in the southern United States and the West Indies, south through Mexico to north-central Peru, and the Guianas.

Tarantula hawks are found in the southern United States and the West Indies, south through Mexico to north-central Peru, and the Guianas. (Illustration by Barbara Duperron. Reproduced by permission.)

Habitat: This species is often found near water where flowering plants grow.

Diet: Adults drink nectar and are especially attracted to the flowers of milkweeds. The larvae feed on spiders.

Behavior and reproduction: Adult males and females are commonly found on flowers. Females are often seen crawling on the ground in search of large spiders, such as tarantulas, to use as food for their larvae. The female will paralyze a spider with her sting and drag it to suitable shelter, such as a burrow in the ground. She then stuffs the spider into a specially prepared chamber in the burrow. She lays a single egg on the living but paralyzed spider, then covers the entrance to the burrow and leaves. The larva pupates after the spider is eaten.

Tarantula hawks and people: Female tarantula hawks have stings that are very painful, but they do not attack people unless they are threatened.

Conservation status: This species is not considered endangered or threatened. ■

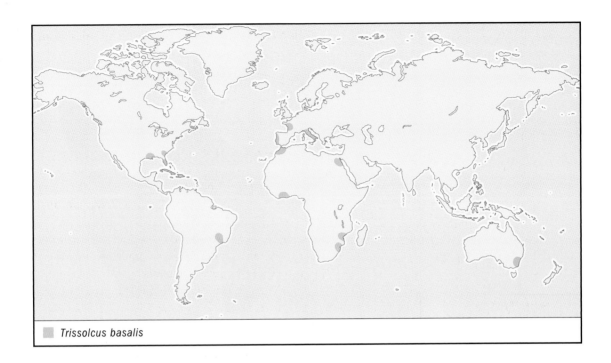

Trissolcus basalis

NO COMMON NAME
Trissolcus basalis

Physical characteristics: The body is black with elbow-shaped antennae that point downward and a flattened abdomen. They measure 0.04 to 0.05 inches (1 to 1.3 millimeters) in length. The wing veins are reduced in size and number.

Geographic range: This species is found in parts of the southeastern United States, the West Indies, Venezuela, Brazil, Australia, Egypt, Ivory Coast, Morocco, South Africa, Zimbabwe, Portugal, France, and Italy.

Habitat: These insects are found in many kinds of crops, including cotton, grains, soybeans, beans, peas, tomatoes, eggplant, peppers, sweet corn, sunflowers, nuts, melons, and other fruits.

Diet: The adults drink nectar, but the larvae are internal parasitoids in the eggs of stink bugs.

Trissolcus basalis *are found in many kinds of crops, including cotton, grains, soybeans, beans, peas, tomatoes, eggplant, peppers, sweet corn, sunflowers, nuts, melons, and other fruits. (Illustration by Barbara Duperron. Reproduced by permission.)*

Behavior and reproduction: The larvae are parasitoids that feed individually within the eggs of stink bugs. They grow and pupate inside the eggs.

Adults mate immediately after they emerge from the pupa. Females use their ovipositor to insert a single egg in the egg of a stink bug. The larva molts three times before pupating inside the host egg.

Trissolcus basalis and people: This species has been introduced into many different countries to control the southern green stink bug, an important pest of cotton, beans, vegetables, and citrus.

Conservation status: _Trissolcus basalis_ is not considered endangered or threatened. ■

Potter wasp *(Eumenes fraternus)*

POTTER WASP
Eumenes fraternus

Physical characteristics   The body of a potter wasp measures 0.51 to 0.66 inches (13 to 17 millimeters) in length. It is black with yellow markings on the thorax and abdomen. The dark smoky wings have a violet iridescence. The first abdominal segment is very slender, but the second is broad and bell-shaped. The middle legs, just before the feet, have only one spur at the tip.

Geographic range: Potter wasps are found in the eastern United States, west to Minnesota, Nebraska, Kansas, Oklahoma, and Texas.

Habitat: Adults are found in open areas or on flowers.

Diet: Adults feed on nectar; larvae eat caterpillars.

Behavior and reproduction: Potter wasps live alone. They build jug-shaped nests out of mud that have narrow necks with an expanded rim.

The female suspends a single egg from the wall of the nest with a slender thread. She then packs the nest with one to twelve paralyzed caterpillars and seals the nest with more mud. The hatching wasp grub eats the living but paralyzed prey provided by its mother. The larva pupates inside the nest. After emerging from the pupa, the adult breaks its way out of the nest.

Potter wasps and people: Because they do not defend their nests, potter wasps are not aggressive and seldom sting people. Their mud nests are believed to have been the models for clay pots made by native Americans.

Conservation status: This species is not considered endangered or threatened. ■

Potter wasps are found in the eastern United States, west to Minnesota, Nebraska, Kansas, Oklahoma, and Texas. (Illustration by Barbara Duperron. Reproduced by permission.)

FOR MORE INFORMATION

Books:

Buchman, S. L., and G. P. Nabhan. *The Forgotten Pollinators.* Washington: The Island Press, 1996.

Hölldobler, B., and E. O. Wilson. *Journey to the Ants: A Story of Scientific Exploration.* Cambridge, MA: Harvard University Press, 1994.

Hoyt, E. *The Earth Dwellers: Adventures in the Land of Ants.* New York: Simon & Schuster, 1996.

Hubbell, S. *A Book of Bees.* New York: Ballantine Books, 1989.

Hubbell, S. *Broadsides from the Other Orders: A Book of Bugs.* New York: Random House, 1993.

Tavolacci, J., ed. *Insects and Spiders of the World.* New York: Marshall Cavendish, 2003.

Wade, N., ed. *The Science Times Book of Insects.* New York: The Lyons Press, 1999.

Periodicals:

Evans, A. V. "The Giant Hornet." *Fauna.* (July/August 2001), pp. 67–68.

Evans, A. V. "Ants. Friend or Foe?" *Bird Talk* (February 2004), pp. 28–37.

Evans, A. V. "Ants: There's Strength in Numbers." *Reptiles Magazine* 12, no. 3 (March 2004): 58–61.

Mairson, A. "America's Beekeepers. Hives for Hire." *National Geographic* 183, no. 5 (May 1993): 73–93.

Moffett, M. W. "Gardeners of the Ant World." *National Geographic* 188, no. 1 (December 1996): 98–11.

Sisson, R. F. "The Wasp that Plays Cupid to a Fig." *National Geographic* 138, no. 5 (November 1970): 690–697.

Web sites:

"Hymenoptera. Wasps, bees, ants." Ecowatch. http://www.ento.csiro. au/Ecowatch/Hymenoptera.html (accessed on November 8, 2004).

"A Scanning Electron Microscope Atlas of the Honey Bee." http://gears .tucson.ars.ag.gov/beebook/bee.html (accessed on November 8, 2004).

"Wasps, bees, ants. Hymenoptera." BioKids. Critter Catalog. http://www .biokids.umich.edu/critters/information/Hymenoptera.html (accessed on November 8, 2004).

Videos:

Bug City. Ants. Wynnewood, PA: Schlessinger Media, 1998.

Bug City. Bees. Wynnewood, PA: Schlessinger Media, 1998.

CENTIPEDES
Chilopoda

Class: Myriapoda
Subclass: Chilopoda
Number of families: 18 or 19
families

subclass
CHAPTER

PHYSICAL CHARACTERISTICS

Adult centipedes vary in length from 0.15 to 11.8 inches (4 to 300 millimeters). Most species are completely yellowish or brownish, but a few species are brightly colored with distinctive bands on their bodies and different colored legs and antennae (an-TEH-nee), or sense organs. These bold colors and patterns may serve as warning colors to potential predators (PREH-duh-ters), or animals that hunt other animals for food. The head is flat or dome-shaped. The antennae are long and slender with fourteen to more than one hundred segments. Centipedes are bristling with tiny hairlike structures that are used for touch and smell. The eyes, if present, vary considerably. They may have one or more simple eyes, or eyes with one lens, on either side of the head, or a pair of compound eyes, or eyes with multiple lenses. The mouthparts are made up of three pairs of structures. The jaws help cut up food, while the remaining mouthparts help move food to the jaws.

Mature centipedes are long and, depending on species, have anywhere from fifteen to 191 pairs of legs, for a total of thirty to 382 legs. Adults always have an odd number of leg pairs, with one pair on each body segment. Centipedes are the only animals that have fanglike legs used to inject venom. All the legs are similar in length and appearance, except for the first and last pair. Located on the side of the head, the first pair of legs contains poison glands. They inject venom through an opening at the base of each fanglike claw. The last pair is often long and thick and is sometimes pincherlike. These legs are used for grasping or defense. The remaining legs are used for walking, running, or digging.

GEOGRAPHIC RANGE

Centipedes are found on all continents except Antarctica. A few species have become widespread, accidentally carried to other parts of the world with plants or soil.

HABITAT

Centipedes are found in all kinds of habitats, from sea level to high mountain peaks. A few species prefer to live in caves. Some individual species are found in a wide variety of situations under bark, in leaf litter, or under rocks.

DIET

All centipedes are predators. They feed on soft-bodied insects, spiders, other centipedes, and worms. Larger species will attack small mice, frogs, toads, birds, lizards, and snakes. Animals are killed by venom injected by the fangs, then grasped by the fangs and the first several pairs of walking legs. A few species may eat plant materials if they cannot find animal prey.

BEHAVIOR AND REPRODUCTION

Most centipedes are active at night. During the day they seek shelter under objects on the ground, inside logs and stumps, or in animal burrows. During the hot dry weather they will usually bury themselves deep in the soil. They are not territorial and move about the environment in search of food and mates.

Centipedes live alone until they are ready to mate or when they are raising their young. When they do meet, they are often very aggressive toward one another and will sometimes eat the other. Some species living along the seashore hunt in packs. Several individuals will feed together on the same animal, usually a barnacle or beach hopper.

When threatened, centipedes protect themselves by running away or biting. Others whip their bodies about or spread their hind legs wide in a threatening manner. Some species fool predators by having markings that make them look as if they have two heads. Others release bad smelling and tasting chemicals from glands on their undersides. In one group of centipedes, these chemicals actually glow in the dark. A few centipedes produce glue that hardens within seconds when exposed to air. This sticky stuff can tangle up the legs of even the largest insect predators.

Most species must mate to reproduce. The male usually places a sperm packet in a web on the ground. He then coaxes the female to the web by tapping her back legs with his antennae. This courtship may last for hours. Eventually the rear of her body comes into contact with the web and she takes the packet into her reproductive organs. A few kinds of centipedes are capable of parthenogenesis (PAR-thuh-no-JEH-nuh-sihs), where the young develop from unfertilized eggs. Only females are produced by this method of reproduction.

Some species of centipedes lay their eggs one at a time. In other species the female digs out chambers in rotten wood or soil and lays up to eighty or more eggs all at once. She wraps her body around her eggs and cleans them constantly so funguses, molds, or hungry predators do not harm them. Of these species some will eventually camouflage the eggs with bits of soil and abandon them. Others will remain with their eggs, even until after they hatch. They are unable to hunt and remain with their mother until after their next molt, or shedding of their hard outer coverings or exoskeletons.

Young centipedes resemble small adults. However, depending on the species, they may not hatch with their full number of legs. Additional pairs of legs and body segments are added as they molt. For example, hatchlings of house centipedes have only four pairs of legs, while the adults have fifteen. Stone centipedes hatch with six to eight pairs of legs, while the adults have fifteen. In other groups of species, such as the earth-loving centipedes and scolopenders, hatchlings come into the world with all the legs they will ever have. All centipedes molt several times before reaching maturity in a matter of months or years.

CENTIPEDES AND PEOPLE

All centipedes are venomous, but smaller species are either unable to pierce human skin, or the effects of their bites are no

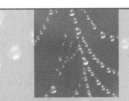

CONSERVING WATER IN THE DESERT

The exoskeletons of insects are coated with a waxy layer that keeps them from drying out, but centipedes don't have this waxy layer. Without their bodies to help them, desert-dwelling centipede species depend instead on their behavior to prevent water loss. They come out only at night when the air is cooler and wetter, and they spend their days hiding in the cool and moist shelters of animal burrows or beneath rocks.

worse than a bee sting. However, larger species are capable of delivering a very painful bite. Children and elderly people or those suffering allergic reactions may need to seek medical attention. The severity of a centipede bite varies with species and may produce moderate to severe pain for several hours or days, and well as localized swelling, discoloration, and numbness. Many people believe that the legs of larger centipedes are also capable of delivering venom, but this is not true. Inflamed punctures or scratches as a result of a centipede walking on human skin are most likely due to bacterial infection. There have been very few human deaths from centipede bites.

Large species are sold as pets and are frequently used as display animals in insect zoos. Only one species is thought to be of any agricultural importance and feeds on roots. Centipedes do not cause or spread disease. Most species are of little consequence to humans or their activities.

CONSERVATION STATUS

Only one species of centipede is listed by the World Conservation Union (IUCN). The Serpent Island centipede (*Scolopendra abnormis*) from the island of Mauritius off the east coast of Africa is listed as Vulnerable, or facing a high risk of extinction in the wild.

Most centipede species are distributed over several continents. But a few apparently have smaller ranges and are known only from single localities. At least one species known only from the Galápagos Islands has not been seen in many years and may be extinct, or no longer alive. The introduction of exotic mammals and snakes has threatened or wiped out many species of island-dwelling animals around the world, including centipedes.

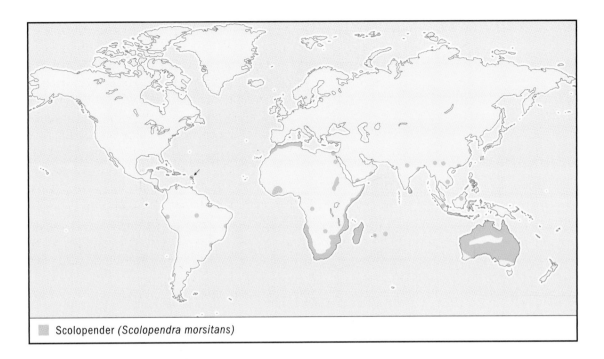

Scolopender (Scolopendra morsitans)

SCOLOPENDER
Scolopendra morsitans

Physical characteristics: Adult scolopenders measure up to 5.1 inches (130 millimeters), with the females usually larger. They are variable in color, with the head and body yellowish or brown with darker bands. Each side of the head has a small cluster of four simple eyes. The antennae have seventeen to twenty-three segments. The body has twenty-one pairs of legs.

Geographic range: This species is found throughout the tropics and other warm regions, including Mexico, Central America, the Caribbean, much of Africa, Madagascar, South and East Asia, and Australia, with a few records in tropical South America.

Habitat: The scolopender's habitat varies; they are found anywhere from desert to rainforest.

Diet: They eat spiders, mites, flies, beetles, ants, termites, cockroaches, and other centipedes. Captive individuals will attack small frogs and toads.

Behavior and reproduction: Scolopenders hunt at night and spend their days in leaf litter, under logs, or beneath loose bark. When threatened they can run fast or burrow quickly in leaf litter. They are active throughout most of the year in the warmer parts of their range.

Males deposit a bean-shaped sperm packet measuring 0.01 inches (2.5 millimeters) onto a web. Females dig brood chambers in soil under rocks and lay twenty-six to eighty-six greenish yellow eggs. In Nigeria, the young reach adulthood within a year, with two generations produced each year.

Scolopenders and people: This species may bite if threatened or carelessly handled.

Conservation status: This species is not considered endangered or threatened. ■

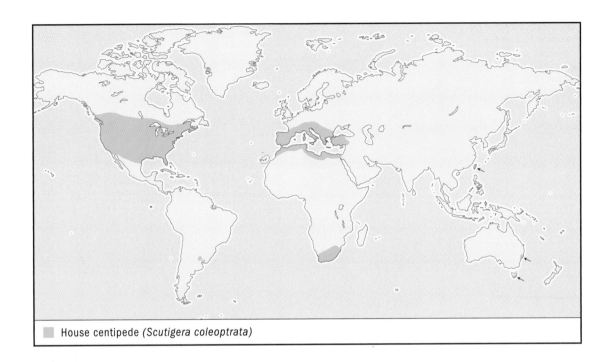

House centipede *(Scutigera coleoptrata)*

HOUSE CENTIPEDE
Scutigera coleoptrata

Physical characteristics: Adult house centipedes measure up to 1.2 inches (35 millimeters) in length. They are yellow or brown with three purplish or bluish bands along the length of the body. They have large compound eyes on each side of the head. The antennae are very long and threadlike with five hundred to six hundred segments. Adults have fifteen pairs of long slender legs that keep the body well above the ground when they are on the move. The last pair of legs are the longest with those of females twice as long as the body.

Geographic range: This species is native to southern Europe, North Africa, and the Near East.

They are widely distributed in North America and South Africa. Populations with limited distributions have been found in Britain, northern Europe, Australia, Argentina, Uruguay, tropical Africa, and Taiwan.

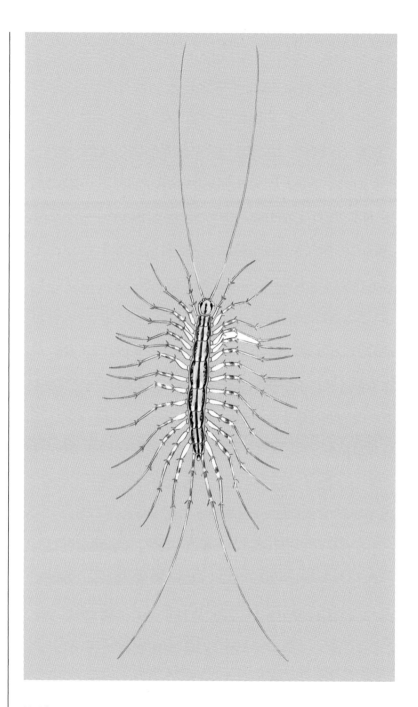

House centipedes eat insects that are considered to be household pests, such as flies and cockroaches. (Illustration by Barbara Duperron. Reproduced by permission.)

Habitat: House centipedes are found in a variety of habitats under wood, in trash, or inside caves. They are often found in homes, especially in places where there is moisture, such as tubs, basins, and basements.

Diet: They eat silverfish, flies, cockroaches, moths, spiders, and other house centipedes.

Behavior and reproduction: House centipedes are usually active day and night and run quickly when threatened. They can run at speeds up to 16 inches (400 millimeters) per second.

Males and females court one another by forming a circle and tapping each other with their antennae. The male eventually deposits a lemon-shaped sperm packet. He guides the female to it, and she removes the sperm from the packet. The eggs are 0.05 inches (1.25 millimeters) long. The female holds a single egg between her reproductive structures, covers it with dirt, and then places it in a crack in the soil. The breeding season lasts about two months. During this time she will lay about four eggs per day. Hatchlings start with four pairs of legs. With each molt the total number of legs increases to five, seven, nine, eleven, and thirteen pairs. There are five more molts after they have all 15 pairs of legs. Adults live nearly three years in captivity.

House centipedes and people: House centipedes eat insects that are considered to be household pests, such as flies and cockroaches. They are delicate animals, and it is unlikely that their fangs can puncture human skin.

Conservation status: This species is not considered endangered or threatened. ■

FOR MORE INFORMATION

Books:

Lewis, J. G. E. *The Biology of Centipedes.* Cambridge, U.K.: Cambridge University Press, 1981.

Tavolacci, J., ed. *Insects and Spiders of the World.* Volume 3: *Carrion Beetle-Earwig.* New York: Marshall Cavendish, 2003.

Walls, J. G. *The Guide to Owning Millipedes and Centipedes.* Neptune City, NJ: T.F.H. Publications, 2000.

Periodicals:

Shelley, R. M. "Centipedes and Millipedes with Emphasis on North American Fauna." *The Kansas School Naturalist* 45, no. 3 (1999).

Web sites:

The Centipede Order Scolopendropmorpha in North America. http://www.naturalsciences.org/research/inverts/centipedes/ (accessed on November 1, 2004).

"Centipedes. Chilopoda." BioKids. Critter Catalog. http://www.biokids .umich.edu/critters/information/Chilopoda.html (accessed on November 1, 2004).

"Chilopoda. Centipedes." Ecowatch. http://www.ento.csiro.au/Ecowatch/ Insects_Invertebrates/Chilopoda.htm (accessed on November 1, 2004).

Myriapoda. http://www.myriapoda.org (accessed on November 18, 2004).

Class: Myriapoda

Subclass: Diplopoda

Number of families: About 121 families

subclass
CHAPTER

PHYSICAL CHARACTERISTICS

Millipedes usually have long wormlike bodies that measure 0.08 to 11.8 inches (2 to 300 millimeters) in length. However, bristly millipedes resemble small (0.16 inches; 4 millimeters) caterpillars that are covered with tufts of stiff hairlike structures. Pill millipedes have short wide bodies that roll up into a ball just like pillbugs. Most millipedes are brownish, blackish, or dark greenish, but many are pale or pinkish. Others are brightly marked with yellow or red. The head has two pairs of jaws. The eyes, if they have any at all, are simple and have only one lens each. The antennae (an-TEH-nee), or sense organs, are short and seven-segmented.

The usually stiff bodies of millipedes are either flattened, rounded, or dome-shaped in cross-section and divided into eleven to 192 segments, depending on age and species. Each segment is formed while the millipede is still in the egg by the joining of two body segments. This is why most of the body segments have two pairs of legs. The first and last body segments are always legless. The first legless segment is a heavily armored collarlike segment that separates the head from the rest of the body. Segments two through four have one or two pair of legs each, except in the males of one group of millipedes where these legs are specialized and used for reproduction. Adults have anywhere from eleven pairs (twenty-two legs) to 375 pairs (750 legs) of legs. Males and females look very similar to one another, but males usually have longer legs so they can grasp the female while mating. The legs of millipedes are

phylum

class

○ **subclass**

order

monotypic order

suborder

family

attached directly underneath the body and are only slightly visible on the sides, if at all. This arrangement gives them the power they need for burrowing and allows them to get into narrow spaces without breaking off legs. The common name millipede, meaning "thousand-legger," refers to the fact that millipedes often have a lot of legs and not to a specific number.

GEOGRAPHIC RANGE

Millipedes are found on all continents except Antarctica. Because they move so slowly on their own, most millipedes have small distributions. However, because many species are burrowers, they have been transported by humans throughout the world in soil and with plants. In fact, half of the species that are native to Britain have been introduced to North America this way. There are about seven thousand species of millipedes worldwide, with about fourteen hundred species in the United States and Canada.

HABITAT

Millipedes usually live in dark damp habitats, but *Archispirostreptus syriacus* and *Orthoporus ornatus* prefer dry habitats and live in deserts. Most species are under leaf litter, woodpiles, and stones. Soil dwellers are usually found in the top inch or two of soil. A few species climb trees. For example, some species of bristly millipedes live in the small cracks in tree bark. Although many millipedes are active at night, pill millipedes, such as *Glomeris marginata*, are usually active during the day.

DIET

Most millipedes eat decaying leaves and other vegetation, but some will eat shoots and roots of living plants. A few species are known to feed on animal remains or funguses. Many species will also eat their own waste pellets. It is believed that they obtain nutrition from funguses growing inside the pellets rather than from the waste itself.

BEHAVIOR AND REPRODUCTION

Most millipedes lack a waxy layer on the outside of their exoskeletons, or hard outer coverings, that helps to prevent the loss of body moisture. Like centipedes, millipedes spend most of their time in cool wet places and become active only at night or after rains.

Many millipedes defend themselves by rolling their bodies up into a ball or spiral. This behavior protects the legs and delicate underside of the animal, leaving only the hard plates of the body segments exposed. Some species also protect themselves by producing toxic or bad-smelling chemicals through a series of openings on the sides of their bodies. Some larger tropical species can actually squirt their attackers with a defensive spray. Bristly millipedes do not produce these defensive chemicals. Other species behave strangely when threatened. For example, *Diopsiulus regressus* alternates between flipping its body into the air and running short distances.

Males and females usually have to mate to produce offspring, with males usually depositing sperm directly into the reproductive organs of the female. There may or may not be any courtship behavior. Bristly millipede males must first spin a web on which they deposit their sperm. The female then approaches the web and puts the sperm into her own reproductive organs. In some pill millipedes a male coaxes a female to mate with squeaking noises made by rubbing the bases of his legs against his body. He then grasps the female's body with his legs. A sperm packet is released behind his head and passed back from one pair of legs to the next like a conveyor belt, until it reaches the reproductive organs of the female. In other pill millipedes the male covers the sperm packet in dirt before passing it back with his legs to his mate's reproductive organs.

Millipedes lay their eggs in the soil. Some species make individual cases for their eggs out of chewed-up leaves. In some species, the female, and occasionally the male, guards the eggs until they hatch. Although young millipedes resemble small adults, they are usually legless when they first hatch from the egg. After they molt, or shed their exoskeleton for the first time, they have six body segments and three pairs of legs. They add additional body segments and pairs of legs with each molt until they reach the maximum adult number. Millipedes molt in sheltered places underground or in cracks in the soil. *Nar-*

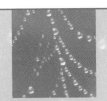

WHY DO BLIND MILLIPEDES HAVE THEIR OWN NIGHT LIGHTS?

Scattered in the mountains of central and southern California are millipedes that glow in the dark. These eight species of *Motyxia* represent the world's only bioluminescent (BI-o-LU-mih-NEH-sent) millipedes. Bioluminscent organisms produce their own light. All but their undersides glow bright white, causing them to resemble small glow sticks. They do not have eyes to see approaching predators, but their obvious glow might warn nighttime predators of their bad taste.

ceus americanus and *Orthoporus ornatus* seal themselves off in special chambers dug for this very delicate stage of their lives. Millipedes reach adulthood in one or two years, sometimes longer. Adults live for one to eleven years, although some individuals may live longer.

MILLIPEDES AND PEOPLE

Millipedes are an important, yet seldom appreciated, group of animals that break down dead plants and recycle them into food for other organisms. It has been estimated that they add two tons of manure per acre (0.40 hectares) of forest floor each year.

Sometimes millipedes damage gardens and crops by eating shoots and roots. In Japan thousands of *Parafontaria laminata* crushed by trains have resulted in the tracks becoming slick, causing railroad cars to lose traction.

Some people have strong allergic reactions to the defensive chemicals of millipedes. The defensive fluids of *Spirobolus* will stain and irritate human skin, whether or not the person is allergic to the chemicals.

CONSERVATION STATUS

No millipedes are considered endangered or threatened.

Pill millipede (*Glomeris marginata*)

PILL MILLIPEDE
Glomeris marginata

Physical characteristics: Pill millipedes are short and either dark brown or black. Their twelve body segments are dome-shaped in cross section. They have light brown or light gray margins toward the rear. Adults have seventeen to nineteen pairs of legs and reach 0.8 inches (20 millimeters) in length and 0.3 inches (8 millimeters) in width.

Geographic range: This species is found in the British Isles and in western and northwestern Europe.

Habitat: Pill millipedes are found in forests, fields, and gardens, usually in leaf litter. Unlike most millipedes, *Glomeris marginata* is better equipped to deal with drier conditions. It is often active on bright, sunny days.

Pill millipedes are found in the British Isles and in western and northwestern Europe. (Illustration by Amanda Humphrey. Reproduced by permission.)

Diet: Pill millipedes eat decaying leaves. A study in France showed that they eat about one of every ten leaves that falls to the forest floor each autumn.

Behavior and reproduction: When threatened they roll up into a ball, just like a pillbug. They also produce a chemical that makes them smell and taste bad to most predators (PREH-duh-ters), or animals that hunt other animals for food.

Males produce pheromones (FEH-re-moans), or chemicals that are attractive to females. They also make a squeaking sound to get females to mate with them.

Females lay six or seven dozen eggs in spring and again in summer. Each egg is deposited in a capsule. The young molt once inside the egg before they hatch about two months later. Cooler temperatures can delay hatching up to several months. The young take several years to reach adulthood. They may live up to a total of eleven years. Females may produce a dozen batches of eggs during their long life.

Pill millipedes and people: This species is important because it breaks down and recycles dead leaves and other vegetable matter.

Conservation status: This species is not considered endangered or threatened. ■

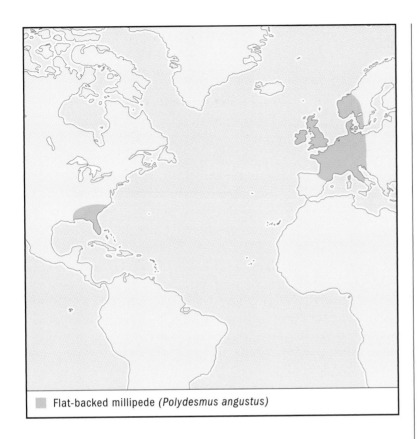

Flat-backed millipede (*Polydesmus angustus*)

FLAT-BACKED MILLIPEDE
Polydesmus angustus

Physical characteristics: Flat-backed millipedes resemble centipedes. The bodies of the adults are flat, dark brown, with about twenty segments. They measure 0.6 to 1.0 inches (14 to 25 millimeters) in length and are about 0.16 inches (0.4 millimeters) wide. The plate segments covering the back are ridged along their lengths. The antennae and legs are longer than in most other millipedes.

Geographic range: This species is found in northwestern Europe and was accidentally introduced to the southeastern United States.

Habitat: Flat-backed millipedes live in compost piles, under tree bark, inside cracks in stumps and logs, or in loose soil with lots of decaying bits of leaves.

Flat-backed millipedes eat roots, dead leaves, and other bits of decayed plant materials, as well as strawberries and other fruits. (Illustration by Amanda Humphrey. Reproduced by permission.)

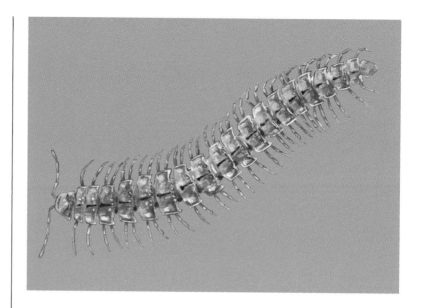

Diet: They eat roots, dead leaves, and other bits of decayed plant materials, as well as strawberries and other fruits.

Behavior and reproduction: The ridged body of this millipede helps it to push its way through the soil.

Mating occurs from late spring through the summer and then again in late summer through mid-fall. Males usually mate only once. The females store the sperm from a single mating and produce several batches of eggs. Young millipedes hatching earlier in the year reach adulthood in one year, while those hatching later require two.

Flat-backed millipedes and people: This species has been studied by scientists to understand the effect of sunlight and day length on millipedes.

Conservation status: This species is not considered endangered or threatened.   ■

FOR MORE INFORMATION

Books:

Hopkin, S. P., and H. J. Read. *The Biology of Millipedes.* Oxford, U.K.: Oxford University Press, 1992.

Tavolacci, J., ed. *Insects and Spiders of the World.* Volume 6: *Locomotion-Orb-web Spider.* New York: Marshall Cavendish, 2003.

Walls, J. G. *The Guide to Owning Millipedes and Centipedes.* Neptune City, NJ: T.F.H. Publications, 2000.

Periodicals:

Evans, A. V. "Minding Millipedes." *Reptiles Magazine* 11, no. 10 (October 2003): 86–91.

Shelley, R. M. "Centipedes and Millipedes with Emphasis on North American Fauna." *Kansas School Naturalist* 45, no. 3 (1999): 1–15.

Web sites:

"Diplopoda. Millipedes." Ecowatch. http://www.ento.csiro.au/Ecowatch/Insects_Invertebrates/Diplopoda.htm (accessed on November 2, 2004).

"Millipedes. Diplopoda." BioKids. Critter Catalog. http://www.biokids.umich.edu/critters/information/Diplopoda.html (accessed on November 2, 2004).

Myriapoda. http://www.myriapoda.org (accessed on November 18, 2004).

subclass

CHAPTER

PHYSICAL CHARACTERISTICS

The soft, whitish bodies of symphylans (sim-FIL-ehns) are long and slender, measuring 0.078 to 0.31 inches (2 to 8 millimeters) in length. The head is distinct, heart-shaped and has three pairs of mouthparts. One pair is fused together to form a lower lip. The antennae (an-TEH-nee), or sense organs, are long and threadlike or beadlike. There are no eyes. The body has fourteen segments. The back of the body is covered with fifteen to twenty-four soft plates. The first twelve body segments each have a pair of legs. At the base of each leg is a short stiff spine and special sac. The spine probably helps the symphylan move through the soil, while the sac probably regulates water and salts in the body. The next-to-last body segment has a pair of projections from which the symphylans produce silk. The last body segment has a pair of long, sensitive hairlike structures.

GEOGRAPHIC RANGE

Symphylans are found on all continents except Antarctica. There are about two hundred species worldwide. The species in the United States and Canada are so poorly studied that it is not known just how many species there are.

HABITAT

Symphylans live in the upper 3.2 foot (1 meter) layers of soil in both natural and agricultural habitats. They prefer moist but not wet soils.

DIET

Symphylans eat mainly roots and rootlike structures of funguses, but most species are probably omnivorous (am-NI-vo-rus), or animals that feed on both plant and animal materials.

BEHAVIOR AND REPRODUCTION

Symphylans are usually found in large numbers and sometimes gather in groups. They move up and down in the soil to maintain the proper moisture levels in their surroundings. Their antennae move constantly as they move about searching for food and mates, but they are held back over the body when feeding. Symphylans run swiftly, especially when threatened.

Males and females are both required for reproduction. Males deposit sperm packets on the ground. The females later pick up the sperm packets in their mouths. Nothing else is known about their courtship behavior or how they might communicate or interact with each other. Females deposit up to twenty-five pearly-white eggs in a mass. The hatchlings have fewer body segments than adults and only six or seven pairs of legs. They are very inactive. Each time they molt, or shed their exoskeleton or hard outer covering, they will add an additional segment and pair of legs until they reach adulthood with twelve pairs.

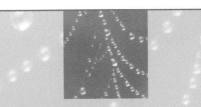

LIKE TWO SHIPS PASSING IN THE NIGHT

Males and females of *Scutigerella* do not have be in the same place at the same time to reproduce. Each male produces up to 450 sperm packets and places them on top of short stalks of silk. Later, females walk through the patches of packets and gobble up to eighteen each day. Most are swallowed and digested, but some are stored in special sacs in her mouth. Afterward she gently removes each egg from her reproductive organs and fertilizes them in her mouth.

SYMPHYLANS AND PEOPLE

Symphylans are small, secretive animals that do not bite or sting and are largely unknown to the public. Garden symphylans damage crops such as pineapple, beets, potatoes, beans, and many others. They are sometimes a pest in greenhouses.

CONSERVATION STATUS

No symphylan is considered endangered or threatened. However, symphylans are not very well known, and it is possible that species found only in limited areas could be vulnerable to extinction if their habitats were spoiled or destroyed.

GARDEN SYMPHYLAN
Scutigerella immaculata

Physical characteristics: This species measures 0.19 to 0.31 inches (5 to 8 millimeters) in length. Their bodies are whitish or light brownish. They are impossible to identify without examination through a microscope.

Geographic range: The true range of this species is unknown because it is often confused with other closely related species.

Habitat: This species lives in leaf litter and rich soil. It is also found in agricultural fields and greenhouses.

Diet: The garden symphylan eats vegetable material, especially small roots and rootlike parts of funguses.

Behavior and reproduction: The adults are especially quick when threatened.

Males leave sperm packets on the ground for females to pick up. Eggs are laid in masses, each mass containing up to twenty-five eggs. The larvae (LAR-vee), or young, hatch with six or seven pairs of legs and add a new pair of legs with each molt.

Garden symphylans and people: This species is sometimes a serious pest in fields, gardens, and greenhouses and hothouses.

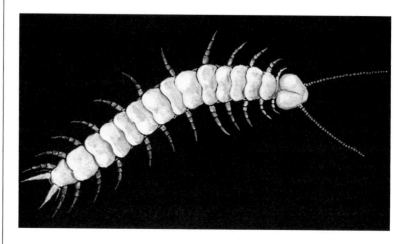

Garden symphylans live in leaf litter and rich soil. They are also found in agricultural fields and greenhouses. (Illustration by Emily Damstra. Reproduced by permission.)

Conservation status: Garden symphylans are not considered endangered or threatened. ■

FOR MORE INFORMATION

Books:

Edwards, C. A. *Symphyla: In Soil Biology Guide*, edited by Daniel L. Dindal. New York: John Wiley and Sons, 1990.

Eisenbeis, G., and W. Wichard, *Atlas on the Biology of Soil Arthropods*. Berlin, Germany: Springer-Verlag, 1987.

Periodicals:

Scheller, U. "Symphyla from the United States and Mexico." *Texas Memorial Museum, Speleological Monographs* 1 (1986): 87–125.

Web sites:

"Symphyla." Tree of Life Web Project. http://tolweb.org/tree?group= Symphyla&contgroup=Arthropoda (accessed on November 3, 2004).

Tasmanian Symphyla. http://www.qvmag.tas.gov.au/zoology/multipedes/ tassymph/symintro.html (accessed on November 3, 2004).

subclass

CHAPTER

PHYSICAL CHARACTERISTICS

Pauropods are very small, measuring only 0.019 to 0.078 inches (0.5 to 2.0 millimeters) in length. Their long slender white or brownish bodies are usually soft and flexible, but some are covered with relatively thick plates. The small head is directed downward. Their chewing mouthparts are small, weak, and made up of two sets of jaws. The first set of jaws has curved teeth that look like a comb. The second pair is joined together to form a flaplike structure. They lack eyes. The antennae (an-TEH-nee), or sense organs, have two branches. The body is twelve-segmented and has eight to eleven pairs of legs, one pair per body segment. There are usually only six plates across their backs, but some species have twelve. Like millipedes, the reproductive organs are located toward the front of the body on the third segment. The last segment has a special plate. The size and texture of the plate is used to distinguish different species.

GEOGRAPHIC RANGE

They are found on all continents except Antarctica. There are about seven hundred species known worldwide. The pauropods of the United States and Canada are so poorly known that it is not possible to give even an approximate number of species found in these countries.

HABITAT

Pauropods live in a variety of habitats and are most common in the upper 7.8 inches (200 millimeters) of soil. They are often found in moist soils under rocks, wood, and clumps of moss.

DIET

The foods of most pauropods are unknown. Some species eat mold or suck fluids from the rootlike structures of funguses. One species is known to eat the tiny hairlike structures on plant roots.

BEHAVIOR AND REPRODUCTION

Populations of pauropods are usually small and widely scattered, but the populations of some species can reach the thousands in both wild areas and agricultural fields. They move through the soil to follow changing moisture levels. Since their bodies are soft and not built for burrowing, pauropods follow roots and crevices deep into the soil as they search for moisture. Most species run very quickly, usually in fits and starts. These species usually change directions with ease, but a few are not so agile. Nothing is known about how they communicate with each other or whether or not they maintain territories.

Both males and females are usually required for reproduction. A few species are known to reproduce by parthenogenesis (PAR-thuh-no-JEH-nuh-sihs), where the larvae (LAR-vee), or young, develop from unfertilized eggs. The eggs go through a short pupalike stage before they hatch. A pupa (PYU-puh) is the life stage between larva and adult. In one group of pauropods the larvae hatch with three pairs of legs. With each molt, or shedding of the exoskeleton, or hard outer covering, the total number of legs changes to five, six, and eight pairs. In all other pauropods the hatching larvae start with six pairs of legs.

PAUROPODS AND PEOPLE

Pauropods are small and secretive animals that are overlooked by most people, even trained scientists. One species (*Saintpaulia*) in the Netherlands is known to damage greenhouse cuttings, but all others do not impact people or their activities.

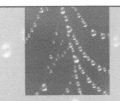

YOU NEVER KNOW UNTIL YOU LOOK

Since 1866 more than seven hundred species of pauropods have been described, but there may be two thousand to three thousand species awaiting discovery, possibly more. In 2002, a retired high school teacher from Sweden, the world's only authority on the group, paid a visit to Great Smoky Mountains National Park. Only five species of pauropods were known from the park, but in just three weeks he found at least forty-four species, twelve of which were new to science.

CONSERVATION STATUS

There are no pauropods considered endangered or threatened. They are so poorly known that little thought has been given to their conservation.

NO COMMON NAME
Allopauropus carolinensis

Physical characteristics: They are white or whitish and measure 0.039 inches (1 millimeter) in length. They can only be identified with the aid of a microscope.

Geographic range: This species is found in the eastern United States, however not enough studies have been completed to determine how many states should be included.

Habitat: This species is found in forests and woodlands.

Diet: They probably feed on funguses.

Behavior and reproduction: This species is very active but not well studied. Nothing is known about their mating or reproductive behavior.

***Allopauropus carolinensis* and people:** This species does not impact people or their activities.

Conservation status: This species is not considered endangered or threatened. ■

Allopauropus carolinensis *are found in forests and woodlands and probably eat funguses. (Ernest Bernard. Reproduced by permission.)*

FOR MORE INFORMATION

Books:

Dindal, D. L., ed. *Soil Biology Guide.* New York: John Wiley and Sons, 1990.

Eisenbeis, G., and W. Wichard. *Atlas on the Biology of Soil Arthropods.* Berlin, Germany: Springer-Verlag, 1987.

Periodicals:

Scheller, U. "The Pauropoda (Myriapoda) of the Savannah River Plant, Aiken, South Carolina." *Savannah River Plant and National Environmental Research Park Program* 17 (1988): 1–99.

Scheller, U. "Pauropoda. The Little Ones Among the Myriapods." *ATBI Quarterly* 3, No. 4 (2002): 3.

Web sites:

"Pauropoda." Tree of Life Web Project. http://tolweb.org/tree?group= Pauropoda&contgroup=Arthropoda (accessed on November 5, 2004).

Tasmanian Pauropoda. http://www.qvmag.tas.gov.au/zoology/multipedes/ taspauro/pauintro.html (accessed on November 5, 2004).

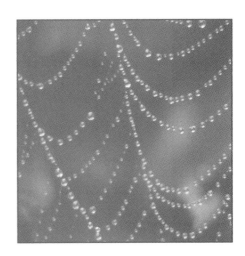

Species List by Biome

CONIFEROUS FOREST
American cockroach
Bed bug
Book louse
Book scorpion
Brown mayfly
European earwig
German cockroach
Giant salmonfly
Giant whip scorpion
Greenhouse camel cricket
Hair follicle mite
Holijapyx diversiuguis
Honeybee
Human head/body louse
Indian mealmoth
Long-bodied cellar spider
Megarhyssa nortoni
Oriental cockroach
Rock-crawler
Rocky Mountain wood tick
Schummel's inocelliid snakefly
Silverfish
Slender pigeon louse
Wandering glider
Zebra jumping spider

CONTINENTAL MARGIN
Colossendeis megalonyx
Horseshoe crab

DECIDUOUS FOREST
Allopauropus carolinensis
American burying beetle
American cockroach
Bed bug
Big black horse fly
Book louse
Book scorpion
Brownbanded cockroach
Brown mayfly
Chigoe
Chiloporter eatoni
Chinese mantid
Common American
  walkingstick
Common harvestman
Devil's coach-horse
Eastern dobsonfly
Eastern subterranean
  termite
European earwig
European mantid
European marsh crane fly
European stag beetle
Flat-backed millipede
Garden symphylan
German cockroach
Giant whip scorpion
Greenhouse camel cricket
Gypsy moth

Hair follicle mite
Halictophagus naulti
Holijapyx diversiuguis
House centipede
Honeybee
Hubbard's angel insect
Human head/body louse
Indian mealmoth
Long-bodied cellar spider
Macleay's spectre
Mediterranean fruit fly
Megarhyssa nortoni
Moth lacewing
Oriental cockroach
Panorpa nuptialis
Pea aphid
Pill millipede
Rock-crawler
Potter wasp
Rocky Mountain wood
  tick
Saunders embiid
Scolopender
Seventeen-year cicada
Silkworm
Silverfish
Sinetomon yoroi
Slender pigeon louse
Spider bat fly
Spoonwing lacewing

Tarantula hawk
Triaenodes bicolor
Trissolcus basalis
Velvet ant
Wandering glider
Western flower thrips
Zebra jumping spider

DESERT

American cockroach
Antlion
Bed bug
Big black horse fly
Book louse
Brownbanded cockroach
Camel spider
European earwig
Hair follicle mite
Honeybee
House centipede
Indian mealmoth
German cockroach
Giant whip scorpion
Greenhouse camel cricket
Long-bodied cellar spider
Oriental cockroach
Sacred scarab
Scolopender
Silverfish
Slender pigeon louse
Spider bat fly
Tarantula hawk
Wandering glider
Western flower thrips
Wide-headed rottenwood
  termite
Zebra jumping spider

GRASSLAND

American burying beetle
American cockroach
Antlion
Backswimmer
Big black horse fly
Bed bug
Book louse
Book scorpion

Brownbanded cockroach
Common harvestman
Death's head hawk moth
Emperor scorpion
European earwig
European marsh crane fly
European mantid
Garden symphylan
German cockroach
Giant whip scorpion
Gladiator
Hair follicle mite
Honeybee
House centipede
Human head/body louse
Indian mealmoth
Indian stick insect
Large blue
Long-bodied cellar spider
Lucerne flea
Oriental cockroach
Pea aphid
Sacred scarab
St. Helena earwig
Scolopender
Sheep and goat flea
Silverfish
Slender pigeon louse
Spider bat fly
Spoonwing lacewing
Tarantula hawk
Trissolcus basalis
Tsetse fly
Variegated grasshopper
Velvet ant
Wandering glider
Western flower thrips
Wide-headed rottenwood
  termite
Yellow fever mosquito
Zebra jumping spider

LAKE AND POND

American cockroach
Brownbanded cockroach
German cockroach
Great water beetle
Hair follicle mite

Honeybee
Oriental cockroach
Wandering glider

OCEAN

Colossendeis megalonyx
Sea skater

RAINFOREST

American cockroach
Atlas moth
Bed bug
Balsam beast
Beetle cricket
Black macrotermes
Black-headed nasute termite
Blue morpho
Book louse
Brownbanded cockroach
Chigoe
Cubacubana spelaea
Dead-leaf mantid
Dead leaf mimetica
Emperor scorpion
European earwig
Forest giant
German cockroach
Giant water bug
Giraffe-necked weevil
Green lacewing
Greenhouse camel cricket
Greenhouse whitefly
Hair follicle mite
Hercules beetle
Hispaniola hooded katydid
Honeybee
House centipede
Human head/body louse
Indian mealmoth
Javan leaf insect
Jungle nymph
Leaf-cutter ant
Linnaeus's snapping termite
Madeira cockroach
Mantid lacewing
Mediterranean fruit fly

Orchid mantid
Oriental cockroach
Pea aphid
Saunders embiid
Scolopender
Silverfish
Slender pigeon louse
Spider bat fly
Stalk-eyed fly
Tailless whip scorpion
Tarantula hawk
Tsetse fly
Wandering glider
Wandering violin mantid
Yellow fever mosquito

RIVER AND STREAM
American cockroach
Brownbanded cockroach

Forest giant
German cockroach
Hair follicle mite
Honeybee
Oriental cockroach
Rocky Mountain wood tick
Triaenodes bicolor
Wandering glider

SEASHORE
Hair follicle mite
Honeybee
Horseshoe crab
Petrobius brevistylis
Wandering glider

TUNDRA
Book louse
Hair follicle mite

Human head/body louse
Slender pigeon louse

WETLAND
American cockroach
Big black horse fly
Brownbanded cockroach
European earwig
German cockroach
Greenhouse camel cricket
Hair follicle mite
Human head/body louse
Long-winged conehead
Oriental cockroach
Rocky Mountain wood
  tick
Slender pigeon louse
Wandering glider

Species List by Geographic Range

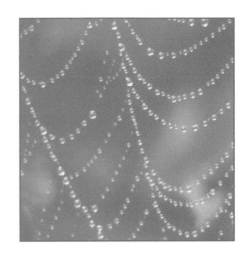

AFGHANISTAN
American cockroach
Bed bug
Brownbanded cockroach
German cockroach
Greenhouse camel cricket
Greenhouse whitefly
Hair follicle mite
Honeybee
Human head/body louse
Indian mealmoth
Liposcelis bostrychophila
Long-bodied cellar spider
Lucerne flea
Pea aphid
Silverfish
Wandering glider
Western flower thrips

ALBANIA
American cockroach
Bed bug
Book scorpion
Brown mayfly
Brownbanded cockroach
Common harvestman
Death's head hawk moth
Devil's coach-horse
European earwig
European mantid

European stag beetle
German cockroach
Great water beetle
Greenhouse camel cricket
Greenhouse whitefly
Gypsy moth
Hair follicle mite
Honeybee
Human head/body louse
Indian mealmoth
Large blue
Liposcelis bostrychophila
Long-bodied cellar spider
Long-winged conehead
Lucerne flea
Mediterranean fruitfly
Pea aphid
Sacred scarab
Silverfish
Slender pigeon louse
Spoonwing lacewing
Triaenodes bicolor
Velvet ant
Western flower thrips
Zebra jumping spider

ALGERIA
American cockroach
Bed bug
Brownbanded cockroach

Camel spider
Death's head hawk moth
Devil's coach-horse
European mantid
German cockroach
Greenhouse camel cricket
Gypsy moth
Hair follicle mite
Honeybee
House centipede
Human head/body louse
Indian mealmoth
Liposcelis bostrychophila
Long-bodied cellar spider
Long-winged conehead
Lucerne flea
Mediterranean fruitfly
Sacred scarab
Scolopender
Silverfish
Slender pigeon louse
Spoonwing lacewing
Wandering glider
Western flower thrips
Yellow fever mosquito

ANDORRA
American cockroach
Antlion
Bed bug

Book scorpion
Brown mayfly
Brownbanded cockroach
Common harvestman
Death's head hawk moth
Devil's coach-horse
European earwig
European mantid
European stag beetle
German cockroach
Great water beetle
Greenhouse camel cricket
Greenhouse whitefly
Gypsy moth
Hair follicle mite
Honeybee
House centipede
Human head/body louse
Indian mealmoth
Large blue
Liposcelis bostrychophila
Long-bodied cellar spider
Long-winged conehead
Lucerne flea
Mediterranean fruitfly
Pea aphid
Sacred scarab
Silverfish
Slender pigeon louse
Spoonwing lacewing
Velvet ant
Western flower thrips
Yellow fever mosquito
Zebra jumping spider

ANGOLA
American cockroach
Bed bug
Brownbanded cockroach
Chigoe
Death's head hawk moth
European mantid
German cockroach
Greenhouse camel cricket
Greenhouse whitefly
Hair follicle mite

Honeybee
Human head/body louse
Indian mealmoth
Liposcelis bostrychophila
Long-bodied cellar spider
Lucerne flea
Madeira cockroach
Scolopender
Silverfish
Tsetse fly
Variegated grasshopper
Wandering glider
Yellow fever mosquito

ANTIGUA AND BARBUDA
Bed bug
German cockroach
Greenhouse camel cricket
Hair follicle mite
Honeybee
Human head/body louse
Indian mealmoth
Liposcelis bostrychophila
Long-bodied cellar spider
Lucerne flea
Silverfish
Wandering glider

ARCTIC
German cockroach

ARGENTINA
American cockroach
Backswimmer
Bed bug
Brownbanded cockroach
Chiloporter eatoni
German cockroach
Greenhouse camel cricket
Greenhouse whitefly
Hair follicle mite
Honeybee
Human head/body louse
Indian mealmoth

Leaf-cutter ant
Liposcelis bostrychophila
Long-bodied cellar spider
Lucerne flea
Oriental cockroach
Pea aphid
Silverfish
Wandering glider

ARMENIA
American cockroach
Bed bug
Brown mayfly
Death's head hawk moth
Devil's coach-horse
European mantid
German cockroach
Greenhouse camel cricket
Greenhouse whitefly
Hair follicle mite
Honeybee
Human head/body louse
Indian mealmoth
Liposcelis bostrychophila
Long-bodied cellar spider
Lucerne flea
Pea aphid
Silverfish
Slender pigeon louse
Yellow fever mosquito

ATLANTIC OCEAN
Colossendeis megalonyx
Sea skater

AUSTRALIA
American cockroach
Balsam beast
Bed bug
European earwig
European mantid
German cockroach
Green lacewing
Greenhouse camel cricket
Greenhouse whitefly

Gypsy moth
Hair follicle mite
House centipede
Human head/body louse
Indian mealmoth
Liposcelis bostrychophila
Long-bodied cellar spider
Lucerne flea
Macleay's specter
Mantid lacewing
Mediterranean fruitfly
Moth lacewing
Oriental cockroach
Pea aphid
Scolopender
Silverfish
Spider bat fly
Trissolcus basalis
Wandering glider
Western flower thrips
Yellow fever mosquito

AUSTRIA

American cockroach
Bed bug
Book scorpion
Brown mayfly
Common harvestman
Devil's coach-horse
European earwig
European mantid
European marsh crane fly
European stag beetle
Flat-backed millipede
German cockroach
Great water beetle
Greenhouse camel cricket
Greenhouse whitefly
Hair follicle mite
Honeybee
House centipede
Human head/body louse
Indian mealmoth
Large blue
Liposcelis bostrychophila
Long-bodied cellar spider

Long-winged conehead
Lucerne flea
Pea aphid
Silverfish
Slender pigeon louse
Spoonwing lacewing
Triaenodes bicolor
Velvet ant
Western flower thrips
Zebra jumping spider

AZERBAIJAN

American cockroach
Bed bug
Brown mayfly
Common harvestman
Death's head hawk moth
Devil's coach-horse
European mantid
German cockroach
Greenhouse camel cricket
Greenhouse whitefly
Hair follicle mite
Honeybee
Human head/body louse
Indian mealmoth
Liposcelis bostrychophila
Long-bodied cellar spider
Lucerne flea
Pea aphid
Silverfish
Slender pigeon louse
Yellow fever mosquito
Zebra jumping spider

BAHAMAS

Bed bug
German cockroach
Greenhouse camel cricket
Hair follicle mite
Honeybee
Human head/body louse
Indian mealmoth
Liposcelis bostrychophila
Long-bodied cellar spider

Lucerne flea
Silverfish
Wandering glider

BAHRAIN

Bed bug
Camel spider
German cockroach
Greenhouse camel cricket
Hair follicle mite
Honeybee
Human head/body louse
Indian mealmoth
Liposcelis bostrychophila
Long-bodied cellar spider
Lucerne flea
Silverfish
Slender pigeon louse
Wandering glider
Yellow fever mosquito

BANGLADESH

American cockroach
Atlas moth
Bed bug
Brownbanded cockroach
German cockroach
Greenhouse camel cricket
Greenhouse whitefly
Hair follicle mite
Honeybee
Human head/body louse
Indian mealmoth
Liposcelis bostrychophila
Long-bodied cellar spider
Lucerne flea
Orchid mantid
Oriental cockroach
Pea aphid
Scolopender
Silkworm
Silverfish
Slender pigeon louse
Wandering glider
Wandering violin mantid
Yellow fever mosquito

BARBADOS

Bed bug
German cockroach
Greenhouse camel cricket
Hair follicle mite
Honeybee
Human head/body louse
Indian mealmoth
Liposcelis bostrychophila
Long-bodied cellar spider
Lucerne flea
Silverfish
Wandering glider

BELARUS

American cockroach
Bed bug
Book scorpion
Brown mayfly
Common harvestman
Devil's coach-horse
European earwig
European stag beetle
German cockroach
Great water beetle
Greenhouse camel cricket
Gypsy moth
Hair follicle mite
Honeybee
Human head/body louse
Indian mealmoth
Large blue
Liposcelis bostrychophila
Long-bodied cellar spider
Long-winged conehead
Lucerne flea
Pea aphid
Schummel's inocelliid
  snakefly
Silverfish
Slender pigeon louse
Spoonwing lacewing
Triaenodes bicolor
Velvet ant
Western flower thrips
Zebra jumping spider

BELGIUM

American cockroach
Antlion
Bed bug
Book scorpion
Brown mayfly
Common harvestman
Devil's coach-horse
European earwig
European marsh crane fly
European stag beetle
Flat-backed millipede
German cockroach
Great water beetle
Greenhouse camel cricket
Gypsy moth
Hair follicle mite
Honeybee
Human head/body louse
Indian mealmoth
Large blue
Liposcelis bostrychophila
Long-bodied cellar spider
Long-winged conehead
Lucerne flea
Oriental cockroach
Petrobius brevistylis
Pill millipede
Silverfish
Slender pigeon louse
Spoonwing lacewing
Triaenodes bicolor
Velvet ant
Western flower thrips
Zebra jumping spider

BELIZE

American cockroach
Bed bug
Black-headed nasute termite
Brownbanded cockroach
Chigoe
Forest giant
German cockroach
Greenhouse camel cricket
Hair follicle mite

Hercules beetle
Honeybee
Horseshoe crab
Human head/body louse
Indian mealmoth
Liposcelis bostrychophila
Long-bodied cellar spider
Lucerne flea
Madeira cockroach
Mediterranean fruitfly
Pea aphid
Silverfish
Tailless whip scorpion
Wandering glider
Yellow fever mosquito

BENIN

American cockroach
Bed bug
Brownbanded cockroach
Chigoe
Death's head hawk moth
Emperor scorpion
European mantid
German cockroach
Greenhouse camel cricket
Greenhouse whitefly
Hair follicle mite
Honeybee
Human head/body louse
Indian mealmoth
Liposcelis bostrychophila
Long-bodied cellar spider
Long-winged conehead
Lucerne flea
Madeira cockroach
Silverfish
Slender pigeon louse
Tsetse fly
Variegated grasshopper
Wandering glider
Yellow fever mosquito

BHUTAN

American cockroach
Atlas moth

Bed bug
Brownbanded cockroach
Chinese mantid
Dead-leaf mantid
German cockroach
Greenhouse camel cricket
Greenhouse whitefly
Hair follicle mite
Honeybee
Human head/body louse
Indian mealmoth
Liposcelis bostrychophila
Long-bodied cellar spider
Lucerne flea
Oriental cockroach
Pea aphid
Silverfish
Wandering glider
Yellow fever mosquito

BOLIVIA

American cockroach
Backswimmer
Bed bug
Blue morpho
Brownbanded cockroach
Chigoe
Forest giant
German cockroach
Giant water bug
Greenhouse camel cricket
Greenhouse whitefly
Hair follicle mite
Hercules beetle
Honeybee
Human head/body louse
Indian mealmoth
Leaf-cutter ant
Liposcelis bostrychophila
Long-bodied cellar spider
Lucerne flea
Mediterranean fruitfly
Pea aphid
Silverfish
Wandering glider

BOSNIA AND HERZEGOVINA

American cockroach
Bed bug
Book scorpion
Brown mayfly
Brownbanded cockroach
Common harvestman
Devil's coach-horse
European mantid
European stag beetle
German cockroach
Great water beetle
Greenhouse camel cricket
Greenhouse whitefly
Gypsy moth
Hair follicle mite
Honeybee
House centipede
Human head/body louse
Indian mealmoth
Large blue
Liposcelis bostrychophila
Long-bodied cellar spider
Long-winged conehead
Lucerne flea
Mediterranean fruitfly
Pea aphid
Silverfish
Slender pigeon louse
Spoonwing lacewing
Triaenodes bicolor
Velvet ant
Western flower thrips
Yellow fever mosquito
Zebra jumping spider

BOTSWANA

American cockroach
Bed bug
Brownbanded cockroach
Death's head hawk moth
European mantid
German cockroach
Greenhouse camel cricket

Greenhouse whitefly
Hair follicle mite
Honeybee
Human head/body louse
Indian mealmoth
Liposcelis bostrychophila
Long-bodied cellar spider
Lucerne flea
Silverfish
Wandering glider
Western flower thrips
Yellow fever mosquito

BRAZIL

American cockroach
Backswimmer
Bed bug
Black-headed nasute termite
Blue morpho
Brownbanded cockroach
Chigoe
Cubacubana spelaea
German cockroach
Giant water bug
Greenhouse camel cricket
Greenhouse whitefly
Hair follicle mite
Hercules beetle
Honeybee
Human head/body louse
Indian mealmoth
Leaf-cutter ant
Linnaeus's snapping termite
Liposcelis bostrychophila
Long-bodied cellar spider
Lucerne flea
Magarhyssa nortoni
Mediterranean fruitfly
Pea aphid
Scolopender
Silverfish
Trissolcus basalis
Wandering glider
Yellow fever mosquito

BRUNEI

American cockroach
Atlas moth
Bed bug
Black macrotermes
Cyrtodiopsis dalmanni
Dead-leaf mantid
European earwig
German cockroach
Greenhouse camel cricket
Greenhouse whitefly
Hair follicle mite
Honeybee
Human head/body louse
Indian mealmoth
Javan leaf insect
Jungle nymph
Liposcelis bostrychophila
Long-bodied cellar spider
Lucerne flea
Orchid mantid
Pea aphid
Silverfish
Wandering glider
Yellow fever mosquito

BULGARIA

American cockroach
Bed bug
Book scorpion
Brown mayfly
Brownbanded cockroach
Common harvestman
Death's head hawk moth
Devil's coach-horse
European mantid
European stag beetle
German cockroach
Great water beetle
Greenhouse camel cricket
Greenhouse whitefly
Gypsy moth
Hair follicle mite
Honeybee
Human head/body louse

Indian mealmoth
Liposcelis bostrychophila
Long-bodied cellar spider
Long-winged conehead
Lucerne flea
Pea aphid
Sacred scarab
Silverfish
Slender pigeon louse
Spoonwing lacewing
Triaenodes bicolor
Velvet ant
Western flower thrips
Zebra jumping spider

BURKINA FASO

American cockroach
Bed bug
Brownbanded cockroach
Chigoe
Death's head hawk moth
Emperor scorpion
German cockroach
Greenhouse camel cricket
Greenhouse whitefly
Hair follicle mite
Honeybee
Human head/body louse
Indian mealmoth
Liposcelis bostrychophila
Long-bodied cellar spider
Lucerne flea
Silverfish
Slender pigeon louse
Tsetse fly
Variegated grasshopper
Wandering glider
Yellow fever mosquito

BURUNDI

American cockroach
Bed bug
Brownbanded cockroach
Chigoe
Death's head hawk moth
European earwig

European mantid
German cockroach
Greenhouse camel cricket
Greenhouse whitefly
Hair follicle mite
Honeybee
Human head/body louse
Indian mealmoth
Liposcelis bostrychophila
Long-bodied cellar spider
Lucerne flea
Silverfish
Slender pigeon louse
Wandering glider
Yellow fever mosquito

CAMBODIA

American cockroach
Atlas moth
Bed bug
Black macrotermes
Brownbanded cockroach
German cockroach
Greenhouse camel cricket
Greenhouse whitefly
Hair follicle mite
Honeybee
Human head/body louse
Indian mealmoth
Liposcelis bostrychophila
Long-bodied cellar spider
Lucerne flea
Oriental cockroach
Pea aphid
Silverfish
Wandering glider
Yellow fever mosquito

CAMEROON

American cockroach
Bed bug
Brownbanded cockroach
Chigoe
Death's head hawk moth
Emperor scorpion

European mantid
German cockroach
Greenhouse camel cricket
Greenhouse whitefly
Hair follicle mite
Honeybee
Human head/body louse
Indian mealmoth
Liposcelis bostrychophila
Long-bodied cellar spider
Long-winged conehead
Lucerne flea
Madeira cockroach
Scolopender
Silverfish
Tsetse fly
Variegated grasshopper
Wandering glider
Yellow fever mosquito

CANADA
American cockroach
American horseshoe crab
Bed bug
Big black horse fly
Brownbanded cockroach
Common American
  walkingstick
Common harvestman
Eastern dobsonfly
Eastern subterranean termite
European earwig
European mantid
European marsh crane fly
German cockroach
Giant salmonfly
Greenhouse camel cricket
Greenhouse whitefly
Gypsy moth
Hair follicle mite
Honeybee
House centipede
Human head/body louse
Indian mealmoth
Liposcelis bostrychophila
Long-bodied cellar spider

Lucerne flea
Oriental cockroach
Pea aphid
Petrobius brevistylis
Potter wasp
Rock-crawler
Rocky Mountain wood tick
Silverfish
Wandering glider
Western flower thrips
Zebra jumping spider

CAPE VERDE
Bed bug
Death's head hawk moth
German cockroach
Greenhouse camel cricket
Hair follicle mite
Honeybee
Human head/body louse
Indian mealmoth
Liposcelis bostrychophila
Long-bodied cellar spider
Lucerne flea
Silverfish
Wandering glider
Yellow fever mosquito

CENTRAL AFRICAN REPUBLIC
American cockroach
Bed bug
Brownbanded cockroach
Chigoe
Death's head hawk moth
Emperor scorpion
European mantid
German cockroach
Greenhouse camel cricket
Greenhouse whitefly
Hair follicle mite
Honeybee
Human head/body louse
Indian mealmoth
Liposcelis bostrychophila

Long-bodied cellar spider
Lucerne flea
Silverfish
Slender pigeon louse
Tsetse fly
Variegated grasshopper
Wandering glider
Yellow fever mosquito

CHAD
American cockroach
Bed bug
Brownbanded cockroach
Camel spider
Chigoe
Death's head hawk moth
Emperor scorpion
German cockroach
Greenhouse camel cricket
Greenhouse whitefly
Hair follicle mite
Honeybee
Human head/body louse
Indian mealmoth
Liposcelis bostrychophila
Long-bodied cellar spider
Lucerne flea
Silverfish
Slender pigeon louse
Tsetse fly
Variegated grasshopper
Wandering glider
Yellow fever mosquito

CHILE
American cockroach
Bed bug
Brownbanded cockroach
Chigoe
Chiloporter eatoni
European earwig
German cockroach
Greenhouse camel cricket
Greenhouse whitefly
Hair follicle mite

Honeybee
Human head/body louse
Indian mealmoth
Liposcelis bostrychophila
Long-bodied cellar spider
Lucerne flea
Oriental cockroach
Pea aphid
Silverfish
Wandering glider

CHINA

American cockroach
Atlas moth
Bed bug
Brownbanded cockroach
Chinese mantid
German cockroach
Greenhouse camel cricket
Greenhouse whitefly
Hair follicle mite
Honeybee
Human head/body louse
Indian mealmoth
Javan leaf insect
Large blue
Liposcelis bostrychophila
Long-bodied cellar spider
Lucerne flea
Oriental cockroach
Pea aphid
Scolopender
Sheep and goat flea
Silkworm
Silverfish
Wandering glider
Yellow fever mosquito
Zebra jumping spider

COLOMBIA

American cockroach
Bed bug
Black-headed nasute termite
Blue morpho
Brownbanded cockroach

Chigoe
Forest giant
German cockroach
Giant water bug
Greenhouse camel cricket
Greenhouse whitefly
Hair follicle mite
Hercules beetle
Honeybee
Human head/body louse
Indian mealmoth
Leaf-cutter ant
Liposcelis bostrychophila
Long-bodied cellar spider
Lucerne flea
Madeira cockroach
Mediterranean fruitfly
Pea aphid
Silverfish
Wandering glider
Western flower thrips
Yellow fever mosquito

COMOROS

Bed bug
Death's head hawk moth
German cockroach
Greenhouse camel cricket
Hair follicle mite
Honeybee
Human head/body louse
Indian mealmoth
Liposcelis bostrychophila
Long-bodied cellar spider
Lucerne flea
Scolopender
Silverfish
Wandering glider
Yellow fever mosquito

COSTA RICA

American cockroach
Bed bug
Black-headed nasute termite
Brownbanded cockroach
Chigoe

Dead leaf mimetica
Forest giant
German cockroach
Greenhouse camel cricket
Hair follicle mite
Hercules beetle
Honeybee
Human head/body louse
Indian mealmoth
Leaf-cutter ant
Liposcelis bostrychophila
Long-bodied cellar spider
Lucerne flea
Madeira cockroach
Mediterranean fruitfly
Pea aphid
Silverfish
Tailless whip scorpion
Tarantula hawk
Wandering glider
Yellow fever mosquito

CROATIA

American cockroach
Bed bug
Book scorpion
Brown mayfly
Brownbanded cockroach
Common harvestman
Death's head hawk moth
Devil's coach-horse
European earwig
European mantid
European stag beetle
German cockroach
Great water beetle
Greenhouse camel cricket
Greenhouse whitefly
Gypsy moth
Hair follicle mite
Honeybee
House centipede
Human head/body louse
Indian mealmoth
Large blue
Liposcelis bostrychophila

Long-bodied cellar spider
Long-winged conehead
Lucerne flea
Mediterranean fruitfly
Pea aphid
Silverfish
Slender pigeon louse
Spoonwing lacewing
Triaenodes bicolor
Velvet ant
Western flower thrips
Yellow fever mosquito
Zebra jumping spider

CUBA
Bed bug
Chigoe
German cockroach
Greenhouse camel cricket
Greenhouse whitefly
Hair follicle mite
Human head/body louse
Indian mealmoth
Liposcelis bostrychophila
Long-bodied cellar spider
Lucerne flea
Madeira cockroach
Mediterranean fruitfly
Pea aphid
Saunders embiid
Silverfish
Tarantula hawk
Trissolcus basalis
Wandering glider
Yellow fever mosquito

CYPRUS
Bed bug
Book scorpion
German cockroach
Greenhouse camel cricket
Hair follicle mite
Honeybee
Human head/body louse
Indian mealmoth
Liposcelis bostrychophila

Long-bodied cellar spider
Lucerne flea
Silverfish

CZECH REPUBLIC
American cockroach
Bed bug
Book scorpion
Brown mayfly
Common harvestman
Devil's coach-horse
European earwig
European marsh crane fly
European stag beetle
Flat-backed millipede
German cockroach
Great water beetle
Greenhouse camel cricket
Greenhouse whitefly
Gypsy moth
Hair follicle mite
Honeybee
Human head/body louse
Indian mealmoth
Large blue
Liposcelis bostrychophila
Long-bodied cellar spider
Long-winged conehead
Lucerne flea
Pea aphid
Pill millipede
Silverfish
Slender pigeon louse
Spoonwing lacewing
Triaenodes bicolor
Velvet ant
Western flower thrips
Zebra jumping spider

DEMOCRATIC REPUBLIC OF THE CONGO
American cockroach
Bed bug
Brownbanded cockroach
Chigoe

Death's head hawk moth
Emperor scorpion
European mantid
German cockroach
Greenhouse camel cricket
Greenhouse whitefly
Hair follicle mite
Honeybee
Human head/body louse
Indian mealmoth
Liposcelis bostrychophila
Long-bodied cellar spider
Lucerne flea
Madeira cockroach
Silverfish
Tsetse fly
Variegated grasshopper
Wandering glider
Yellow fever mosquito

DENMARK
American cockroach
Antlion
Bed bug
Book scorpion
Brown mayfly
Devil's coach-horse
European earwig
European marsh crane fly
European stag beetle
Flat-backed millipede
German cockroach
Great water beetle
Greenhouse camel cricket
Gypsy moth
Hair follicle mite
Honeybee
Human head/body louse
Indian mealmoth
Large blue
Liposcelis bostrychophila
Long-bodied cellar spider
Long-winged conehead
Lucerne flea
Oriental cockroach
Petrobius brevistylis

Pill millipede
Silverfish
Slender pigeon louse
Spoonwing lacewing
Triaenodes bicolor
Velvet ant
Western flower thrips

DJIBOUTI
Bed bug
Chigoe
Death's head hawk moth
European earwig
German cockroach
Greenhouse camel cricket
Hair follicle mite
Honeybee
Human head/body louse
Indian mealmoth
Liposcelis bostrychophila
Long-bodied cellar spider
Lucerne flea
Silverfish
Wandering glider
Yellow fever mosquito

DOMINICAN REPUBLIC
Bed bug
Chigoe
German cockroach
Greenhouse camel cricket
Greenhouse whitefly
Hair follicle mite
Hispaniola hooded catydid
Human head/body louse
Indian mealmoth
Liposcelis bostrychophila
Long-bodied cellar spider
Lucerne flea
Madeira cockroach
Mediterranean fruitfly
Pea aphid
Scolopender
Silverfish
Trissolcus basalis

Wandering glider
Yellow fever mosquito

ECUADOR
American cockroach
Bed bug
Black-headed nasute termite
Blue morpho
Brownbanded cockroach
Chigoe
Forest giant
German cockroach
Giant water bug
Greenhouse camel cricket
Greenhouse whitefly
Hair follicle mite
Honeybee
Human head/body louse
Indian mealmoth
Leaf-cutter ant
Liposcelis bostrychophila
Long-bodied cellar spider
Lucerne flea
Mediterranean fruitfly
Pea aphid
Silverfish
Tarantula hawk
Wandering glider
Western flower thrips
Yellow fever mosquito

EGYPT
American cockroach
Bed bug
Brownbanded cockroach
Camel spider
Death's head hawk moth
European earwig
German cockroach
Greenhouse camel cricket
Greenhouse whitefly
Hair follicle mite
Honeybee
House centipede
Human head/body louse

Indian mealmoth
Liposcelis bostrychophila
Long-bodied cellar spider
Long-winged conehead
Lucerne flea
Mediterranean fruitfly
Sacred scarab
Scolopender
Silverfish
Slender pigeon louse
Trissolcus basalis
Wandering glider
Yellow fever mosquito

EL SALVADOR
American cockroach
Bed bug
Black-headed nasute termite
Brownbanded cockroach
Chigoe
Forest giant
German cockroach
Greenhouse camel cricket
Greenhouse whitefly
Hair follicle mite
Hercules beetle
Honeybee
Human head/body louse
Indian mealmoth
Liposcelis bostrychophila
Long-bodied cellar spider
Lucerne flea
Madeira cockroach
Mediterranean fruitfly
Pea aphid
Silverfish
Wandering glider
Yellow fever mosquito

EQUATORIAL GUINEA
American cockroach
Bed bug
Brownbanded cockroach
Chigoe
Death's head hawk moth

Emperor scorpion
German cockroach
Greenhouse camel cricket
Greenhouse whitefly
Hair follicle mite
Honeybee
Human head/body louse
Indian mealmoth
Liposcelis bostrychophila
Long-bodied cellar spider
Lucerne flea
Madeira cockroach
Silverfish
Tsetse fly
Variegated grasshopper
Wandering glider
Yellow fever mosquito

ERITREA
Bed bug
Chigoe
Death's head hawk moth
European earwig
German cockroach
Greenhouse camel cricket
Hair follicle mite
Honeybee
Human head/body louse
Indian mealmoth
Liposcelis bostrychophila
Long-bodied cellar spider
Lucerne flea
Silverfish
Slender pigeon louse
Wandering glider
Yellow fever mosquito

ESTONIA
American cockroach
Bed bug
Brown mayfly
Common harvestman
European earwig
European marsh crane fly
German cockroach
Great water beetle

Greenhouse camel cricket
Gypsy moth
Hair follicle mite
Honeybee
Human head/body louse
Indian mealmoth
Large blue
Liposcelis bostrychophila
Long-bodied cellar spider
Long-winged conehead
Lucerne flea
Petrobius brevistylis
Schummel's inocelliid
snakefly
Silverfish
Slender pigeon louse
Spoonwing lacewing
Triaenodes bicolor
Velvet ant
Western flower thrips
Zebra jumping spider

ETHIOPIA
Bed bug
Brownbanded cockroach
Chigoe
Death's head hawk moth
European earwig
German cockroach
Greenhouse camel cricket
Greenhouse whitefly
Hair follicle mite
Honeybee
Human head/body louse
Indian mealmoth
Liposcelis bostrychophila
Long-bodied cellar spider
Lucerne flea
Silverfish
Slender pigeon louse
Wandering glider
Yellow fever mosquito

FIJI
Bed bug
German cockroach

Greenhouse camel cricket
Hair follicle mite
Honeybee
Human head/body louse
Indian mealmoth
Liposcelis bostrychophila
Long-bodied cellar spider
Lucerne flea
Silverfish
Wandering glider

FINLAND
American cockroach
Bed bug
Brown mayfly
Common harvestman
European marsh crane fly
German cockroach
Great water beetle
Greenhouse camel cricket
Gypsy moth
Hair follicle mite
Honeybee
Human head/body louse
Indian mealmoth
Liposcelis bostrychophila
Long-bodied cellar spider
Lucerne flea
Petrobius brevistylis
Schummel's inocelliid
  snakefly
Silverfish
Slender pigeon louse
Triaenodes bicolor
Velvet ant
Zebra jumping spider

FRANCE
American cockroach
Antlion
Bed bug
Book scorpion
Brown mayfly
Brownbanded cockroach
Common harvestman

Death's head hawk moth
Devil's coach-horse
European earwig
European mantid
European marsh crane fly
European stag beetle
Flat-backed millipede
German cockroach
Great water beetle
Greenhouse camel cricket
Greenhouse whitefly
Gypsy moth
Hair follicle mite
Honeybee
House centipede
Human head/body louse
Indian mealmoth
Large blue
Liposcelis bostrychophila
Long-bodied cellar spider
Long-winged conehead
Lucerne flea
Mediterranean fruitfly
Oriental cockroach
Pea aphid
Petrobius brevistylis
Pill millipede
Sacred scarab
Silverfish
Slender pigeon louse
Spoonwing lacewing
Triaenodes bicolor
Trissolcus basalis
Velvet ant
Western flower thrips
Yellow fever mosquito
Zebra jumping spider

FRENCH GUIANA
American cockroach
Bed bug
Black-headed nasute termite
Blue morpho
Brownbanded cockroach
Chigoe
German cockroach

Giant water bug
Greenhouse camel cricket
Greenhouse whitefly
Hair follicle mite
Honeybee
Human head/body louse
Indian mealmoth
Linnaeus's snapping termite
Liposcelis bostrychophila
Long-bodied cellar spider
Lucerne flea
Madeira cockroach
Mediterranean fruitfly
Pea aphid
Silverfish
Tarantula hawk
Wandering glider
Western flower thrips

GABON
American cockroach
Bed bug
Brownbanded cockroach
Chigoe
Death's head hawk moth
Emperor scorpion
German cockroach
Greenhouse camel cricket
Greenhouse whitefly
Hair follicle mite
Honeybee
Human head/body louse
Indian mealmoth
Liposcelis bostrychophila
Long-bodied cellar spider
Lucerne flea
Madeira cockroach
Silverfish
Tsetse fly
Variegated grasshopper
Wandering glider
Yellow fever mosquito

GAMBIA
American cockroach
Bed bug

Brownbanded cockroach
Chigoe
Death's head hawk moth
Emperor scorpion
German cockroach
Greenhouse camel cricket
Hair follicle mite
Honeybee
Human head/body louse
Indian mealmoth
Liposcelis bostrychophila
Long-bodied cellar spider
Lucerne flea
Madeira cockroach
Oriental cockroach
Silverfish
Slender pigeon louse
Tsetse fly
Wandering glider
Yellow fever mosquito

GEORGIA
American cockroach
Bed bug
Brown mayfly
Death's head hawk moth
Devil's coach-horse
European mantid
German cockroach
Greenhouse camel cricket
Greenhouse whitefly
Hair follicle mite
Honeybee
Human head/body louse
Indian mealmoth
Liposcelis bostrychophila
Long-bodied cellar spider
Long-winged conehead
Lucerne flea
Pea aphid
Silverfish
Slender pigeon louse
Yellow fever mosquito
Zebra jumping spider

GERMANY

American cockroach
Antlion
Bed bug
Book scorpion
Brown mayfly
Common harvestman
Devil's coach-horse
European earwig
European mantid
European marsh crane fly
European stag beetle
Flat-backed millipede
German cockroach
Great water beetle
Greenhouse camel cricket
Greenhouse whitefly
Gypsy moth
Hair follicle mite
Honeybee
Human head/body louse
Indian mealmoth
Large blue
Liposcelis bostrychophila
Long-bodied cellar spider
Long-winged conehead
Lucerne flea
Oriental cockroach
Pea aphid
Petrobius brevistylis
Pill millipede
Schummel's inocelliid
  snakefly
Silverfish
Slender pigeon louse
Spoonwing lacewing
Triaenodes bicolor
Velvet ant
Western flower thrips
Zebra jumping spider

GHANA

American cockroach
Bed bug
Brownbanded cockroach
Chigoe

Death's head hawk moth
Emperor scorpion
European mantid
German cockroach
Greenhouse camel cricket
Greenhouse whitefly
Hair follicle mite
Honeybee
Human head/body louse
Indian mealmoth
Liposcelis bostrychophila
Long-bodied cellar spider
Long-winged conehead
Lucerne flea
Madeira cockroach
Oriental cockroach
Silverfish
Slender pigeon louse
Tsetse fly
Variegated grasshopper
Wandering glider
Yellow fever mosquito

GREECE

American cockroach
Bed bug
Book scorpion
Brown mayfly
Brownbanded cockroach
Common harvestman
Death's head hawk moth
European earwig
European mantid
European stag beetle
German cockroach
Great water beetle
Greenhouse camel cricket
Greenhouse whitefly
Gypsy moth
Hair follicle mite
Honeybee
House centipede
Human head/body louse
Indian mealmoth
Liposcelis bostrychophila
Long-bodied cellar spider

Long-winged conehead
Lucerne flea
Mediterranean fruitfly
Pea aphid
Sacred scarab
Silverfish
Slender pigeon louse
Spoonwing lacewing
Velvet ant
Western flower thrips
Yellow fever mosquito
Zebra jumping spider

GREENLAND

German cockroach
Greenhouse camel cricket
Hair follicle mite
Human head/body louse
Indian mealmoth
Liposcelis bostrychophila

GRENADA

Bed bug
German cockroach
Greenhouse camel cricket
Hair follicle mite
Honeybee
Human head/body louse
Indian mealmoth
Liposcelis bostrychophila
Long-bodied cellar spider
Lucerne flea
Silverfish
Wandering glider

GUAM

Bed bug
German cockroach
Greenhouse camel cricket
Hair follicle mite
Honeybee
Human head/body louse
Indian mealmoth
Liposcelis bostrychophila
Long-bodied cellar spider

Lucerne flea
Silverfish

GUATEMALA
American cockroach
Bed bug
Black-headed nasute termite
Brownbanded cockroach
Chigoe
Forest giant
German cockroach
Greenhouse camel cricket
Greenhouse whitefly
Hair follicle mite
Hercules beetle
Honeybee
Human head/body louse
Indian mealmoth
Liposcelis bostrychophila
Long-bodied cellar spider
Lucerne flea
Madeira cockroach
Mediterranean fruitfly
Pea aphid
Silverfish
Tailless whip scorpion
Wandering glider
Yellow fever mosquito

GUINEA
American cockroach
Bed bug
Beetle cricket
Brownbanded cockroach
Chigoe
Death's head hawk moth
Emperor scorpion
German cockroach
Greenhouse camel cricket
Greenhouse whitefly
Hair follicle mite
Honeybee
Human head/body louse
Indian mealmoth
Liposcelis bostrychophila

Long-bodied cellar spider
Lucerne flea
Madeira cockroach
Oriental cockroach
Silverfish
Slender pigeon louse
Tsetse fly
Variegated grasshopper
Wandering glider
Yellow fever mosquito

GUINEA-BISSAU
American cockroach
Bed bug
Brownbanded cockroach
Chigoe
Death's head hawk moth
Emperor scorpion
German cockroach
Greenhouse camel cricket
Greenhouse whitefly
Hair follicle mite
Honeybee
Human head/body louse
Indian mealmoth
Liposcelis bostrychophila
Long-bodied cellar spider
Lucerne flea
Madeira cockroach
Oriental cockroach
Silverfish
Slender pigeon louse
Tsetse fly
Variegated grasshopper
Wandering glider
Yellow fever mosquito

GUYANA
American cockroach
Bed bug
Black-headed nasute termite
Blue morpho
Brownbanded cockroach
Chigoe
German cockroach

Giant water bug
Greenhouse camel cricket
Greenhouse whitefly
Hair follicle mite
Honeybee
Human head/body louse
Indian mealmoth
Leaf-cutter ant
Linnaeus's snapping termite
Liposcelis bostrychophila
Long-bodied cellar spider
Lucerne flea
Madeira cockroach
Mediterranean fruitfly
Pea aphid
Silverfish
Tarantula hawk
Wandering glider
Western flower thrips

HAITI
Bed bug
Chigoe
German cockroach
Greenhouse camel cricket
Greenhouse whitefly
Hair follicle mite
Human head/body louse
Indian mealmoth
Liposcelis bostrychophila
Long-bodied cellar spider
Lucerne flea
Madeira cockroach
Mediterranean fruitfly
Pea aphid
Scolopender
Silverfish
Trissolcus basalis
Wandering glider
Yellow fever mosquito

HONDURAS
American cockroach
Bed bug
Black-headed nasute termite

Brownbanded cockroach
Chigoe
Forest giant
German cockroach
Greenhouse camel cricket
Greenhouse whitefly
Hair follicle mite
Hercules beetle
Honeybee
Human head/body louse
Indian mealmoth
Liposcelis bostrychophila
Long-bodied cellar spider
Lucerne flea
Madeira cockroach
Mediterranean fruitfly
Pea aphid
Silverfish
Wandering glider
Yellow fever mosquito

HUNGARY
American cockroach
Bed bug
Book scorpion
Brown mayfly
Common harvestman
Devil's coach-horse
European earwig
European mantid
European stag beetle
German cockroach
Great water beetle
Greenhouse camel cricket
Greenhouse whitefly
Gypsy moth
Hair follicle mite
Honeybee
Human head/body louse
Indian mealmoth
Large blue
Liposcelis bostrychophila
Long-bodied cellar spider
Long-winged conehead
Lucerne flea
Pea aphid

Silverfish
Slender pigeon louse
Spoonwing lacewing
Triaenodes bicolor
Velvet ant
Western flower thrips
Zebra jumping spider

ICELAND
German cockroach
Greenhouse camel cricket
Hair follicle mite
Human head/body louse
Indian mealmoth
Liposcelis bostrychophila
Long-bodied cellar spider
Lucerne flea
Petrobius brevistylis

INDIA
American cockroach
Atlas moth
Bed bug
Brownbanded cockroach
German cockroach
Greenhouse camel cricket
Greenhouse whitefly
Hair follicle mite
Honeybee
Human head/body louse
Indian mealmoth
Indian stick insect
Javan leaf insect
Liposcelis bostrychophila
Long-bodied cellar spider
Lucerne flea
Oriental cockroach
Pea aphid
Saunders embiid
Silkworm
Silverfish
Slender pigeon louse
Wandering glider
Wandering violin mantid
Western flower thrips
Yellow fever mosquito

INDIAN OCEAN
Colossendeis megalonyx
Sea skater

INDONESIA
Atlas moth
Bed bug
Cyrtodiopsis dalmanni
Dead-leaf mantid
European earwig
European mantid
German cockroach
Greenhouse camel cricket
Greenhouse whitefly
Hair follicle mite
Honeybee
Human head/body louse
Indian mealmoth
Javan leaf insect
Liposcelis bostrychophila
Long-bodied cellar spider
Lucerne flea
Orchid mantid
Pea aphid
Saunders embiid
Scolopender
Silverfish
Stalk-eyed fly
Wandering glider

IRAN
American cockroach
Bed bug
Brownbanded cockroach
Death's head hawk moth
German cockroach
Greenhouse camel cricket
Greenhouse whitefly
Hair follicle mite
Honeybee
Human head/body louse
Indian mealmoth
Liposcelis bostrychophila
Long-bodied cellar spider
Lucerne flea
Silverfish

Slender pigeon louse
Wandering glider
Yellow fever mosquito

IRAQ
Bed bug
Brownbanded cockroach
Camel spider
Death's head hawk moth
German cockroach
Greenhouse camel cricket
Greenhouse whitefly
Hair follicle mite
Honeybee
Human head/body louse
Indian mealmoth
Liposcelis bostrychophila
Long-bodied cellar spider
Lucerne flea
Mediterranean fruitfly
Pea aphid
Sacred scarab
Silverfish
Slender pigeon louse
Wandering glider
Yellow fever mosquito

IRELAND
American cockroach
Antlion
Bed bug
Book scorpion
Common harvestman
Devil's coach-horse
European earwig
European marsh crane fly
Flat-backed millipede
German cockroach
Great water beetle
Greenhouse camel cricket
Greenhouse whitefly
Gypsy moth
Hair follicle mite
Honeybee
Human head/body louse

Indian mealmoth
Large blue
Liposcelis bostrychophila
Long-bodied cellar spider
Lucerne flea
Oriental cockroach
Petrobius brevistylis
Silverfish
Slender pigeon louse
Spoonwing lacewing
Triaenodes bicolor
Zebra jumping spider

ISRAEL
American cockroach
Bed bug
Brownbanded cockroach
Camel spider
German cockroach
Greenhouse camel cricket
Greenhouse whitefly
Hair follicle mite
Honeybee
Human head/body louse
Indian mealmoth
Liposcelis bostrychophila
Long-bodied cellar spider
Long-winged conehead
Lucerne flea
Mediterranean fruitfly
Oriental cockroach
Sacred scarab
Silverfish
Slender pigeon louse
Wandering glider
Yellow fever mosquito

ITALY
American cockroach
Antlion
Bed bug
Book scorpion
Brown mayfly
Brownbanded cockroach
Common harvestman

Death's head hawk moth
Devil's coach-horse
European earwig
European mantid
European stag beetle
Flat-backed millipede
German cockroach
Great water beetle
Greenhouse camel cricket
Greenhouse whitefly
Gypsy moth
Hair follicle mite
Honeybee
House centipede
Human head/body louse
Indian mealmoth
Large blue
Liposcelis bostrychophila
Long-bodied cellar spider
Long-winged conehead
Lucerne flea
Mediterranean fruitfly
Pea aphid
Sacred scarab
Silverfish
Slender pigeon louse
Spoonwing lacewing
Triaenodes bicolor
Trissolcus basalis
Velvet ant
Western flower thrips
Yellow fever mosquito
Zebra jumping spider

IVORY COAST
American cockroach
Bed bug
Brownbanded cockroach
Chigoe
Death's head hawk moth
Emperor scorpion
German cockroach
Greenhouse camel cricket
Greenhouse whitefly
Hair follicle mite

Honeybee
Human head/body louse
Indian mealmoth
Liposcelis bostrychophila
Long-bodied cellar spider
Long-winged conehead
Lucerne flea
Madeira cockroach
Oriental cockroach
Silverfish
Slender pigeon louse
Trissolcus basalis
Tsetse fly
Variegated grasshopper
Wandering glider
Yellow fever mosquito

JAMAICA
Bed bug
Chigoe
German cockroach
Greenhouse camel cricket
Greenhouse whitefly
Hair follicle mite
Human head/body louse
Indian mealmoth
Liposcelis bostrychophila
Long-bodied cellar spider
Lucerne flea
Madeira cockroach
Mediterranean fruitfly
Pea aphid
Silverfish
Wandering glider
Yellow fever mosquito

JAPAN
American cockroach
Bed bug
Chinese mantid
European mantid
German cockroach
Greenhouse camel cricket
Greenhouse whitefly

Gypsy moth
Hair follicle mite
Human head/body louse
Indian mealmoth
Liposcelis bostrychophila
Long-bodied cellar spider
Lucerne flea
Pea aphid
Silkworm
Silverfish
Sinetomon yoroi
Wandering glider

JORDAN
American cockroach
Bed bug
Brownbanded cockroach
Camel spider
German cockroach
Greenhouse camel cricket
Greenhouse whitefly
Hair follicle mite
Honeybee
Human head/body louse
Indian mealmoth
Liposcelis bostrychophila
Long-bodied cellar spider
Lucerne flea
Mediterranean fruitfly
Sacred scarab
Scolopender
Silverfish
Slender pigeon louse
Wandering glider
Yellow fever mosquito

KAZAKHSTAN
Bed bug
Brown mayfly
Common harvestman
European mantid
German cockroach
Greenhouse camel cricket
Hair follicle mite
Honeybee

Human head/body louse
Indian mealmoth
Large blue
Liposcelis bostrychophila
Long-bodied cellar spider
Lucerne flea
Silverfish
Slender pigeon louse
Zebra jumping spider

KENYA
American cockroach
Bed bug
Brownbanded cockroach
Chigoe
Death's head hawk moth
European earwig
European mantid
German cockroach
Greenhouse camel cricket
Greenhouse whitefly
Hair follicle mite
Honeybee
Human head/body louse
Indian mealmoth
Liposcelis bostrychophila
Long-bodied cellar spider
Lucerne flea
Saunders embiid
Scolopender
Silverfish
Slender pigeon louse
Trissolcus basalis
Wandering glider
Yellow fever mosquito

KIRIBATI
Bed bug
German cockroach
Greenhouse camel cricket
Hair follicle mite
Honeybee
Human head/body louse
Indian mealmoth
Liposcelis bostrychophila
Long-bodied cellar spider

Lucerne flea
Silverfish
Wandering glider

KUWAIT
Bed bug
Camel spider
German cockroach
Greenhouse camel cricket
Hair follicle mite
Honeybee
Human head/body louse
Indian mealmoth
Liposcelis bostrychophila
Long-bodied cellar spider
Lucerne flea
Silverfish
Slender pigeon louse
Wandering glider
Yellow fever mosquito

KYRGYZSTAN
Atlas moth
Bed bug
Brownbanded cockroach
European mantid
German cockroach
Greenhouse camel cricket
Hair follicle mite
Honeybee
Human head/body louse
Indian mealmoth
Large blue
Liposcelis bostrychophila
Long-bodied cellar spider
Lucerne flea
Silverfish
Wandering glider
Western flower thrips
Zebra jumping spider

LAOS
American cockroach
Atlas moth

Bed bug
Brownbanded cockroach
German cockroach
Greenhouse camel cricket
Greenhouse whitefly
Hair follicle mite
Honeybee
Human head/body louse
Indian mealmoth
Liposcelis bostrychophila
Long-bodied cellar spider
Lucerne flea
Oriental cockroach
Pea aphid
Scolopender
Silverfish
Wandering glider
Yellow fever mosquito

LATVIA
American cockroach
Bed bug
Book scorpion
Brown mayfly
Common harvestman
European earwig
European marsh crane fly
German cockroach
Great water beetle
Greenhouse camel cricket
Gypsy moth
Hair follicle mite
Honeybee
Human head/body louse
Indian mealmoth
Large blue
Liposcelis bostrychophila
Long-bodied cellar spider
Long-winged conehead
Lucerne flea
Oriental cockroach
Petrobius brevistylis
Schummel's inocelliid
  snakefly
Silverfish
Slender pigeon louse

Spoonwing lacewing
Triaenodes bicolor
Velvet ant
Western flower thrips
Zebra jumping spider

LEBANON
American cockroach
Bed bug
Brownbanded cockroach
Camel spider
German cockroach
Greenhouse camel cricket
Greenhouse whitefly
Hair follicle mite
Honeybee
Human head/body louse
Indian mealmoth
Liposcelis bostrychophila
Long-bodied cellar spider
Long-winged conehead
Lucerne flea
Mediterranean fruitfly
Sacred scarab
Silverfish
Slender pigeon louse
Wandering glider
Yellow fever mosquito

LESOTHO
American cockroach
Bed bug
Brownbanded cockroach
Death's head hawk moth
European mantid
German cockroach
Greenhouse camel cricket
Greenhouse whitefly
Hair follicle mite
Honeybee
House centipede
Human head/body louse
Indian mealmoth
Liposcelis bostrychophila
Long-bodied cellar spider

Lucerne flea
Oriental cockroach
Silverfish
Wandering glider
Western flower thrips
Yellow fever mosquito

LESSER ANTILLES
Bed bug
German cockroach
Greenhouse camel cricket
Hair follicle mite
Honeybee
Human head/body louse
Indian mealmoth
Liposcelis bostrychophila
Long-bodied cellar spider
Lucerne flea
Silverfish

LIBERIA
American cockroach
Bed bug
Brownbanded cockroach
Chigoe
Death's head hawk moth
Emperor scorpion
European mantid
German cockroach
Greenhouse camel cricket
Greenhouse whitefly
Hair follicle mite
Honeybee
Human head/body louse
Indian mealmoth
Liposcelis bostrychophila
Long-bodied cellar spider
Long-winged conehead
Lucerne flea
Madeira cockroach
Scolopender
Silverfish
Slender pigeon louse
Tsetse fly
Variegated grasshopper

Wandering glider
Yellow fever mosquito

LIBYA
American cockroach
Bed bug
Brownbanded cockroach
Camel spider
Death's head hawk moth
European earwig
German cockroach
Greenhouse camel cricket
Greenhouse whitefly
Gypsy moth
Hair follicle mite
Honeybee
House centipede
Human head/body louse
Indian mealmoth
Liposcelis bostrychophila
Long-bodied cellar spider
Long-winged conehead
Lucerne flea
Mediterranean fruitfly
Sacred scarab
Silverfish
Slender pigeon louse
Wandering glider
Yellow fever mosquito

LIECHTENSTEIN
American cockroach
Antlion
Bed bug
Book scorpion
Brown mayfly
Common harvestman
Devil's coach-horse
European earwig
European marsh crane fly
European stag beetle
Flat-backed millipede
German cockroach
Great water beetle
Greenhouse camel cricket

Gypsy moth
Hair follicle mite
Honeybee
House centipede
Human head/body louse
Indian mealmoth
Large blue
Liposcelis bostrychophila
Long-bodied cellar spider
Long-winged conehead
Lucerne flea
Pill millipede
Silverfish
Slender pigeon louse
Spoonwing lacewing
Triaenodes bicolor
Velvet ant
Western flower thrips
Zebra jumping spider

LITHUANIA
American cockroach
Bed bug
Book scorpion
Brown mayfly
Common harvestman
European earwig
European marsh crane fly
German cockroach
Great water beetle
Greenhouse camel cricket
Gypsy moth
Hair follicle mite
Honeybee
Human head/body louse
Indian mealmoth
Large blue
Liposcelis bostrychophila
Long-bodied cellar spider
Long-winged conehead
Lucerne flea
Oriental cockroach
Petrobius brevistylis
Schummel's inocelliid
  snakefly
Silverfish

Slender pigeon louse
Spoonwing lacewing
Triaenodes bicolor
Velvet ant
Western flower thrips
Zebra jumping spider

LUXEMBOURG
American cockroach
Antlion
Bed bug
Book scorpion
Brown mayfly
Common harvestman
Devil's coach-horse
European earwig
European stag beetle
Flat-backed millipede
German cockroach
Great water beetle
Greenhouse camel cricket
Gypsy moth
Hair follicle mite
Honeybee
Human head/body louse
Indian mealmoth
Large blue
Liposcelis bostrychophila
Long-bodied cellar spider
Long-winged conehead
Lucerne flea
Pill millipede
Silverfish
Slender pigeon louse
Spoonwing lacewing
Triaenodes bicolor
Velvet ant
Western flower thrips
Zebra jumping spider

MACEDONIA
American cockroach
Bed bug
Book scorpion
Brown mayfly
Brownbanded cockroach

Common harvestman
Death's head hawk moth
Devil's coach-horse
European earwig
European mantid
European stag beetle
German cockroach
Great water beetle
Greenhouse camel cricket
Greenhouse whitefly
Gypsy moth
Hair follicle mite
Honeybee
House centipede
Human head/body louse
Indian mealmoth
Liposcelis bostrychophila
Long-bodied cellar spider
Long-winged conehead
Lucerne flea
Mediterranean fruitfly
Pea aphid
Sacred scarab
Silverfish
Slender pigeon louse
Spoonwing lacewing
Triaenodes bicolor
Velvet ant
Western flower thrips
Yellow fever mosquito
Zebra jumping spider

MADAGASCAR
Chigoe
Death's head hawk moth
German cockroach
Giraffe-necked weevil
Greenhouse camel cricket
Greenhouse whitefly
Hair follicle mite
Human head/body louse
Indian mealmoth
Indian stick insect
Javan leaf insect
Liposcelis bostrychophila
Lucerne flea

Saunders embiid
Scolopender
Silverfish
Wandering glider
Yellow fever mosquito

MALAWI
American cockroach
Bed bug
Brownbanded cockroach
Chigoe
Death's head hawk moth
European mantid
German cockroach
Greenhouse camel cricket
Greenhouse whitefly
Hair follicle mite
Honeybee
Human head/body louse
Indian mealmoth
Liposcelis bostrychophila
Long-bodied cellar spider
Lucerne flea
Silverfish
Wandering glider
Yellow fever mosquito

MALAYSIA
American cockroach
Atlas moth
Bed bug
Black macrotermes
Cyrtodiopsis dalmanni
Dead-leaf mantid
European earwig
German cockroach
Greenhouse camel cricket
Greenhouse whitefly
Hair follicle mite
Honeybee
Human head/body louse
Indian mealmoth
Javan leaf insect
Jungle nymph
Liposcelis bostrychophila
Long-bodied cellar spider

Lucerne flea
Orchid mantid
Pea aphid
Silverfish
Stalk-eyed fly
Wandering glider
Yellow fever mosquito

MALDIVES
Bed bug
German cockroach
Greenhouse camel cricket
Hair follicle mite
Honeybee
Human head/body louse
Indian mealmoth
Liposcelis bostrychophila
Long-bodied cellar spider
Lucerne flea
Silverfish
Wandering glider

MALI
American cockroach
Bed bug
Brownbanded cockroach
Chigoe
Death's head hawk moth
Emperor scorpion
German cockroach
Greenhouse camel cricket
Hair follicle mite
Honeybee
Human head/body louse
Indian mealmoth
Liposcelis bostrychophila
Long-bodied cellar spider
Lucerne flea
Mediterranean fruitfly
Silverfish
Slender pigeon louse
Tsetse fly
Variegated grasshopper
Wandering glider
Yellow fever mosquito

MALTA
Bed bug
German cockroach
Greenhouse camel cricket
Gypsy moth
Hair follicle mite
Honeybee
Human head/body louse
Indian mealmoth
Large blue
Liposcelis bostrychophila
Long-bodied cellar spider
Lucerne flea
Silverfish
Velvet ant
Western flower thrips

MARIANA ISLANDS
Bed bug
German cockroach
Greenhouse camel cricket
Hair follicle mite
Honeybee
Human head/body louse
Indian mealmoth
Liposcelis bostrychophila
Long-bodied cellar spider
Lucerne flea
Silverfish

MARSHALL ISLANDS
Bed bug
German cockroach
Greenhouse camel cricket
Hair follicle mite
Honeybee
Human head/body louse
Indian mealmoth
Liposcelis bostrychophila
Long-bodied cellar spider
Lucerne flea
Silverfish
Wandering glider

MAURITANIA
Bed bug
Chigoe
Death's head hawk moth
German cockroach
Greenhouse camel cricket
Hair follicle mite
Honeybee
Human head/body louse
Indian mealmoth
Liposcelis bostrychophila
Long-bodied cellar spider
Lucerne flea
Mediterranean fruitfly
Sacred scarab
Silverfish
Slender pigeon louse
Tsetse fly
Wandering glider
Western flower thrips
Yellow fever mosquito

MAURITIUS
Bed bug
Death's head hawk moth
German cockroach
Greenhouse camel cricket
Hair follicle mite
Honeybee
Human head/body louse
Indian mealmoth
Javan leaf insect
Liposcelis bostrychophila
Long-bodied cellar spider
Lucerne flea
Scolopender
Silverfish
Wandering glider
Yellow fever mosquito

MEXICO
American cockroach
Bed bug
Black-headed nasute termite
Brownbanded cockroach

Chigoe
Common harvestman
European earwig
Forest giant
German cockroach
Giant whip scorpion
Greenhouse camel cricket
Greenhouse whitefly
Hair follicle mite
Halictophagus naulti
Honeybee
Horseshoe crab
Human head/body louse
Indian mealmoth
Liposcelis bostrychophila
Long-bodied cellar spider
Lucerne flea
Madeira cockroach
Oriental cockroach
Panorpa nuptialis
Pea aphid
Rocky Mountain wood tick
Saunders embiid
Scolopender
Silverfish
Tarantula hawk
Wandering glider
Western flower thrips
Wide-headed rottenwood
  termite
Yellow fever mosquito
Zebra jumping spider

MICRONESIA
Bed bug
German cockroach
Greenhouse camel cricket
Hair follicle mite
Honeybee
Human head/body louse
Indian mealmoth
Liposcelis bostrychophila
Long-bodied cellar spider
Lucerne flea
Silverfish
Wandering glider

MOLDOVA
American cockroach
Bed bug
Book scorpion
Brown mayfly
Common harvestman
Death's head hawk moth
Devil's coach-horse
European earwig
European stag beetle
German cockroach
Great water beetle
Greenhouse camel cricket
Greenhouse whitefly
Gypsy moth
Hair follicle mite
Honeybee
Human head/body louse
Indian mealmoth
Large blue
Liposcelis bostrychophila
Long-bodied cellar spider
Long-winged conehead
Lucerne flea
Pea aphid
Silverfish
Slender pigeon louse
Spoonwing lacewing
Triaenodes bicolor
Velvet ant
Western flower thrips
Zebra jumping spider

MONACO
American cockroach
Antlion
Bed bug
Book scorpion
Brown mayfly
Brownbanded cockroach
Death's head hawk moth
Devil's coach-horse
European earwig
European mantid
European stag beetle
Flat-backed millipede

German cockroach
Great water beetle
Greenhouse camel cricket
Greenhouse whitefly
Gypsy moth
Hair follicle mite
Honeybee
House centipede
Human head/body louse
Indian mealmoth
Large blue
Liposcelis bostrychophila
Long-bodied cellar spider
Long-winged conehead
Lucerne flea
Mediterranean fruitfly
Pea aphid
Silverfish
Slender pigeon louse
Spoonwing lacewing
Triaenodes bicolor
Velvet ant
Western flower thrips
Yellow fever mosquito

MONGOLIA
Bed bug
Chinese mantid
Common harvestman
European mantid
German cockroach
Greenhouse camel cricket
Hair follicle mite
Honeybee
Human head/body louse
Indian mealmoth
Large blue
Liposcelis bostrychophila
Long-bodied cellar spider
Lucerne flea
Sheep and goat flea
Silverfish
Wandering glider
Western flower thrips
Zebra jumping spider

MOROCCO

American cockroach
Bed bug
Brownbanded cockroach
Chigoe
Death's head hawk moth
Devil's coach-horse
European earwig
European mantid
German cockroach
Greenhouse camel cricket
Greenhouse whitefly
Gypsy moth
Hair follicle mite
Honeybee
House centipede
Human head/body louse
Indian mealmoth
Liposcelis bostrychophila
Long-bodied cellar spider
Long-winged conehead
Lucerne flea
Mediterranean fruitfly
Sacred scarab
Scolopender
Silverfish
Slender pigeon louse
Spoonwing lacewing
Trissolcus basalis
Velvet ant
Wandering glider
Western flower thrips
Yellow fever mosquito

MOZAMBIQUE

American cockroach
Bed bug
Brownbanded cockroach
Chigoe
Death's head hawk moth
European mantid
German cockroach
Greenhouse camel cricket
Greenhouse whitefly
Hair follicle mite
Honeybee

Human head/body louse
Indian mealmoth
Liposcelis bostrychophila
Long-bodied cellar spider
Lucerne flea
Oriental cockroach
Saunders embiid
Scolopender
Silverfish *Trissolcus basalis*
Wandering glider
Western flower thrips
Yellow fever mosquito

MYANMAR

American cockroach
Atlas moth
Bed bug
Brownbanded cockroach
Dead-leaf mantid
European mantid
German cockroach
Greenhouse camel cricket
Greenhouse whitefly
Hair follicle mite
Honeybee
Human head/body louse
Indian mealmoth
Liposcelis bostrychophila
Long-bodied cellar spider
Lucerne flea
Orchid mantid
Oriental cockroach
Pea aphid
Silverfish
Wandering glider
Wandering violin mantid
Yellow fever mosquito

NAMIBIA

American cockroach
Bed bug
Brownbanded cockroach
Death's head hawk moth
European mantid
German cockroach
Gladiator

Greenhouse camel cricket
Greenhouse whitefly
Hair follicle mite
Honeybee
Human head/body louse
Indian mealmoth
Liposcelis bostrychophila
Long-bodied cellar spider
Lucerne flea
Scolopender
Silverfish
Wandering glider
Western flower thrips
Yellow fever mosquito

NAURU

Bed bug
German cockroach
Greenhouse camel cricket
Hair follicle mite
Honeybee
Human head/body louse
Indian mealmoth
Liposcelis bostrychophila
Long-bodied cellar spider
Lucerne flea
Silverfish
Wandering glider

NEPAL

American cockroach
Atlas moth
Bed bug
Brownbanded cockroach
German cockroach
Greenhouse camel cricket
Greenhouse whitefly
Hair follicle mite
Honeybee
Human head/body louse
Indian mealmoth
Liposcelis bostrychophila
Long-bodied cellar spider
Lucerne flea
Pea aphid
Scolopender

Silkworm
Silverfish
Slender pigeon louse
Wandering glider
Western flower thrips
Yellow fever mosquito

NETHERLANDS
American cockroach
Antlion
Bed bug
Book scorpion
Brown mayfly
Common harvestman
Devil's coach-horse
European earwig
European marsh crane fly
European stag beetle
Flat-backed millipede
German cockroach
Great water beetle
Greenhouse camel cricket
Gypsy moth
Hair follicle mite
Honeybee
Human head/body louse
Indian mealmoth
Large blue
Liposcelis bostrychophila
Long-bodied cellar spider
Long-winged conehead
Lucerne flea
Oriental cockroach
Petrobius brevistylis
Pill millipede
Schummel's inocelliid
  snakefly
Scolopender
Silverfish
Slender pigeon louse
Spoonwing lacewing
Triaenodes bicolor
Velvet ant
Western flower thrips
Zebra jumping spider

NEW ZEALAND
Colossendeis megalonyx
European earwig
German cockroach
Greenhouse camel cricket
Greenhouse whitefly
Hair follicle mite
Human head/body louse
Indian mealmoth
Liposcelis bostrychophila
Long-bodied cellar spider
Lucerne flea
Megarhyssa nortoni
Pea aphid
Silverfish
Wandering glider
Western flower thrips

NICARAGUA
American cockroach
Bed bug
Black-headed nasute termite
Brownbanded cockroach
Chigoe
Forest giant
German cockroach
Greenhouse camel cricket
Greenhouse whitefly
Hair follicle mite
Hercules beetle
Honeybee
Human head/body louse
Indian mealmoth
Liposcelis bostrychophila
Long-bodied cellar spider
Lucerne flea
Madeira cockroach
Mediterranean fruitfly
Pea aphid
Scolopender
Silverfish
Yellow fever mosquito

NIGER
American cockroach
Bed bug

Brownbanded cockroach
Camel spider
Chigoe
Death's head hawk moth
Emperor scorpion
German cockroach
Greenhouse camel cricket
Hair follicle mite
Honeybee
Human head/body louse
Indian mealmoth
Liposcelis bostrychophila
Long-bodied cellar spider
Lucerne flea
Silverfish
Slender pigeon louse
Tsetse fly
Variegated grasshopper
Wandering glider
Yellow fever mosquito

NIGERIA
American cockroach
Bed bug
Brownbanded cockroach
Chigoe
Death's head hawk moth
Emperor scorpion
European mantid
German cockroach
Greenhouse camel cricket
Greenhouse whitefly
Hair follicle mite
Honeybee
Human head/body louse
Indian mealmoth
Liposcelis bostrychophila
Long-bodied cellar spider
Long-winged conehead
Lucerne flea
Madeira cockroach
Silverfish
Slender pigeon louse
Tsetse fly
Variegated grasshopper

Wandering glider
Yellow fever mosquito

NORTH KOREA
American cockroach
Bed bug
Chinese mantid
Common harvestman
European mantid
German cockroach
Greenhouse camel cricket
Hair follicle mite
Honeybee
Human head/body louse
Indian mealmoth
Large blue
Liposcelis bostrychophila
Long-bodied cellar spider
Lucerne flea
Pea aphid
Silkworm
Silverfish
Wandering glider
Western flower thrips
Zebra jumping spider

NORWAY
American cockroach
Bed bug
Brown mayfly
Common harvestman
European marsh crane fly
Flat-backed millipede
German cockroach
Great water beetle
Greenhouse camel cricket
Gypsy moth
Hair follicle mite
Honeybee
Human head/body louse
Indian mealmoth
Liposcelis bostrychophila
Long-bodied cellar spider
Lucerne flea
Oriental cockroach

Petrobius brevistylis
Pill millipede
Silverfish
Slender pigeon louse
Spoonwing lacewing
Triaenodes bicolor
Velvet ant
Zebra jumping spider

OMAN
Bed bug
Camel spider
German cockroach
Greenhouse camel cricket
Hair follicle mite
Honeybee
Human head/body louse
Indian mealmoth
Liposcelis bostrychophila
Long-bodied cellar spider
Lucerne flea
Scolopender
Silverfish
Slender pigeon louse
Wandering glider
Yellow fever mosquito

PACIFIC OCEAN
Colossendeis megalonyx
Sea skater

PAKISTAN
American cockroach
Atlas moth
Bed bug
Brownbanded cockroach
German cockroach
Greenhouse camel cricket
Greenhouse whitefly
Hair follicle mite
Honeybee
Human head/body louse
Indian mealmoth
Liposcelis bostrychophila

Long-bodied cellar spider
Lucerne flea
Pea aphid
Silkworm
Silverfish
Slender pigeon louse
Wandering glider
Western flower thrips
Yellow fever mosquito

PALAU
Bed bug
German cockroach
Greenhouse camel cricket
Hair follicle mite
Honeybee
Human head/body louse
Indian mealmoth
Liposcelis bostrychophila
Long-bodied cellar spider
Lucerne flea
Silverfish
Wandering glider

PANAMA
American cockroach
Bed bug
Black-headed nasute termite
Brownbanded cockroach
Chigoe
Dead leaf mimetica
Forest giant
German cockroach
Greenhouse camel cricket
Greenhouse whitefly
Hair follicle mite
Hercules beetle
Honeybee
Human head/body louse
Indian mealmoth
Leaf-cutter ant
Liposcelis bostrychophila
Long-bodied cellar spider
Lucerne flea
Madeira cockroach

Mediterranean fruitfly
Pea aphid
Silverfish
Tarantula hawk
Wandering glider
Yellow fever mosquito

PAPUA NEW GUINEA
Bed bug
Cyrtodiopsis dalmanni
German cockroach
Greenhouse camel cricket
Greenhouse whitefly
Hair follicle mite
Honeybee
Human head/body louse
Indian mealmoth
Liposcelis bostrychophila
Long-bodied cellar spider
Lucerne flea
Mantid lacewing
Pea aphid
Silverfish
Stalk-eyed fly
Wandering glider
Yellow fever mosquito

PARAGUAY
American cockroach
Backswimmer
Bed bug
Blue morpho
Brownbanded cockroach
Chigoe
German cockroach
Greenhouse camel cricket
Greenhouse whitefly
Hair follicle mite
Honeybee
Human head/body louse
Indian mealmoth
Leaf-cutter ant
Liposcelis bostrychophila
Long-bodied cellar spider
Lucerne flea

Mediterranean fruitfly
Pea aphid
Silverfish
Wandering glider

PERU
American cockroach
Bed bug
Black-headed nasute termite
Blue morpho
Brownbanded cockroach
Chigoe
Forest giant
German cockroach
Greenhouse camel cricket
Greenhouse whitefly
Hair follicle mite
Honeybee
Human head/body louse
Indian mealmoth
Leaf-cutter ant
Liposcelis bostrychophila
Long-bodied cellar spider
Lucerne flea
Mediterranean fruitfly
Pea aphid
Scolopender
Silverfish
Tarantula hawk
Wandering glider
Yellow fever mosquito

PHILIPPINES
American cockroach
Atlas moth
Bed bug
European earwig
German cockroach
Greenhouse camel cricket
Greenhouse whitefly
Hair follicle mite
Honeybee
Human head/body louse
Indian mealmoth
Liposcelis bostrychophila

Long-bodied cellar spider
Lucerne flea
Oriental cockroach
Pea aphid
Scolopender
Silverfish
Wandering glider

POLAND
American cockroach
Bed bug
Book scorpion
Brown mayfly
Common harvestman
Devil's coach-horse
European earwig
European marsh crane fly
European stag beetle
German cockroach
Great water beetle
Greenhouse camel cricket
Greenhouse whitefly
Gypsy moth
Hair follicle mite
Honeybee
Human head/body louse
Indian mealmoth
Large blue
Liposcelis bostrychophila
Long-bodied cellar spider
Long-winged conehead
Lucerne flea
Oriental cockroach
Pea aphid
Petrobius brevistylis
Pill millipede
Schummel's inocelliid
  snakefly
Silverfish
Slender pigeon louse
Spoonwing lacewing
Triaenodes bicolor
Velvet ant
Western flower thrips
Zebra jumping spider

PORTUGAL

American cockroach
Antlion
Bed bug
Book scorpion
Brown mayfly
Brownbanded cockroach
Common harvestman
Death's head hawk moth
Devil's coach-horse
European earwig
European mantid
German cockroach
Greenhouse camel cricket
Greenhouse whitefly
Gypsy moth
Hair follicle mite
Honeybee
House centipede
Human head/body louse
Indian mealmoth
Large blue
Liposcelis bostrychophila
Long-bodied cellar spider
Long-winged conehead
Lucerne flea
Mediterranean fruitfly
Oriental cockroach
Pea aphid
Sacred scarab
Silverfish
Slender pigeon louse
Spoonwing lacewing
Trissolcus basalis
Velvet ant
Western flower thrips
Yellow fever mosquito
Zebra jumping spider

PUERTO RICO

Bed bug
German cockroach
Greenhouse camel cricket
Hair follicle mite
Honeybee
Human head/body louse

Indian mealmoth
Liposcelis bostrychophila
Long-bodied cellar spider
Lucerne flea
Silverfish
Wandering glider

QATAR

Bed bug
Camel spider
German cockroach
Greenhouse camel cricket
Hair follicle mite
Honeybee
Human head/body louse
Indian mealmoth
Liposcelis bostrychophila
Long-bodied cellar spider
Lucerne flea
Silverfish
Slender pigeon louse
Wandering glider
Yellow fever mosquito

REPUBLIC OF THE CONGO

American cockroach
Bed bug
Brownbanded cockroach
Chigoe
Death's head hawk moth
Emperor scorpion
German cockroach
Greenhouse camel cricket
Greenhouse whitefly
Hair follicle mite
Honeybee
Human head/body louse
Indian mealmoth
Liposcelis bostrychophila
Long-bodied cellar spider
Lucerne flea
Madeira cockroach
Silverfish
Tsetse fly

Variegated grasshopper
Wandering glider
Yellow fever mosquito

ROMANIA

American cockroach
Bed bug
Book scorpion
Brown mayfly
Common harvestman
Death's head hawk moth
Devil's coach-horse
European earwig
European mantid
European stag beetle
German cockroach
Great water beetle
Greenhouse camel cricket
Greenhouse whitefly
Gypsy moth
Hair follicle mite
Honeybee
Human head/body louse
Indian mealmoth
Large blue
Liposcelis bostrychophila
Long-bodied cellar spider
Long-winged conehead
Lucerne flea
Pea aphid
Silverfish
Slender pigeon louse
Spoonwing lacewing
Triaenodes bicolor
Velvet ant
Western flower thrips
Zebra jumping spider

RUSSIA

American cockroach
Bed bug
Brown mayfly
Common harvestman
Death's head hawk moth
Devil's coach-horse

European earwig
European mantid
European marsh crane fly
European stag beetle
German cockroach
Great water beetle
Greenhouse camel cricket
Greenhouse whitefly
Gypsy moth
Hair follicle mite
Honeybee
Human head/body louse
Indian mealmoth
Large blue
Liposcelis bostrychophila
Long-bodied cellar spider
Long-winged conehead
Lucerne flea
Pea aphid
Sacred scarab
Schummel's inocelliid
  snakefly
Sheep and goat flea
Silverfish
Slender pigeon louse
Triaenodes bicolor
Velvet ant
Western flower thrips
Zebra jumping spider

RWANDA
American cockroach
Bed bug
Brownbanded cockroach
Chigoe
Death's head hawk moth
European earwig
European mantid
German cockroach
Greenhouse camel cricket
Greenhouse whitefly
Hair follicle mite
Honeybee
Human head/body louse
Indian mealmoth

Liposcelis bostrychophila
Long-bodied cellar spider
Lucerne flea
Silverfish
Slender pigeon louse
Wandering glider
Yellow fever mosquito

ST. KITTS-NEVIS
Bed bug
German cockroach
Greenhouse camel cricket
Hair follicle mite
Honeybee
Human head/body louse
Indian mealmoth
Liposcelis bostrychophila
Long-bodied cellar spider
Lucerne flea
Silverfish
Wandering glider

ST. LUCIA
Bed bug
German cockroach
Greenhouse camel cricket
Hair follicle mite
Honeybee
Human head/body louse
Indian mealmoth
Liposcelis bostrychophila
Long-bodied cellar spider
Lucerne flea
Silverfish
Wandering glider

ST. VINCENT
Bed bug
German cockroach
Greenhouse camel cricket
Hair follicle mite
Honeybee
Human head/body louse
Indian mealmoth
Liposcelis bostrychophila

Long-bodied cellar spider
Lucerne flea
Silverfish
Wandering glider

SAMOA
Bed bug
German cockroach
Greenhouse camel cricket
Hair follicle mite
Honeybee
Human head/body louse
Indian mealmoth
Liposcelis bostrychophila
Long-bodied cellar spider
Lucerne flea
Silverfish
Wandering glider

SAN MARINO
American cockroach
Antlion
Bed bug
Book scorpion
Brown mayfly
Brownbanded cockroach
Common harvestman
Death's head hawk moth
Devil's coach-horse
European earwig
European mantid
European stag beetle
Flat-backed millipede
German cockroach
Great water beetle
Greenhouse camel cricket
Greenhouse whitefly
Gypsy moth
Hair follicle mite
Honeybee
House centipede
Human head/body louse
Indian mealmoth
Large blue
Liposcelis bostrychophila

Long-bodied cellar spider
Long-winged conehead
Lucerne flea
Mediterranean fruitfly
Pea aphid
Sacred scarab
Silverfish
Slender pigeon louse
Spoonwing lacewing
Triaenodes bicolor
Velvet ant
Western flower thrips
Yellow fever mosquito
Zebra jumping spider

SÃO TOMÉ AND PRÍNCIPE

Bed bug
Death's head hawk moth
Emperor scorpion
German cockroach
Greenhouse camel cricket
Hair follicle mite
Honeybee
Human head/body louse
Indian mealmoth
Liposcelis bostrychophila
Long-bodied cellar spider
Lucerne flea
Silverfish
Wandering glider
Yellow fever mosquito

SAUDI ARABIA

Bed bug
Brownbanded cockroach
Camel spider
German cockroach
Greenhouse camel cricket
Hair follicle mite
Honeybee
Human head/body louse
Indian mealmoth
Liposcelis bostrychophila
Long-bodied cellar spider

Lucerne flea
Mediterranean fruitfly
Sacred scarab
Silverfish
Slender pigeon louse
Wandering glider
Yellow fever mosquito

SENEGAL

American cockroach
Bed bug
Brownbanded cockroach
Chigoe
Death's head hawk moth
Devil's coach-horse
Emperor scorpion
German cockroach
Greenhouse camel cricket
Greenhouse whitefly
Hair follicle mite
Honeybee
Human head/body louse
Indian mealmoth
Liposcelis bostrychophila
Long-bodied cellar spider
Lucerne flea
Madeira cockroach
Oriental cockroach
Silverfish
Slender pigeon louse
Tsetse fly
Variegated grasshopper
Wandering glider
Yellow fever mosquito

SERBIA AND MONTENEGRO

American cockroach
Bed bug
Book scorpion
Brown mayfly
Brownbanded cockroach
Common harvestman
Death's head hawk moth
Devil's coach-horse

European earwig
European mantid
European stag beetle
German cockroach
Great water beetle
Greenhouse camel cricket
Greenhouse whitefly
Gypsy moth
Hair follicle mite
Honeybee
House centipede
Human head/body louse
Indian mealmoth
Large blue
Liposcelis bostrychophila
Long-bodied cellar spider
Long-winged conehead
Lucerne flea
Mediterranean fruitfly
Pea aphid
Sacred scarab
Silverfish
Slender pigeon louse
Spoonwing lacewing
Triaenodes bicolor
Velvet ant
Western flower thrips
Yellow fever mosquito
Zebra jumping spider

SEYCHELLES

Bed bug
Death's head hawk moth
German cockroach
Greenhouse camel cricket
Hair follicle mite
Honeybee
Human head/body louse
Indian mealmoth
Javan leaf insect
Liposcelis bostrychophila
Long-bodied cellar spider
Lucerne flea
Scolopender
Silverfish
Wandering glider
Yellow fever mosquito

SIERRA LEONE

American cockroach
Bed bug
Brownbanded cockroach
Chigoe
Death's head hawk moth
Emperor scorpion
European mantid
German cockroach
Greenhouse camel cricket
Greenhouse whitefly
Hair follicle mite
Honeybee
Human head/body louse
Indian mealmoth
Liposcelis bostrychophila
Long-bodied cellar spider
Lucerne flea
Madeira cockroach
Oriental cockroach
Silverfish
Slender pigeon louse
Tsetse fly
Variegated grasshopper
Wandering glider
Yellow fever mosquito

SINGAPORE

American cockroach
Atlas moth
Bed bug
Black macrotermes
Brownbanded cockroach
Cyrtodiopsis dalmanni
Dead-leaf mantid
European earwig
European mantid
German cockroach
Greenhouse camel cricket
Greenhouse whitefly
Hair follicle mite
Honeybee
Human head/body louse
Indian mealmoth
Javan leaf insect

Jungle nymph
Liposcelis bostrychophila
Lucerne flea
Orchid mantid
Silverfish
Stalk-eyed fly
Wandering glider
Yellow fever mosquito

SLOVAKIA

American cockroach
Bed bug
Book scorpion
Brown mayfly
Common harvestman
Devil's coach-horse
European earwig
European mantid
European stag beetle
German cockroach
Great water beetle
Greenhouse camel cricket
Greenhouse whitefly
Gypsy moth
Hair follicle mite
Honeybee
Human head/body louse
Indian mealmoth
Large blue
Liposcelis bostrychophila
Long-bodied cellar spider
Long-winged conehead
Lucerne flea
Pea aphid
Silverfish
Slender pigeon louse
Spoonwing lacewing
Triaenodes bicolor
Velvet ant
Western flower thrips
Zebra jumping spider

SLOVENIA

American cockroach
Bed bug

Book scorpion
Brown mayfly
Brownbanded cockroach
Common harvestman
Death's head hawk moth
Devil's coach-horse
European earwig
European mantid
European stag beetle
Flat-backed millipede
German cockroach
Great water beetle
Greenhouse camel cricket
Greenhouse whitefly
Gypsy moth
Hair follicle mite
Honeybee
House centipede
Human head/body louse
Indian mealmoth
Large blue
Liposcelis bostrychophila
Long-bodied cellar spider
Long-winged conehead
Lucerne flea
Mediterranean fruitfly
Pea aphid
Pill millipede
Silverfish
Slender pigeon louse
Spoonwing lacewing
Triaenodes bicolor
Velvet ant
Western flower thrips
Yellow fever mosquito
Zebra jumping spider

SOLOMON ISLANDS

Bed bug
German cockroach
Greenhouse camel cricket
Hair follicle mite
Honeybee
Human head/body louse
Indian mealmoth
Liposcelis bostrychophila

Long-bodied cellar spider
Lucerne flea
Silverfish
Wandering glider

SOMALIA
Bed bug
Brownbanded cockroach
Chigoe
Death's head hawk moth
European earwig
European mantid
German cockroach
Greenhouse camel cricket
Greenhouse whitefly
Hair follicle mite
Honeybee
Human head/body louse
Indian mealmoth
Liposcelis bostrychophila
Long-bodied cellar spider
Lucerne flea
Saunders embiid
Scolopender
Silverfish
Slender pigeon louse
Wandering glider
Yellow fever mosquito

SOUTH AFRICA
American cockroach
Bed bug
Brownbanded cockroach
Death's head hawk moth
European mantid
German cockroach
Gladiator
Greenhouse camel cricket
Greenhouse whitefly
Hair follicle mite
Honeybee
House centipede
Human head/body louse
Indian mealmoth
Liposcelis bostrychophila

Long-bodied cellar spider
Lucerne flea
Oriental cockroach
Scolopender
Silverfish
Wandering glider
Western flower thrips
Yellow fever mosquito

SOUTH KOREA
American cockroach
Bed bug
Chinese mantid
Common harvestman
German cockroach
Greenhouse camel cricket
Hair follicle mite
Honeybee
Human head/body louse
Indian mealmoth
Liposcelis bostrychophila
Long-bodied cellar spider
Lucerne flea
Pea aphid
Silkworm
Silverfish
Wandering glider
Western flower thrips
Zebra jumping spider

SPAIN
American cockroach
Antlion
Bed bug
Book scorpion
Brown mayfly
Brownbanded cockroach
Common harvestman
Death's head hawk moth
Devil's coach-horse
European earwig
European mantid
European marsh crane fly
European stag beetle
German cockroach

Great water beetle
Greenhouse camel cricket
Greenhouse whitefly
Gypsy moth
Hair follicle mite
Honeybee
House centipede
Human head/body louse
Indian mealmoth
Large blue
Liposcelis bostrychophila
Long-bodied cellar spider
Long-winged conehead
Lucerne flea
Mediterranean fruitfly
Oriental cockroach
Pea aphid
Sacred scarab
Silverfish
Slender pigeon louse
Spoonwing lacewing
Velvet ant
Western flower thrips
Yellow fever mosquito
Zebra jumping spider

SRI LANKA
Atlas moth
Bed bug
Brownbanded cockroach
German cockroach
Greenhouse camel cricket
Greenhouse whitefly
Hair follicle mite
Honeybee
Human head/body louse
Indian mealmoth
Javan leaf insect
Liposcelis bostrychophila
Long-bodied cellar spider
Lucerne flea
Scolopender
Silverfish
Wandering glider
Wandering violin mantid

SUDAN

Bed bug
Brownbanded cockroach
Camel spider
Chigoe
Death's head hawk moth
European mantid
German cockroach
Greenhouse camel cricket
Hair follicle mite
Honeybee
Human head/body louse
Indian mealmoth
Liposcelis bostrychophila
Long-bodied cellar spider
Lucerne flea
Scolopender
Silverfish
Slender pigeon louse
Tsetse fly
Wandering glider
Yellow fever mosquito

SURINAME

American cockroach
Bed bug
Black-headed nasute termite
Blue morpho
Brownbanded cockroach
Chigoe
German cockroach
Giant water bug
Greenhouse camel cricket
Greenhouse whitefly
Hair follicle mite
Honeybee
Human head/body louse
Indian mealmoth
Linnaeus's snapping termite
Liposcelis bostrychophila
Long-bodied cellar spider
Lucerne flea
Madeira cockroach
Mediterranean fruitfly
Pea aphid
Silverfish

Tarantula hawk
Wandering glider
Western flower thrips

SWAZILAND

American cockroach
Bed bug
Brownbanded cockroach
Death's head hawk moth
European mantid
German cockroach
Greenhouse camel cricket
Greenhouse whitefly
Hair follicle mite
Honeybee
House centipede
Human head/body louse
Indian mealmoth
Liposcelis bostrychophila
Long-bodied cellar spider
Lucerne flea
Oriental cockroach
Silverfish
Wandering glider
Western flower thrips
Yellow fever mosquito

SWEDEN

American cockroach
Bed bug
Brown mayfly
Common harvestman
Devil's coach-horse
European marsh crane fly
Flat-backed millipede
German cockroach
Great water beetle
Greenhouse camel cricket
Gypsy moth
Hair follicle mite
Honeybee
Human head/body louse
Indian mealmoth
Liposcelis bostrychophila
Long-bodied cellar spider
Long-winged conehead
Lucerne flea

Oriental cockroach
Petrobius brevistylis
Pill millipede
Schummel's inocelliid
   snakefly
Silverfish
Slender pigeon louse
Spoonwing lacewing
Triaenodes bicolor
Velvet ant
Zebra jumping spider

SWITZERLAND

American cockroach
Antlion
Bed bug
Book scorpion
Brown mayfly
Brownbanded cockroach
Common harvestman
Devil's coach-horse
European earwig
European mantid
European marsh crane fly
European stag beetle
Flat-backed millipede
German cockroach
Great water beetle
Greenhouse camel cricket
Greenhouse whitefly
Gypsy moth
Hair follicle mite
Honeybee
House centipede
Human head/body louse
Indian mealmoth
Large blue
Liposcelis bostrychophila
Long-bodied cellar spider
Long-winged conehead
Lucerne flea
Pea aphid
Pill millipede
Silverfish
Slender pigeon louse
Spoonwing lacewing
Triaenodes bicolor

Velvet ant
Western flower thrips
Zebra jumping spider

SYRIA
American cockroach
Bed bug
Brownbanded cockroach
Camel spider
Death's head hawk moth
German cockroach
Greenhouse camel cricket
Greenhouse whitefly
Hair follicle mite
Honeybee
Human head/body louse
Indian mealmoth
Liposcelis bostrychophila
Long-bodied cellar spider
Long-winged conehead
Lucerne flea
Mediterranean fruitfly
Pea aphid
Sacred scarab
Silverfish
Slender pigeon louse
Wandering glider
Yellow fever mosquito

TAIWAN
Bed bug
German cockroach
Greenhouse camel cricket
Hair follicle mite
Honeybee
Human head/body louse
Indian mealmoth
Liposcelis bostrychophila
Long-bodied cellar spider
Lucerne flea
Silverfish

TAJIKISTAN
American cockroach
Atlas moth

Bed bug
Brownbanded cockroach
German cockroach
Greenhouse camel cricket
Greenhouse whitefly
Hair follicle mite
Honeybee
Human head/body louse
Indian mealmoth
Liposcelis bostrychophila
Long-bodied cellar spider
Lucerne flea
Silverfish
Slender pigeon louse
Wandering glider
Western flower thrips

TANZANIA
American cockroach
Bed bug
Brownbanded cockroach
Chigoe
Death's head hawk moth
European earwig
European mantid
German cockroach
Gladiator
Greenhouse camel cricket
Greenhouse whitefly
Hair follicle mite
Honeybee
Human head/body louse
Indian mealmoth
Liposcelis bostrychophila
Long-bodied cellar spider
Lucerne flea
Saunders embiid
Scolopender
Silverfish
Slender pigeon louse
Wandering glider
Yellow fever mosquito

THAILAND
American cockroach
Atlas moth

Bed bug
Black macrotermes
Brownbanded cockroach
German cockroach
Greenhouse camel cricket
Greenhouse whitefly
Hair follicle mite
Honeybee
Human head/body louse
Indian mealmoth
Jungle nymph
Liposcelis bostrychophila
Long-bodied cellar spider
Lucerne flea
Oriental cockroach
Pea aphid
Silverfish
Wandering glider
Yellow fever mosquito

TIMOR-LESTE
Bed bug
Dead-leaf mantid
German cockroach
Greenhouse camel cricket
Honeybee
Human head/body louse
Indian mealmoth
Liposcelis bostrychophila
Long-bodied cellar spider
Lucerne flea
Silverfish

TOGO
American cockroach
Bed bug
Brownbanded cockroach
Chigoe
Death's head hawk moth
Emperor scorpion
European mantid
German cockroach
Greenhouse camel cricket
Greenhouse whitefly
Hair follicle mite
Honeybee

Human head/body louse
Indian mealmoth
Liposcelis bostrychophila
Long-bodied cellar spider
Long-winged conehead
Lucerne flea
Madeira cockroach
Silverfish
Slender pigeon louse
Tsetse fly
Variegated grasshopper
Wandering glider
Yellow fever mosquito

TONGA
Bed bug
German cockroach
Greenhouse camel cricket
Hair follicle mite
Honeybee
Human head/body louse
Indian mealmoth
Liposcelis bostrychophila
Long-bodied cellar spider
Lucerne flea
Silverfish
Wandering glider

TRINIDAD AND TOBAGO
Bed bug
German cockroach
Greenhouse camel cricket
Hair follicle mite
Honeybee
Human head/body louse
Indian mealmoth
Linnaeus's snapping termite
Liposcelis bostrychophila
Long-bodied cellar spider
Lucerne flea
Silverfish
Wandering glider

TUNISIA
American cockroach
Bed bug

Brownbanded cockroach
Death's head hawk moth
Devil's coach-horse
European earwig
European mantid
German cockroach
Greenhouse camel cricket
Greenhouse whitefly
Gypsy moth
Hair follicle mite
Honeybee
House centipede
Human head/body louse
Indian mealmoth
Liposcelis bostrychophila
Long-bodied cellar spider
Long-winged conehead
Lucerne flea
Mediterranean fruitfly
Sacred scarab
Scolopender
Silverfish
Slender pigeon louse
Spoonwing lacewing
Wandering glider
Western flower thrips
Yellow fever mosquito

TURKEY
American cockroach
Bed bug
Book scorpion
Brown mayfly
Devil's coach-horse
European earwig
European mantid
European stag beetle
German cockroach
Great water beetle
Greenhouse camel cricket
Greenhouse whitefly
Gypsy moth
Hair follicle mite
Honeybee
House centipede
Human head/body louse

Indian mealmoth
Liposcelis bostrychophila
Long-bodied cellar spider
Long-winged conehead
Lucerne flea
Mediterranean fruitfly
Pea aphid
Sacred scarab
Silverfish
Slender pigeon louse
Velvet ant
Western flower thrips
Yellow fever mosquito
Zebra jumping spider

TURKMENISTAN
Bed bug
Brownbanded cockroach
German cockroach
Greenhouse camel cricket
Greenhouse whitefly
Hair follicle mite
Honeybee
Human head/body louse
Indian mealmoth
Liposcelis bostrychophila
Long-bodied cellar spider
Lucerne flea
Pea aphid
Silverfish
Wandering glider
Zebra jumping spider

TUVALU
Bed bug
German cockroach
Greenhouse camel cricket
Hair follicle mite
Honeybee
Human head/body louse
Indian mealmoth
Liposcelis bostrychophila
Long-bodied cellar spider
Lucerne flea
Silverfish
Wandering glider

UGANDA

American cockroach
Bed bug
Brownbanded cockroach
Chigoe
Death's head hawk moth
European earwig
European mantid
German cockroach
Greenhouse camel cricket
Greenhouse whitefly
Hair follicle mite
Honeybee
Human head/body louse
Indian mealmoth
Liposcelis bostrychophila
Long-bodied cellar spider
Lucerne flea
Silverfish
Slender pigeon louse
Wandering glider
Yellow fever mosquito

UKRAINE

American cockroach
Bed bug
Book scorpion
Brown mayfly
Common harvestman
Death's head hawk moth
Devil's coach-horse
European earwig
European mantid
European stag beetle
German cockroach
Great water beetle
Greenhouse camel cricket
Greenhouse whitefly
Gypsy moth
Hair follicle mite
Honeybee
Human head/body louse
Indian mealmoth
Large blue
Liposcelis bostrychophila
Long-bodied cellar spider

Long-winged conehead
Lucerne flea
Pea aphid
Sacred scarab
Schummel's inocelliid
  snakefly
Silverfish
Slender pigeon louse
Spoonwing lacewing
Velvet ant
Western flower thrips
Zebra jumping spider

UNITED ARAB EMIRATES

Bed bug
Camel spider
German cockroach
Great water beetle
Greenhouse camel cricket
Hair follicle mite
Honeybee
Human head/body louse
Indian mealmoth
Large blue
Liposcelis bostrychophila
Long-bodied cellar spider
Lucerne flea
Silverfish
Slender pigeon louse
Wandering glider
Yellow fever mosquito

UNITED KINGDOM

American cockroach
Antlion
Bed bug
Book scorpion
Common harvestman
Devil's coach-horse
European earwig
European marsh crane fly
Flat-backed millipede
German cockroach
Greenhouse camel cricket

Greenhouse whitefly
Gypsy moth
Hair follicle mite
Honeybee
Human head/body louse
Indian mealmoth
Liposcelis bostrychophila
Long-bodied cellar spider
Long-winged conehead
Lucerne flea
Oriental cockroach
Petrobius brevistylis
Pill millipede
Silverfish
Slender pigeon louse
Spoonwing lacewing
St. Helena earwig
Triaenodes bicolor
Velvet ant
Western flower thrips
Zebra jumping spider

UNITED STATES

Allopauropus carolinensis
American burying beetle
American cockroach
Bed bug
Big black horse fly
Brownbanded cockroach
Chinese mantid
Common American
  walkingstick
Common harvestman
Devil's coach-horse
Eastern dobsonfly
Eastern subterranean termite
European earwig
European mantid
European marsh crane fly
Flat-backed millipede
German cockroach
Giant salmonfly
Giant whip scorpion
Greenhouse camel cricket
Greenhouse whitefly
Gypsy moth

Hair follicle mite
Holijapyx diversiuguis
Honeybee
Horseshoe crab
House centipede
Hubbard's angel insect
Human head/body louse
Indian mealmoth
Liposcelis bostrychophila
Long-bodied cellar spider
Lucerne flea
Megarhyssa nortoni
Northern rock-crawler
Oriental cockroach
Panorpa nuptialis
Pea aphid
Potter wasp
Rocky Mountain wood tick
Saunders embiid
Seventeen-year cicada
Silverfish
Tarantula hawk
Trissolcus basalis
Wandering glider
Western flower thrips
Wide-headed rottenwood
  termite
Yellow fever mosquito
Zebra jumping spider

UNKNOWN
Garden symphylan

URUGUAY
American cockroach
Backswimmer
Bed bug
Brownbanded cockroach
German cockroach
Greenhouse camel cricket
Greenhouse whitefly
Hair follicle mite
Honeybee
Human head/body louse
Indian mealmoth
Liposcelis bostrychophila

Long-bodied cellar spider
Lucerne flea
Oriental cockroach
Pea aphid
Silverfish
Wandering glider
Yellow fever mosquito

UZBEKISTAN
Bed bug
Brownbanded cockroach
European mantid
German cockroach
Greenhouse camel cricket
Hair follicle mite
Honeybee
Human head/body louse
Indian mealmoth
Liposcelis bostrychophila
Long-bodied cellar spider
Lucerne flea
Silverfish
Wandering glider
Zebra jumping spider

VANUATU
Bed bug
German cockroach
Greenhouse camel cricket
Hair follicle mite
Honeybee
Human head/body louse
Indian mealmoth
Liposcelis bostrychophila
Long-bodied cellar spider
Lucerne flea
Silverfish
Wandering glider

VATICAN CITY
Bed bug
German cockroach
Greenhouse camel cricket
Hair follicle mite
Honeybee

Human head/body louse
Indian mealmoth
Liposcelis bostrychophila
Long-bodied cellar spider
Lucerne flea
Silverfish

VENEZUELA
American cockroach
Bed bug
Black-headed nasute termite
Blue morpho
Brownbanded cockroach
Chigoe
German cockroach
Giant water bug
Greenhouse camel cricket
Greenhouse whitefly
Hair follicle mite
Hercules beetle
Honeybee
Human head/body louse
Indian mealmoth
Leaf-cutter ant
Liposcelis bostrychophila
Long-bodied cellar spider
Lucerne flea
Madeira cockroach
Mediterranean fruitfly
Pea aphid
Saunders embiid
Silverfish
Tarantula hawk
Wandering glider
Western flower thrips
Yellow fever mosquito

VIETNAM
American cockroach
Atlas moth
Bed bug
Black macrotermes
Brownbanded cockroach
German cockroach
Greenhouse camel cricket

Greenhouse whitefly
Hair follicle mite
Honeybee
Human head/body louse
Indian mealmoth
Liposcelis bostrychophila
Long-bodied cellar spider
Lucerne flea
Oriental cockroach
Pea aphid
Silverfish
Wandering glider
Yellow fever mosquito

YEMEN
Bed bug
Camel spider
German cockroach
Greenhouse camel cricket
Hair follicle mite
Honeybee
Human head/body louse
Indian mealmoth
Liposcelis bostrychophila

Long-bodied cellar spider
Lucerne flea
Scolopender
Silverfish
Slender pigeon louse
Wandering glider
Yellow fever mosquito

ZAMBIA
American cockroach
Bed bug
Brownbanded cockroach
Chigoe
Death's head hawk moth
European mantid
German cockroach
Greenhouse camel cricket
Greenhouse whitefly
Hair follicle mite
Honeybee
Human head/body louse
Indian mealmoth
Liposcelis bostrychophila
Long-bodied cellar spider

Lucerne flea
Silverfish
Wandering glider
Yellow fever mosquito

ZIMBABWE
American cockroach
Bed bug
Brownbanded cockroach
Death's head hawk moth
European mantid
German cockroach
Greenhouse camel cricket
Greenhouse whitefly
Hair follicle mite
Honeybee
Human head/body louse
Indian mealmoth
Liposcelis bostrychophila
Long-bodied cellar spider
Lucerne flea
Silverfish
Wandering glider
Yellow fever mosquito

Index

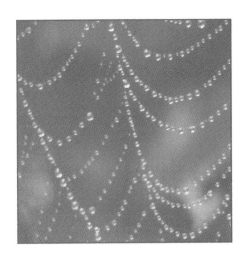

Italic type indicates volume number; **boldface** type indicates entries and their pages; (ill.) indicates illustrations.

T

Tabanus punctifer. See Big black horse flies

Tachycines asynamorus. See Greenhouse camel crickets

Tailless whip scorpions, *1:* 24–26, 24 (ill.), 25 (ill.)

Tarantula hawks, *2:* 407–8, 407 (ill.), 408 (ill.)

Tasmanian devils, *2:* 328

Tasmanian torrent midges, *2:* 341

Telson tails. *See* Proturans

Tenodera aridifolia sinensis. See Chinese mantids

Tent caterpillars, *2:* 372

Termes fatalis. See Linnaeus's snapping termites

Termites, *1:* 99, **117–34,** 136, *2:* 395

Thousandleggers. *See* Millipedes

Thrips, *2:* **257–61**

Thysanoptera. *See* Thrips

Thysanura. *See* Fire brats; Silverfish

Ticks, *1:* **15–44**

Tiger beetles, *2:* 293, 295

Tiger moths, *2:* 370

Timemas, 1: **193–210**

Tipula paludosa. See European marsh crane flies

Toktokkies, *2:* 295

Tortoise beetles, *2:* 296

Trachelophorus giraffa. See Giraffenecked weevils

Tree crickets, *1:* 168

Triaenodes bicolor, 2: 363–64, 363 (ill.), 364 (ill.)

Trichogramma species, *2:* 372

Trichoptera. *See* Caddisflies

Trissolcus basalis, 2: 409–11, 409 (ill.), 410 (ill.)

Troides species. *See* Birdwing butterflies

True bugs, *2:* **236–56**

Tsetse flies, *2:* 340, 346–47, 346 (ill.), 347 (ill.)

Tunga penetrans. See Chigoes

Twistedwing parasites, *2:* **315–19,** 318 (ill.), 319 (ill.)

U

United States Fish and Wildlife Service. *See* Fish and Wildlife Service (U.S.)

Uropsylla tasmanica, 2: 328

V

Varied springtails. *See* Lucerne fleas

Variegated grasshoppers, *1:* 175–76, 175 (ill.), 176 (ill.)

Velvet ants, *2:* 405–6, 405 (ill.), 406 (ill.)

Vine borers, *2:* 372

Vinegaroons. *See* Giant whip scorpions

W

Walkingsticks, common American, *1:* 202–4, 202 (ill.), 203 (ill.)

Wandering gliders, *1:* 86–87, 86 (ill.), 87 (ill.)

Wandering violin mantids, *1:* 139–41, 139 (ill.), 140 (ill.)

Waspmimicking katydids, *1:* 169

Wasps, *2:* 339, **390–414**

Water beetles, *2:* 298, 301–2, 301 (ill.), 302 (ill.)

Water boatmen, *2:* 240

Water bugs, giant, *2:* 239, 240, 248–49, 248 (ill.), 249 (ill.)

Water loss, centipedes and, *2:* 417

Water quality, stoneflies for, *1:* 94

Water scavengers, *2:* 294

Water scorpions, *2:* 238

Water striders, *2:* 238

Webs, spider, *1:* 17

Webspinners, *2:* **211–15**

Webworms, *2:* 372

Weevils, *2:* **289–314**

Western flower thrips, *2:* 260–61, 260 (ill.), 261 (ill.)

Western pygmy blues, *2:* 366

Wetas, giant, *1:* 166, 170

Whip scorpions, *1:* 16 giant, *1:* 39–41, 39 (ill.), 40 (ill.) tailless, *1:* 24–26, 24 (ill.), 25 (ill.)

Whip spiders. *See* Tailless whip scorpions

Whirligig beetles, *2:* 290, 291, 294

White ants. *See* Termites

Whiteflies, *2:* 236, 237, 241–42, 241 (ill.), 242 (ill.)

Wideheaded rottenwood termites, *1:* 132–33, 132 (ill.), 133 (ill.)

Wingless wood cockroaches, *1:* 117

Woodboring beetles, *2:* 293, 298

Wood ticks, Rocky Mountain, *1:* 21–23, 21 (ill.), 22 (ill.)

Woodworms. *See* Thrips

World Conservation Union (IUCN) Red List of Threatened Species on arachnids, *1:* 18 on beetles, *2:* 298, 311 on caddisflies, *2:* 361–62 on centipedes, *2:* 418 on *Chiloporter eatoni, 1:* 77 on cicadas, *2:* 247 on damselflies, *1:* 85 on dragonflies, *1:* 85 on earwigs, *1:* 160, 164 on emperor scorpions, *1:* 44 on flies, *2:* 341 on hemiptera, *2:* 240

on horseshoe crabs, *1:* 11
on hymenoptera, *2:* 396
on large blues, *2:* 377
on lepidoptera, *2:* 372,
  377
on lice, *2:* 229, 230
on Lord Howe stick
  insects, *1:* 196
on mantids, *1:* 138
on mayflies, *1:* 74
on midges, *2:* 341
on orthopterans, *1:* 171–72

on rockcrawlers, *1:* 154
on stoneflies, *1:* 94–95
Worms, blood, *2:* 340
Wound infection, maggots for,
  2: 340
Wrinkled beetles, *2:* 289

Y

Yellow fever mosquitoes,
  2: 342–43, 342 (ill.), 343
  (ill.)
Yellow jackets, *2:* 393, 395

Z

Zebra jumping spiders,
  1: 29–31, 29 (ill.), 30 (ill.)
Zonocerus variegatus. See
  Variegated grasshoppers
Zootermopsis laticeps. See
  Wideheaded rottenwood
  termites
Zoraptera. *See* Angel insects
Zorapterans, *2:* **216–21**
Zorotypus hubbardi. See
  Hubbard's angel insects